Heresy

WITHDRAWN

Rescuing Jesus

Rescuing Jesus

HOW People of Color, Women & Queer Christians Are Reclaiming Evangelicalism

DEBORAH JIAN LEE

BEACON PRESS
BOSTON

BEACON PRESS
Boston, Massachusetts
www.beacon.org

Beacon Press books
are published under the auspices of
the Unitarian Universalist Association of Congregations.

© 2015 by Deborah Jian Lee
All rights reserved
Printed in the United States of America

18 17 16 15   8 7 6 5 4 3 2 1

This book is printed on acid-free paper that meets the uncoated paper
ANSI/NISO specifications for permanence as revised in 1992.

Text design and composition by Kim Arney

Library of Congress Cataloging-in-Publication Data
Lee, Deborah Jian.
   Rescuing Jesus : how people of color, women, and queer
Christians are reclaiming evangelicalism / Deborah Jian Lee.
      pages   cm
   Includes bibliographical references.
   ISBN 978-0-8070-3347-0 (hardcover : alk. paper)
   ISBN 978-0-8070-3348-7 (ebook)
   1. Church and minorities. 2. Social integration—Religious
aspects—Christianity. 3. Evangelicalism. I. Title.
   BV639.M56L44 2015
   277.3'083—dc23
                                        2015013052

For Andrew

Contents

Introduction

THE FIRST BEGINNING

This book had many beginnings. Officially, it began in the run-up to the 2008 elections when I was reporting on the evangelical movement for journalism school and then for public radio. I traveled to suburban South Carolina, where conservative believers had emerged as champions for Barack Obama. I met people like Patricia Moseley, a middle-aged woman with red hair and a silky Southern drawl who had previously campaigned for Strom Thurmond and both George Bushes. But her desire for better public-education policy and an end to the wars abroad brought her out of the Right and into the Obama camp. I followed Robin Lucas, a late-twenties evangelical mother, as she canvassed surrounding neighborhoods with Obama fliers. She regretted what she now saw as a misguided vote for George W. Bush, cast partly out of pressure from fellow Christians, and was trying to redeem herself. I found seminary professors offering guidance to Democratic advisors, busing evangelicals to swing states in order to drum up support for the Democratic candidate. In the postelection analysis, it became clear that these inroads had boosted Obama, who ended up with the same percentage of evangelical support that Bill Clinton had received in 1992.

Though my beat was politics, I could also see that some evangelicals were carving a new path for the movement, one focused not on political labels, but on social justice. As a former true believer, I was intrigued—even more so when they told me *this* is the true heart of the evangelical movement. I met Lisa Sharon Harper, who was launching a faith coalition to combat police brutality and mobilize evangelicals behind immigration reform. I met Southern Baptist-raised Jennifer Crumpton, who was pressing old-school leaders to back policies that advanced women's access to contraception. I also met a slew of young believers challenging the Right's unwavering opposition to LGBTQ equality.

The more people I spoke to, the more I realized that something big was happening. In interview after interview, devout evangelicals told me they were ditching the Religious Right and backing progressive causes. Some were angry at the loud, conservative, self-appointed gatekeepers of evangelicalism; others were hopeful that change was afoot. Even as conservatives were making gains of their own—launching the Tea Party, claiming seats in Congress, doubling down on blocking reproductive rights—the growing progressive minority of evangelicals insisted that their movement, which encompassed priorities far beyond partisan politics and elections, was here to stay. They were declaring a new era, vowing to reclaim the disgraced moniker "evangelical." By redefining their faith on their own terms, they began to brandish the label with pride. Some added minor variations, and one that has stuck is "progressive evangelical."

This is their story.

THE SECOND BEGINNING

The other beginning, more personal and unofficial, dates back to an earlier election: 2000, Bush versus Gore. A college student, I had just awoken to a startling reality: I was living in the middle of the culture wars.

Growing up, the terms "culture wars" and "evangelical" meant nothing to me. I was raised in a loving nonreligious household. My parents, immigrants from Hong Kong via Taiwan, taught me the values of kindness, hard work, and accepting others. When I expressed spiritual curiosity, they didn't offer answers. Instead my mother repeated a mantra: "Every religion has some good in it. Find it. Learn from it." So I did.

I prayed with my Hindu friend and her parents by their weeping willow. I asked questions about my grandmother's Buddhism. I read books. I attended church with my older brother, whose classmate was evangelizing to him.

In our mostly white Chicago suburb, just a handful of school friends were like me, children of immigrants. Their origins ranged from Puerto Rico and Korea to India, West Africa, and other far-flung regions. We kids were so focused on assimilating to white America that we rarely discussed our ethnic identities. But I did notice that everyone, both kids of immigrants and not, had some sort of faith identity. My friends were Hindu, Muslim, Jewish, Baha'i, and nearly every kind of Christian. They had traditions and holidays and sacred texts that spoke meaning into their lives. I wanted that.

For much of my childhood I felt like an outsider, always toggling between Chinese and American culture. At home, the cultural gap between my parents and me grew year by year. I spoke English exclusively, having lost my native Cantonese. My bedroom walls became a shrine to white and black celebrities. My parents felt they were losing me to American culture, and the widening cultural distance between us made home life tense at times.

Even at school, that tension never left my body. I was the kid faking it to fit in. I rarely invited friends over, worried that they'd make hurtful observations about my "weird" Chinese home (they often did). I was picked on for being Chinese and sometimes for no reason at all. Most of it was run-of-the-mill kid stuff that I recovered from—bullies with their taunts, mean girls playing outlandish mind games—but the habitual drive-by racial slurs (the kind of street harassment that has followed me into adulthood) and one particular assault haunt me to this day. These memories sting not because I value the opinions of those idiots any longer, but because I can remember how, at such an impressionable age, those people made me believe I was worthless.

Eventually, I joined the youth group at the immigrant Chinese church my older brother had attended. There, I felt I had found my people. My peers lived in similar split worlds. They embraced me. They told me about their God, about how he made me the way I am and accepted me unconditionally. As a teenager praying quietly in my bedroom alone, I often felt a deep rush of joy swell within, like a fire igniting. I just knew that I was loved.

At fifteen I asked to be baptized. Immersed in a warm tub on the sanctuary stage, I said a few words about how I couldn't imagine my life without Jesus, about the immensity of God's love. I heard the splash as my body went down, then that calm, underwater muteness and the cheers from my new friends as I emerged, my white robe and long black hair drenched, my face smiling. I became a youth group leader and led Bible study sessions. I danced at concerts, planned sleepovers and volunteer events, and started an occasional gathering we called "coffee house," which was a kind of talent-show-meets-night-of-snacking with other teens in a candle-lit gymnasium.

Culture war rhetoric barely touched our immigrant church. We were apolitical, and our elders were conservative in a turn-down-that-crazy-music kind of way, not a partisan politics way. I didn't identify as an "evangelical," and nobody talked about elections or abortion.

Hoping for a similar sense of community, I joined a campus Christian club soon after I arrived at the University of Illinois, Urbana-Champaign. InterVarsity Christian Fellowship is one of the largest evangelical campus ministries in the country, and at my school they had big crimson-bannered booths during freshman orientation, a blowout welcome party, and packed weekly meetings with a lot of smiling faces. It seemed like the place to be.

The group was mostly white, with a strong Asian contingent and a sprinkling of black and Latino students. Part of me felt at home, with the shared faith language and new friends to bond with. But another part of me felt uneasy: something was off. An unspoken cultural undercurrent seemed to be sweeping us all along in the same direction. I couldn't place my finger on it until the 2000 presidential election.

By this point, at the beginning of my junior year, I was a leader in InterVarsity. I thought I knew my community well, yet I could not understand why my Christian peers quivered with delight over the possibility of electing an evangelical president. I asked around. A cheerful Bible study friend explained it this way: Christians had total freedom to vote for whomever they preferred, but they ought not to cast a ballot for anyone who supported legalized abortion.

Two of my closest friends in college were Toby and Rebecca (their names have been changed), who had been dating since high school. Toby was in my freshman year Bible study. Rebecca and I eventually became roommates. Over the years the three of us climbed the ranks of leadership within InterVarsity, eventually leading the group, shaping its vision and planning many of its events.

During the 2000 election, I listened to Toby and Rebecca's political banter with a mixture of confusion and fascination. Toby scrunched his nose when he referred to "those liberals." Just a few nights before we all cast our votes, I sat with Rebecca in our dorm room as she agonized over her choice. I was nineteen, trying an unkempt indie look—shaggy pixie cut, patchwork corduroys—and my feet hung over the side of the bunk bed. Rebecca pulled at her long, golden hair as she compared campaign fliers from the Bush and Gore camps. I argued that many of Bush's policies would contradict certain tenets of her faith she valued most. She listened and agreed, but struggled to shake the message of the Right. She finally burst out, "But with Gore, babies will die!"

That moment may have been this book's true beginning. It was during that election season that I came to understand the power of the "abortion trump card" and the culture's deep aversion to liberalism. I considered myself a budding liberal (I had wavered between the Gore and Nader camps and, eventually, picked Nader), but quietly retreated from that label as I felt disapproval from evangelicals, both in my community and beyond. Why did Toby scrunch his nose when he said "those liberals"? Why did that traveling evangelist condemn gay people? Why did people equate supporting choice with loving abortion? Was the blood of unborn babies really on my hands?

Not long after I cast my ballot, an acquaintance pressed a plastic fetus into my palm.

"This is a baby twelve weeks into a pregnancy," she told me softly, adding that his eyelids had formed and he could make a fist with his tiny fingers. I did not have the language to respond.

A NEW ERA

Over the years, I stayed in touch with Rebecca. I stood in a line of bridesmaids and watched her marry Toby. Toby would go on to join InterVarsity staff, and the two would settle close to campus.

When I called Rebecca in the run-up to the 2008 election, we reminisced about our long conversations in 2000. She remembered how she had felt compelled as if by Christian imperative to vote for George W. Bush, the pro-life candidate. But as the years passed and our country launched two wars, she had become increasingly conflicted about her decision. In 2004, she quietly voted for John Kerry. By 2008, she openly voted for Barack Obama. This shift coincided with her evolving views on abortion: while she personally objects to it and continues to identify as pro-life, she believes the procedure should remain legal. "I don't have to base my vote on pro-life issues anymore," she told me.

In many ways, Rebecca is emblematic of many believers in her generation who now define their faith apart from the dictums of the conservative Right. As part of my reporting during the 2008 elections, I spoke to Matt Dunbar, a mid-twenties evangelical at the time. He told me that he abandoned Christian Right ideology when President Bush launched the war in Iraq. To Matt, war is a "life" issue, one that has changed his generation's definition of what it means to be pro-life. Theirs carries a more nuanced interpretation: believers ought to have a "consistent ethic of life," one that seeks to protect life "from the womb to the tomb," he explained. That means he cares equally about abortion as he does about war and peace, the death penalty, and the environment.

"All of these things are life issues," he said.

Matt, who has no qualms voting for a pro-choice candidate, supports policies that "reduce the need for abortion," such as comprehensive sex education, access to contraception, and programs that help pregnant women, especially those from poor communities. He lost interest long ago in the fight to overturn *Roe v. Wade*, and when asked about his political priorities he said, "To dislodge Christians from the Religious Right."

Matt, Rebecca, and other progressive evangelicals are part of a larger cultural shift away from the Right. In 2007, John Green, a senior fellow of the Pew Forum on Religion and Public Life, revealed that the percentage of white evangelicals who self-identified as Republicans had declined notably since 2004. According to his research at the time, roughly 40 percent of the country's voting evangelicals are now considered "freestyle evangelicals" who increasingly care about progressive issues.[1] Another Pew study in 2007 found that significant numbers of young white evangelicals were departing from the Republican Party while remaining conservative on certain issues like abortion.[2] More recently, a 2013 report by the Public Religion Research Institute found that millennials are twice as likely to be religious progressives than those sixty-eight and older.[3] These young believers want to hold on to their faith while they let go of conservative values. (Furthermore, research shows that most millennials are overwhelmingly nonreligious and are leaving the church[4] and that, after evangelicals, the second-largest major "religious" group is the rapidly growing cohort of religiously unaffiliated adults.[5])

Long known for its sprawling megachurches, its multimillion-dollar media empires, and its stadium-packed conferences, the evangelical movement has reached a tipping point in this new religious landscape. Faced with the choice of changing or dying out, the movement has seen some of its leaders make significant shifts toward embracing progressive values, in part to appeal to the rising generation.

THE THIRD BEGINNING

When I first started reporting this book, I trained my lens on the stories of mega-evangelical leaders making shifts. Their proclamations are a big deal, potentially swaying hundreds of thousands of followers—and maybe it's just human nature to gravitate toward stories of superstars.

But I quickly realized that the real story—the action—propelling this cultural shift came not from the top, but from the grass roots.

My reporting revealed something exciting and counterintuitive, yet it made sense once I saw it plainly: evangelical leaders are not leading but following their dramatically diversifying constituency. As people of color flock to the church, as women rise in leadership, and as LGBTQ believers come out of the closet, faith communities have begun to elevate voices historically marginalized by mainstream evangelicalism. In doing so, these once-ostracized groups are not only filling church pews, they are also advancing a progressive movement within.

Meanwhile, white millennials are rapidly leaving the church permanently or for extended periods (nearly 60 percent leave after age fifteen), yet people of color are taking those vacated seats just as quickly.[6] Soong-Chan Rah, a scholar who focuses on the growth of evangelical churches, predicts the faith's demographic picture will broadly follow general population trends. A recent US census report indicates that minority groups will grow from 33 percent of the country's population in 2008 to 50 percent in 2042. Already, we see evangelical churches moving in this direction. A 2015 study by the Pew Research Center reveals that racial and ethnic minorities grew to 24 percent of evangelical Protestants in 2014, up from 19 percent in 2007.[7] Meanwhile, the face of global Christianity has flipped, with Europe and the United States seeing a rapid decline in church attendance as Latin America, Africa, and Asia explode with Christian (much of it evangelical) fervor. As many of these Christians immigrate to America, they are breathing new life into the American evangelical church.[8]

At the same time, women continue to advance in evangelical leadership, even among theologically conservative communities. Opposition persists, to be sure, but a growing gender equality movement within the conservative ranks has taken hold, in step with the broader American public's acceptance of women's leadership. Today the majority of white evangelicals support women's ordination even if they belong to denominations or congregations that deny it, according to a 2013 report by the Public Religion Research Institute.[9]

Even more striking, the tide is shifting on another hot topic in evangelicalism today: LGBTQ equality. Statistics from the General Social Survey show that while evangelicals remain largely opposed to same-sex marriage, that opposition has declined from 85 percent in the late 1980s to 59 percent in 2010.[10] Among the younger generation, acceptance is even stronger, with the majority of evangelicals under age thirty-four supporting some form of legal recognition for same-sex couples.[11]

While some of this shift can be attributed to sweeping social change, a great deal of credit must also be given to those who are driving this progress from deep within evangelicalism. I met black evangelical leaders marching in Ferguson and telling conservative white evangelicals why their shared faith should compel them to action. I met evangelical feminists rejecting the subservience script they had been taught, advocating for women's equality at the pulpit and in the home, speaking out for reproductive rights and against "purity culture." I found secret queer societies in conservative enclaves such as Christian colleges, where young believers connected with each other for emotional support and on-campus advocacy. (Note: I use "queer" and "LGBTQ" as umbrella terms that encompass the diverse landscape of sexual and gender minorities, as these terms are both inclusive and preferred by many leaders and members of the LGBTQ community now.)

Ultimately, this book is about how, in this new era, people of color, women, and queer Christians are reclaiming evangelicalism to create the kind of community they believe the gospel promises them. They invited me into their world, and when I saw what they were doing, I knew I had to tell their story.

That was the book's third beginning.

OVERVIEW

I've divided the book into three parts, reflecting the journeys of these brave individuals and the movements they represent: first sprouting from conservative surroundings (part 1), then building bridges to reconcile their faith with their minority identity (part 2), and finally forging new paths to transform evangelicalism from within (part 3).

Within the larger parts, each chapter tackles a different identity—race, gender, and sexual orientation and gender identity—and focuses on the journey of a particular evangelical who embodies much of the movement. You will meet Lisa Sharon Harper, a black leader bridging the racial gap while mobilizing conservatives to support immigration reform and combat racial profiling by police. You will meet the Reverend Jennifer Crumpton, a former pageant queen turned feminist minister working to dismantle patriarchal church structures, build an evangelical feminist theology, and coax older leaders to support reproductive rights. You will meet Will Haggerty and Tasha Magness, sexual minority students combating the explicitly anti-queer policies at their conservative evangelical university. The work of these primary characters dovetails into many other believers' stories, all of which have culminated into a major movement sweeping the American evangelical church.

DEFINING THE EVANGELICAL CHURCH

"Evangelical" is a broad term that covers a variety of Protestant denominations, traditions, organizations, and congregations. Some denominations, like the Southern Baptist Convention, the largest Protestant denomination in the country, overwhelmingly embody evangelicalism and heavily influence the subculture. Other denominations are split, with some members and congregations embracing the evangelical label and others eschewing it; many Episcopalians, Presbyterians, Pentecostals, Methodists, and other Christians from a range of denominations identify as evangelical, while others within those denominations do not.

Furthermore, much of evangelical subculture cannot be accounted for by looking at denominations. In the independent spirit of the movement, many churches identify as nondenominational or postdenominational, or even nothing at all. Evangelicalism is anything but a monolith; it is a vastly diverse landscape.

Whatever their theological and cultural differences, evangelicals are often characterized by their belief in four main tenets of the faith:

the authority of the Bible, salvation through Jesus Christ, the importance of a personal relationship with God, and the imperative to share the gospel.

Quantifying such a diverse movement is difficult. Due to the lack of a central governing body and the varied survey methods counting evangelicals, it is impossible to nail down a precise number. Some estimates limit evangelicals to those who identify as "born again" or "evangelical," while others exclude black Protestants, even though they might overwhelmingly identify with evangelical theology. Estimates also face consistency issues when some restrict their definition of evangelicals to certain behavioral benchmarks (frequency of church attendance, scripture reading, prayer, and so on), which ignores those considered "cultural evangelicals." The Institute for the Study of American Evangelicals, acknowledging these limitations when analyzing a broad cross section of data, includes both the devout and the "cultural evangelicals" (many of whom populate Southern white and African American communities), which puts the institute's general estimate of the nation's evangelicals at around one-third of the population, or ninety million to one hundred million Americans.[12] Others offer different estimates; for example, from looking at churches in the evangelical Protestant tradition, the Pew Research Center puts the number of adult evangelicals closer to sixty-two million.[13] While no one can offer a definitive number, we know that tens of millions of evangelicals exist—and, more importantly, that their movement wields tremendous influence in America.

SURPRISES IN HISTORY

In addition to bringing to light stories from modern-day evangelicalism, this book delves into key moments in the faith's history, revealing the roots of the progressive evangelical movement and ways conservatives overpowered activists' early efforts, along with surprising twists in the narrative that often have been obscured, sometimes intentionally. I was surprised to learn of the countless examples of evangelicals advancing progressive values in the 1970s, just before the Religious Right launched. The birth of the modern progressive evangelical movement can be traced to November 1973, with an intimate conference that is now referred to as the Thanksgiving Workshop. Years before the Religious Right came to be, a motley group of evangelicals gathered in a run-down Chicago YMCA hotel over the Thanksgiving weekend, called together by a little-known leader named Ron Sider. His gathering of friends and associates numbered about forty, including older evangelical stalwarts like premier theologian Carl Henry and young evangelicals such as Jim Wallis, an influential antiwar activist with a shaggy mop of hair and overgrown beard. That weekend, the group devised a strategy for asserting its progressive values through political action and hashed out a public statement called the Chicago Declaration of Evangelical Social Concern.

At the time, evangelical Protestants were part of Richard Nixon's "Silent Majority," passively backing the status quo. The Chicago Declaration made a significant departure by plainly condemning the country's militarism, patriarchy, systemic racism, and economic inequality. The *Washington Post* wrote that the group behind the declaration "could shake both political and religious life in America."[14]

Those present would go on to widen their influence: Sider formed the progressive think tank Evangelicals for Social Action and wrote *Rich Christians in an Age of Hunger*, which *Christianity Today* heralded as one of the top fifty books that have shaped the evangelical movement. Jim Wallis's periodical the *Post-American* would later become the influential Washington, DC, lobbying group and magazine *Sojourners*. At the time, it seemed entirely possible that the progressives could shift the direction of evangelical politics.

But in the end, they lost their momentum, in part, because they were unable to incorporate identity politics. "Following its secular counterpart, the evangelical left fragmented along gender, racial and ideological lines," writes historian David Swartz in his book *Moral Minority: The Evangelical Left in an Age of Conservatism*.[15]

Today, a new era is upon us. After decades of trudging along in the shadow of the Religious Right, progressive evangelicals are facing similar questions of identity—but are handling these questions in a very different way. Due to major demographic and generational shifts, minority groups once on the margins have actually bolstered the movement and have become key assets to forging a new kind of evangelicalism.

THE LAST BEGINNING

These very issues of race, gender, and sexuality are what drove me away from evangelicalism as a young woman. Once I started asserting my whole humanity, including my ethics as a Chinese American woman with LGBTQ friends, I felt sidelined, my loyalty to the faith questioned.

In my senior year of college I accepted an executive officer position at InterVarsity with the naive dream that I could change this subculture from within and shake its dated outlook. I was tired of hearing people casually say that they were glad our few black members weren't "too black," or that women should submit to men, or that homosexuality was a disease. I sparred with peers, male and female, who argued for traditional gender roles. I crafted a teaching series that explored the history of racism in the church. I offered my support to a closeted gay member before he came out to the group. To an outsider, this was all basic liberal discourse; I wasn't breaking any new ground. But among some Christian peers, I was a wild-eyed hippie wading in the waters of blasphemy.

When I was in college, and in the years that followed, few people were outright mean to me; evangelicals are some of the most polite people I've met. Instead, they asked me why I needed to talk about race so much, or questioned whether my racial identity had become more important than my identity as a Christian. A few told me that my views bothered them, but mostly friends grew distant without seeking to hash out our conflict. It hurt to see my friends drift away; I loved my evangelical community and wanted to work through the issues. But as I expressed my mostly liberal views, more and more evangelicals told me I was transgressing. One of my closest friends asked me, "Are you even a Christian anymore?" Like any human being, I was looking for a place where I belonged and was valued in my entirety, and I was no longer finding that in the evangelical world.

I can't point to a precise moment when I made my exit from evangelicalism, but by the end of college I was outright rejecting the conservatism of the culture. Gradually, I stopped believing key evangelical theological tenets: I no longer accepted biblical inerrancy (the belief that the Bible is without error), and the idea that one could find salvation only through Christianity contradicted the heart of the God I knew. I cast off evangelicalism to preserve my own faith. The decision came slowly and with a lot of deliberation, but it ultimately granted me some of the most profound spiritual freedom I've ever felt. My faith, that flame within, burned bright, despite the heartache I felt from losing my community.

By the time I started my graduate program in journalism, I was not evangelical and was reluctant to reenter evangelicalism, even as a reporter. I was still working to disentangle from the subculture, skeptical of promises that things were changing. But something compelled me to seek out and stick to the story. Though I had given up on evangelical culture personally, a part of me wanted to believe it was redeemable. That hope sustained me through the years of reporting this book. As a reporter, I had the opportunity to ask tough questions and dig beyond the standard aphorisms in a way I was too polite—or too invested—to do before. And in the process I found a new progressive evangelical movement, one so compelling that even a defector like me paused for another glimpse.

After all of those beginnings, let us begin.

PART 1

Conformists

ONE

Assimilate to Survive

LISA

Seven-year-old Lisa Sharon Harper held her mother's hand as they canvassed their street in the West Oak Lane neighborhood of Philadelphia.
It was the autumn of 1976, election season, and the leaves had begun
to scatter across the sloped lawns leading up to the historic brick row
houses. Lisa's family was one of many African American families in
their predominantly black middle-class neighborhood where everyone
knew everyone.

A decade earlier, Lisa's mother, Sharon, had been a founding member of the Philadelphia chapter of the Student Nonviolent Coordinating
Committee, the civil rights organization that agitated for, among other
things, the right to vote. Now she was an election official in her pre-
cinct, charged with educating local residents on how to register to vote.
She had planted "Jimmy Carter for President" signs on her front lawn
and took Lisa door to door, eager to give her daughter a lesson in civic
engagement. Armed with smiles and papers, the two took turns rapping
on each door.

"Mom, why are we Democrats?" Lisa wondered aloud as they
strolled up to another house. They paused as Sharon explained, "Jimmy
Carter is a Democrat. President Ford is a Republican. The Democrats

are like Robin Hood; they take back money from the rich and give it to the poor. The Republicans steal money from the poor and give it to the rich. That's why we're Democrats."[1] As Lisa grew older, her mother spoke more about the complexity of politics and race. She hoped Lisa would understand the impact that national policy had on the family for generations. She also hoped to instill in Lisa an unshakable belief in her identity, beauty, and value as a black American.

Neither Lisa nor Sharon had any idea how far Lisa would depart from these lessons.

Lisa recalls the first half of her childhood, when she lived in West Oak Lane, as idyllic: summer days lying in the shade of her neighbor's blue spruce, playing with her posse who ruled the street with their games of double Dutch and hide-and-seek. But beneath the surface, trauma haunted her. She was sexually abused at the age of three, an experience that "gutted" her and left her fragile for the rest of her childhood. She felt constantly unsure of herself, unable even to stand up to the bully who punched her. At home, her parents' marriage began to fall apart, bringing more instability to Lisa's life.

When Lisa's father left, her mother moved the children away from West Oak Lane and a fresh start seemed to be on the horizon. But adolescence brought more challenges. Sharon eventually settled Lisa and her siblings in Cape May, a New Jersey county with a strong Southern culture and a legacy of slavery and segregation. Lisa was an outsider in Cape May County, where 93 percent of residents were white and only 6 percent black.[2] She struggled to fit in among her white peers. Home life was also tough. Her mother eventually remarried. Her new stepfather had children of his own, and blending the families was a challenge. Lisa began to look to the world outside for comfort and stability.

In the summer of 1983, when Lisa was thirteen, a friend invited her to an evangelical youth group. On a whim, Lisa attended a meeting and was startled to find all the popular kids there—including a boy she had a crush on. Suddenly, this whole church thing seemed very interesting.

"Getting in with the cool kids was one of my strategies to being accepted into this all-white world," she told me. At thirteen, being popular was a survival strategy. "If you were popular, race didn't matter."

On a deeper level, what ultimately kept her coming back to the all-white group was the sense that everybody genuinely loved her. She had long felt like an outcast in Cape May, but in youth group, everyone called one another brother and sister. They listened to Lisa's heartfelt questions about God. When they told her that God loved her, would protect her, and wanted a personal relationship with her, she felt welcomed into a divine family. For the first time since arriving at Cape May, she felt as though she belonged. Through the witness of white evangelicals, and to the dismay of her family, Lisa responded to a minister's altar call, prayed a prayer of repentance, and became a born-again Christian in 1983.

Later, a friend from youth group told Lisa that being Christian and Republican was a package deal. To be a true believer, you had to be both. Eager to prove her faith, Lisa made another conversion, and began to identify as both Christian and Republican. Her new identities filled her with a sense of purpose. She listened to her youth leader's musings against liberalism, and she loved that her generation of young Christians could guard against those threats. The more her friends and the leaders invested time in Lisa, the more Lisa felt like she was becoming part of something bigger than herself. She knew God personally, and he had brought her into this grand movement.

When President Ronald Reagan ran against former vice president Walter Mondale in 1984, Lisa was in high school, and she solidified her evangelical bona fides by racing home with church tracts detailing the horrors Mondale would inflict. She told her younger sister Merry, "Mom and Dad better vote for Reagan or else all the children will be rounded up in concentration camps and made into slaves by Mondale, because he's the Antichrist."[3] Merry burst into tears and begged her parents to vote for Reagan. Sharon began to worry about Lisa's declarations about Antichrists and trickle-down economics. She threatened to keep her from church, but Lisa dug her heels in. At that moment, Lisa's relationship with her family began to fracture.

Without knowing it at the time, Lisa had mastered the art of assimilation. Like so many minority American youth before and after her, she learned to identify the majority culture's expectations quickly and prove that she could exceed them. She muted the parts of herself that set her apart and amplified the qualities that the culture celebrated. Though a handful of other black students attended her school, Lisa surrounded herself exclusively with white friends. She was one of only a few black students enrolled in college-prep courses, and she listened to heavy metal, straightened her hair, and enthusiastically threw herself into such activities as three-legged races.

In her high school yearbook, Lisa's self-assured smile is splashed across page after page—Key Club, Octagon Club, band, theater, and more. But she had challenges: she never dated, for example. At one point, she and a white boy seemed to like each other. They were close friends, they went to the same parties, they even kissed over games of spin the bottle. But neither her crush, nor any other boy for that matter, asked Lisa out on a date. Then one day her best friend set her crush up with another girl. When Lisa found out, "I went to the backyard and cried my head off. I imagined I was holding a magic knife that could carve the blackness off my skin."

Lisa's skin color stood in the way of her high school theater ambitions, too. Though she excelled at acting and had won prestigious awards, she never got a leading role until her senior year; the director had to argue with the producer to give her the role of Antigone. "It was because I was black and would have to play opposite a white guy," she explained.

Despite the challenges, Lisa flourished and achieved her goal of becoming popular. "It wasn't a conscious thing," she explained. "It was more like I had to overachieve to be seen as normal."

But even as she did her best to assimilate, she found ways to maintain her individuality. She wore colorful clothing and rocked an asymmetrical haircut—a counterculture signifier in the 1980s, when many of the girls were expressing themselves through hair. She directed the school play, *Our Town*. She fell in love with theater and rolled with the drama kids. She was beginning to find herself.

But in college, Lisa's conservatism and longing to fit in intensified to such a degree that she began to silence herself. As a student at Rutgers University, she joined Campus Crusade for Christ.[4] Lisa was one of just two students of color in the two-hundred-member club, and her new friends were white, modestly dressed, and conservative. Once again, Lisa found herself taking cues from white peers for how to act, dress, and believe. She banished bright colors from her wardrobe and began to dress in white, beige, and khaki. She joined her peers at pro-life rallies and in crashing pro-choice demonstrations, where they'd jeer from the sidelines and distribute fliers emblazoned with images of aborted fetuses. When it came to the conservative evangelical agenda, she was all in.

"You're going to be blown away when you see my college picture," Lisa told me one morning when I visited her at her uptown Manhattan apartment in 2010. We were sitting in her cozy living room surrounded by social justice and spirituality books, flipping through the pages of her old yearbooks. She was dressed casually in fitted jeans, a colorful blouse, and weighty metallic earrings that quivered beneath a voluminous mane of lively curls. It was breakfast time, so she took a bite of her grapefruit as she searched for the photograph, letting out a belly laugh when she found it. Her senior yearbook portrait shows a shockingly transformed Lisa, especially when compared to her photos from high school. Her asymmetrical haircut had been replaced with a 1950s bob hairdo. Her fun sense of style had been stamped out by a stuffy, high-collared shirt. Her confident smile had fallen to the wayside. "I was used to blending in, so I just blended in in college and this was the effect," she said with a chuckle. Even though she was a theater major, the yearbook editors listed her major as accounting. "I think they guessed that because I looked like an accountant."

Beneath the jesting, though, there is a deep sadness in how Lisa speaks about this time in her life. "In the process of assimilating, I lost myself," she said. Her borrowed conservatism divided her from her family, and those relationships are "still being rebuilt and restored."

Sharon recalls this time in her daughter's life with similar remorse. From the sidelines, she watched as Lisa shed the proud African American identity her mother had worked so hard to instill in her. They sparred at times, and Sharon sought advice from family members and friends, including her family's Baptist minister. Sharon saw a vast chasm between the black church and the white theology Lisa had embraced. Sharon explained the theological differences between white and black theology this way: "White evangelicals look for redemption—people who have sinned against each other look for redemption, whereas people who have been sinned against look for salvation. In the black church there is not so much an emphasis on redemption from sin—[the emphasis is on] salvation from the sinner."

In college, Lisa did not pay attention to these lessons; fitting in among her peer group dominated her focus. Ultimately, though, Sharon knew Lisa had to find her own way—even if that meant losing Lisa for a time and watching her grapple with the anguish of rejecting her own identity.

As I interviewed Lisa over a period of seven years, I found it easy to identify with her story. As a Chinese American growing up in white America, I felt the same kind of isolation. I assimilated to survive. I saw whiteness as aspirational. Pop culture and my white suburb reinforced this, lodging a barely detectable kernel of self-loathing inside of me. Being different made me feel inferior, less beautiful, less interesting, and less worthy. Over time, I came to reject my Chinese heritage, only much later realizing that this meant I had rejected myself.

I began to wonder if I somehow deserved the racial ridicule that came my way. I remember being eight or nine years old, playing on my lawn or picking green onions from my mother's garden; white kids would regularly walk by and loudly shout "ching-chong" jeers. They'd dissolve into laughter and stroll away. In junior high, two boys beat me up at recess after I won at a game. One grabbed me from behind and locked my arms behind my back. The other pummeled me with basketballs, shouting, "Chink!" Each ball struck me squarely in the chest, knocking the wind out. They threw me to the pavement and left me there, unable to breathe for what felt like forever.

Such experiences left me with questions I could neither answer nor ask anyone else about: What did it mean to be a "chink"? Why did those boys leave me on the asphalt when I was clearly in pain? Why did those white people in a pickup truck try to run over me and my Japanese American friend? Why did they angrily yell out the truck window, "Go back to your country, you fucking gooks!" Without answers, somehow, a terrible idea snuck into my psyche: part of me came to believe that I deserved all this, that my ethnicity made me a lesser person.

Faith challenged that idea. I found it in high school through my Chinese American youth group, and clung to Jesus's words about outcasts finding a home in God and subverting the unjust status quo: *The last will be first. The meek shall inherit the earth.* I loved Matthew 25: 34–40, where Jesus equates himself to "the least of these." His words called his listeners to cast aside their prejudices and love each other, and spoke to the inherent value of every human being—even me.

In college I began to reclaim my ethnic identity in earnest. I made Asian American friends, studied Mandarin, and traveled to Taiwan and China over two summers and one semester abroad. I took classes that explored minority experiences: Asian American literature, postcolonial studies, black history through the books of Toni Morrison. I began to speak more openly about my heritage and about how being an ethnic minority had affected my life and worldview. Slowly, I began to untangle from that growing weed of self-hatred. Seeing my own experiences in the context of a broader historical narrative, I understood I was not to blame for the racist abuse, street harassment, or microaggressions; I lived in a woefully ignorant society.

This ethnic awakening ran parallel to my work in InterVarsity Christian Fellowship, whose large ministry on my campus was mostly white with a good number of Asian American participants and a few black and Hispanic students. InterVarsity seemed intentionally multiethnic, which I liked, but the group's diversity often felt decorative.

Once in a while we sang a Christian song in Spanish or Mandarin, but when I invited my off-campus church's mostly black gospel choir to lead a meeting's worship session, many of my InterVarsity peers stiffened uncomfortably in their seats and seemed unwelcoming to our guests, their arms crossed and faces unsmiling. In the tradition of white evangelicalism, our Bible studies and guest speakers focused primarily on teaching lessons about praying and reading the Bible more, converting others to Christianity, or fighting personal sin such as gossip or sexual thoughts. Minority students assimilated to white theology, which focused on personal piety and conversion; white worship styles, including contemporary Christian rock (think syrupy ballads set to rhythmic guitars and drums); and white evangelical culture, which bought into the capitalistic framework of conferences, merchandising, books, T-shirts, and trendy bracelets. InterVarsity sermons and Bibles studies ignored traditions such as black theology and liberation theology, both of which had sprung out of the belief that the gospel calls Christians to dismantle oppressive social structures.

Meanwhile, I noticed a steady stream of tone-deaf comments about race. Friends would reassure me that I was basically white because I wasn't "one of *those* Asians." One fellowship peer said directly to my black friend, "Haven't we met? No? I guess you all look alike." It was intended as a joke, but it didn't land well. In spite of the disappointed look I shot him, my Christian friend just shrugged as if to say, "Ha-ha, whoops!"

These incidents don't represent InterVarsity as a whole and aren't exclusive to evangelical Christianity, as American culture at large is often racially tone deaf. But, despite the number of astute InterVarsity students and staff, the frequency of these incidents and the free pass they were given underscore the ongoing default to white perspectives common within evangelical circles. I expected more from my Christian peers.

When I became an InterVarsity leader, I strove to address these issues head-on—only to face pushback from those who politely suggested that my speaker series and presentations focused too much on race and gender issues. Some worried that I had steered the group away from core gospel values of evangelism; others insisted that our group didn't have a race problem. Nobody was hostile, but they were dismissive.

During the second semester of my senior year, I learned that another leader at InterVarsity was hosting a "servant auction" to raise money for the club. The title, meant to invoke the Christian principle of service, seemed to continue the tradition of the group's tone-deafness. I couldn't attend, but a few days before the "auction" I asked Rebecca, my old roommate, what kinds of "services" were up for bidding. She excitedly told me about one plan in motion: her small group Bible study intended to bid on another group's "service" of an Indian dance. A group of white students planned to wrap their heads in turbans and perform a "hilarious" dance to an Indian music video. I told her that sounded offensive. She replied that it was a pop video; it was like making fun of 'N Sync. I insisted that it was a bad idea and that she should talk to the group about offering something else up for auction. Rebecca was extremely nice about listening to me, but the two groups went ahead with their plan. When I realized even my closest friends viewed my opinions as trivial, I expressed my disappointment, but walked away thinking, *What more can I do?* Neither Rebecca nor I had any idea how that moment would come back to haunt the entire group at the end of the year.

DIVIDED BY RACE

The rift Lisa and I both felt in white Christian communities harks back to the very roots of the evangelical movement. Although the church's stated doctrine has always been equality through Christ, the gap between teaching and practice has created a fraught relationship between white Christians and people of color, black Americans in particular. In the seventeenth century, European Christians hotly debated the spiritual status of those enslaved. Some Quakers criticized slavery, but many other Christian leaders construed enslaved Africans as only partially human, soulless and therefore disqualified from salvation. Opinion shifted at the turn of the eighteenth century, as white clergy began to seek African conversions. In the attempt to gain converts while appeasing masters, clergy presented an amended theology that granted blacks baptism and salvation while maintaining blacks' status as slaves. During an era known as the First Great Awakening, in the 1730s and 1740s, evangelicalism exploded in British America. George Whitefield, who led revivals across American provinces, operated with a two-pronged agenda: converting enslaved people and establishing slavery in Georgia, where it was not yet allowed.[5] White clergy by and large effectively elevated the institution of slavery to a central tenet of the faith—God's ordained system.

After the American Revolution, a contingent of evangelicals began to see slavery as antithetical to the language of freedom. Still seeing blacks as inferior, they were sympathetic to the economic losses slaveholders might face, and favored a gradual dismantling of slavery. Southern evangelicals, meanwhile, fiercely argued that the Bible supported slavery. Seeking to hold on to their constituencies, both churches and politicians avoided any forceful proclamations against slavery.[6]

In the 1830s, a new generation of abolitionists began to bluntly condemn the institution of slavery as immoral. Charles Finney, a lawyer turned evangelist, with piercing eyes and a receding hairline, led the Second Great Awakening by inspiring his throngs of converts toward social reform efforts, including abolition. He provided the theological framework for the abolitionist movement, making the fight against slavery an integral part of Christian faith; he went so far as to deny communion to slaveholders.[7]

Eventually the movement split, with radical abolitionists on one side and moderate-to-conservative evangelicals on the other. Although he helped advance the abolition movement, Finney was emblematic of the moderates: he viewed ownership of enslaved people as sinful, but did not object to racial prejudice and segregation. He became uncomfortable with the way, as he saw it, abolition efforts had grown demanding, focusing on slavery as a paramount sin and even accepting the blending of the races. Abolitionism detracted from evangelism, he concluded, so he drew back his support.[8]

In the run-up to the Civil War, many denominations subdivided over slavery: first the Presbyterians, then the Methodist Episcopal Church, the Baptists, and so on. The Southern Baptist Convention, for example, formed in 1845 to continue its defense of slavery.

The church also split along racial lines, as African Americans sought to forge faith institutions that fully upheld their rights and humanity. In the 1780s, an enslaved man named Andrew Bryan began preaching to fellow enslaved people in a shack he built in Savannah, Georgia. He eventually attracted hundreds and, once freed, he formed the First African Baptist Church of Savannah, one of the oldest black churches in the country.[9] Other former enslaved people formed black congregations, including the African Methodist Episcopal Church and the African Episcopal Church of St. Thomas. This trend of defecting from white churches continued over the next century, especially after slavery was abolished.

By the end of the nineteenth century, another major split took place as the liberal social gospel movement formed around the idea that God wanted Christians to fight systemic inequality. The social gospel movement grew in the nineteenth and early twentieth centuries under leaders such as white Baptist theologian Walter Rauschenbusch, who sought to eradicate institutional immorality: racial discrimination, unfair labor practices, and economic inequality.[10] Rauschenbusch pastored a church at the edge of Hell's Kitchen in Manhattan, where he confronted the harsh realities industrialization inflicted on the urban underclass, including poor working conditions, chronic unemployment, crime, malnutrition, disease, and inescapable poverty. While remaining faithful to evangelical piety principles, Rauschenbusch called believers to confront society's sins with Christian social action.

In the early twentieth century, fissures within the faith deepened. Mainline Protestant denominations embraced a more flexible theology and liberal ethos. In response, conservative fundamentalists—those who believe that the Bible is without error—forged their own Bible colleges and institutions to spread their message, which sprung from the 1910 publication of *The Fundamentals*, a twelve-volume set of essays defining Protestant orthodoxy.[11] Abandoning the justice work of the social gospel movement, they instead favored the exclusive pursuit of personal piety and evangelism.

Their movement crossed over and became a political force when William Jennings Bryan, a Christian politician who had embraced social gospel ideas during his three presidential campaigns, joined the fundamentalists in his drive against teaching the scientific theory of evolution. Bryan's forceful prosecution won the famous 1925 Scopes trial in Dayton, Tennessee, in which teacher John Scopes was found guilty of violating the state's Butler Act, which forbade the teaching of evolution in public schools. The media spectacle around the trial put the fundamentalist-modernist divide on national display, and public opinion mocked the American fundamentalists, driving the movement underground soon after. Though many modern evangelicals distinguish themselves from fundamentalists, the fundamentalists' focused pursuit of personal piety, biblical inerrancy, and evangelism would emerge as the enduring values of the evangelical faith for the next century.

Today, the black-white divide among evangelicals is far greater than it is among the broader American population. Sociologists Michael Emerson and Christian Smith explain why in their seminal book *Divided by Faith: Evangelical Religion and the Problem of Race in America*. In researching the book, the sociologists interviewed more than 2,500 Americans by phone and nearly 200 evangelicals in person across twenty-three states.[12] They also drew from the University of Chicago's General Social Survey. They found that historic patterns of inequality between white and black evangelicals continue to play out today, even though the groups share many faith principles and an evangelical heritage. Why? Because of the starkly different ways black and white evangelicals interpret the world.

What the schism comes down to is a gap between how much weight each side gives to individual responsibility, on the one hand, and systemic oppression, on the other. Evangelicals focus on personal responsibility as a core element of their faith, Emerson and Smith note: if you want to live a positive, moral life, you and you alone are responsible for maintaining a healthy personal relationship first with Christ, and then with others.

For white evangelicals, this position is absolute; any social problems are seen as rooted in negative relationships and poor choices. There is little room for any way of thinking that places the blame for social conditions outside the individual. We see this in the multitude of worship songs and sermons that focus on the individual's personal faith narrative; collective sin is typically ignored.

On the other hand, black evangelicals value personal responsibility but also understand that unfair systems and history deeply impact social circumstances and the fate of those subject to these systems. This is evidenced in theology that emphasizes deliverance for the oppressed and a salvation that not only offers freedom from the enemy, but a salvation that is collective—as opposed to individual—in nature. These themes have translated into the language of civil rights and cohesive community action, which has its origins in the black church.

The segregation of churches around these radically different perspectives has given rise to a white theology that, developed in isolation, routinely invalidates black beliefs. This, in turn, has helped feed white evangelical support of policies and institutions that carry out black oppression.[13]

It was during the civil rights movement that these tensions, long simmering, erupted. As black churches led a nationwide movement to end Jim Crow segregation, white evangelicals disengaged or actively fought the movement. In the South, white evangelicals stood firmly for segregation; in the North, they focused on battling communism and theological liberalism.

In 1954, Billy Graham banned segregated seating at his crusades and invited fellow preacher Martin Luther King Jr. to deliver a crusade meeting's opening prayer. But Graham rejected King's public protest tactics and believed that changing laws could not change sinful individuals.

Other evangelical leaders, such as Jerry Falwell, spent much of the 1950s and 1960s galvanizing Southern evangelicals toward preserving segregation.[14] After the US Supreme Court mandated school integration in *Brown v. Board of Education* in 1954, Falwell urged whites to form private "segregation academies" in order to keep their children out of integrated schools. He called the separation of the races a "line of distinction" drawn by God.

As the civil rights movement heated up in the 1960s, evangelicals remained largely ambivalent and silent, if not opposed to the dramatic progress unfolding across the country. Even Billy Graham declined the 1963 invitation to King's famous "I Have a Dream" speech, responding, "Only when Christ comes again will little white children of Alabama walk hand in hand with little black children."[15]

By the 1970s, the Internal Revenue Service began targeting private Christian schools for racially discriminatory practices by threatening to revoke their tax-exempt status. In the resulting outrage from white evangelicals, conservative operatives saw their opportunity to form a new political coalition. By the decade's end, the contemporary Religious Right was born, in the form of Falwell's Moral Majority—a national organization that campaigned on issues important to conservative Christians.[16]

I have long wondered why white evangelicals—steeped in Jesus's messages of equality, justice, and neighborly love—routinely sided with our country's most oppressive systems throughout history. Drawing from their research, Emerson and Smith offer this damning conclusion: "Evangelicals usually fail to challenge the system . . . because they support the American system and enjoy its fruits. They share the Protestant work ethic, support laissez-faire economics, and sometimes fail to evaluate whether the social system is consistent with their Christianity."[17]

BETWEEN TWO WORLDS

For the college-age Lisa, these ideas filtered through the background; they were not concepts that she critically engaged. She did not know how to reconcile the evangelical emphasis on personal responsibility with what her family had taught her about their own history: how sometimes the government or a larger force acts upon you in ways that you can't control. Racially based policies had profoundly affected the destiny of her ancestors: Under the Indian Removal Act of 1830, her maternal grandfather's ancestors, Cherokee and Chickasaw Native Americans, were forced out of the land they had known for thousands of years. Her maternal grandmother had descended from enslaved Africans. On her father's side, the 1917 Jones Act allowed Lisa's great-grandfather to bring his family from Puerto Rico to the United States.

"Policies either helped my family flourish or limited its liberty to the point of oppression," Lisa would later write in *Left, Right, and Christ*, a book coauthored with conservative D. C. Innes.[18]

But for most of college, subconsciously aware of the white evangelical values around her, she ignored this heritage. When her mother, Sharon, reminded Lisa of the differences in white and black theology (white people spoke about salvation from their personal sins while black people spoke about salvation from institutional oppression), Sharon emphasized the gospel's promise of deliverance from systemic evil—now *that* was good news to black people. Sharon was the first person to introduce this framework to Lisa. But Lisa rejected this.

"I think what I was probably doing was trying to say, 'Mom, I can be black and also evangelical.' But what I didn't understand was how my way of being evangelical . . . was not recognizing the ways that evangelical theology and politics had actually worked to reinforce black oppression over the last century, especially in the twentieth century."

Lisa held so firmly to the white evangelical marriage of faith and politics that she pushed her mother away. Once, in a debate about abortion, Lisa insisted that her mother's pro-choice position was immoral. She argued that no circumstance made abortion allowable, even if the mother's life was at stake.

Then Sharon told Lisa about the time a recent pregnancy had threatened her survival and how the doctors aborted the baby to save her life. Lisa looked out the window and began to cry. She thought about the sibling she would never know. Then she looked her mother in the eyes and said, "They should have saved the baby."

Lisa and her mother had long sparred over issues of black identity, white evangelicalism, and politics, but this moment drove the sword deep. Decades would pass before they restored their relationship and before Lisa would understand the lessons her mother had tried to impart to her.

But in that moment, as a college student swept up in the conservative evangelical movement, Lisa distanced herself from her mother's concept of black identity and made herself—her beliefs, her politics, her mannerisms, and her attire—as indistinguishable from her white evangelical peers as possible. It was easy to reject her mother's values. Why? Because in that era of her life, she equated white faith values with truth, authority, and orthodoxy.

THE EVANGELICAL RAINBOW

White evangelicals have a long history of discrediting and distancing themselves from black evangelical values. They've been so effective at defining Christian orthodoxy by white values and white identity that today "evangelical" tends to conjure images of a conservative, white Christian, despite the fact that there is a deep heritage of black, Hispanic, Asian, and Native American evangelical faith in our country.

News coverage of evangelicals routinely turns only to white evangelical voices. The same goes for the use of polling figures. In the 2012 elections, media outlets typically reported survey results that looked exclusively at "white evangelicals," excluding from their figures black Protestants, the majority of whom identify with evangelical theology but vote overwhelmingly for Democrats. These figures also left out Latino evangelical Protestants, who make up 16 percent of all Latino registered voters, account for a fast-growing religious segment, and are typically split politically, with about half inclined toward the Democrats and a third inclined toward Republicans.[19] Asian Protestants are also omitted, even though they make up 22 percent of US Asian adults, and those identifying as evangelical count among the most religious groups in the country; they lean toward the GOP, but to a lesser degree than white evangelicals.[20] Furthermore, while many minorities don't call themselves "evangelical," they should be counted as evangelical based on shared faith values and the affiliation of many minority churches with evangelical denominations. By excluding this huge population of minority evangelicals, media outlets miss a major part of the evangelical story.

Of course, the Religious Right wants this habit to continue. By dominating the news cycle, it perpetuates the illusion that its values define all of evangelicalism. It appears dominant, unified, and unchallenged, even though it actually stands for just one segment of a broader group.

Keep the media focused on the conservative white evangelical population, and they'll miss the fact that the minority population is redefining evangelicalism with its escalating numbers and strong cultural values.

PROGRESSIVE EVANGELICAL HISTORY

There was a moment in the 1970s, before the Religious Right launched, when evangelical leaders tried bridging the black-white divide. Recall the birth of the progressive evangelical movement, when leaders met at a run-down YMCA hotel in Chicago in 1973 for the Thanksgiving Workshop.

By this time, black evangelicals had made steep departures from their white counterparts, writes historian David Swartz in *Moral Minority: The Evangelical Left in an Age of Conservatism*.[21] Coalitions such as the National Black Evangelical Association, founded in 1963 as the National Negro Evangelical Association, openly criticized white denominations for their silence on civil rights. The younger generation of black evangelicals took its cue from the civil rights movement, voicing dissent with vigor, criticizing discrimination by evangelical colleges, dismissing older and more moderate black thinkers as "too white," and protesting the lack of black representation and leadership in groups like InterVarsity.

But at the Thanksgiving Workshop, racial reconciliation seemed possible. Black evangelical leaders like John Perkins and William Pannell began conversations about racial justice with progressive white evangelical leaders. Perkins felt encouraged by these white believers of like-minded "precious faith." The leaders of the Thanksgiving Workshop continued hosting conferences throughout the 1970s, and from the get-go they had acknowledged in their Chicago Declaration "the conspicuous responsibility of the evangelical community for perpetuating the personal attitudes and institutional structures that have divided the body of Christ along color lines."[22]

But optimism faded when action did not follow. The black leaders wanted the white leaders to craft a game plan for combating racism within white evangelical culture that involved "decisive and immediate action"—including promotion of minorities to the boards and policy-making bodies of evangelical organizations, implementation of affirmative action programs that encouraged the "full incorporation" of minorities at all levels of evangelical organizations, and incorporation of minority teaching materials in white evangelical structures. But the conversations in the 1974 and 1975 workshops failed to secure commitments, with discussions focusing instead on social action theory while omitting black theology and black activism.[23] At the 1975 workshop, NBEA founder William Bentley listened to the long, theoretical presentations offered by white leaders and grew frustrated by the exclusion of black concerns. He finally stood to say, "I question whether you people can even see us blacks."[24]

In the years that followed, sentiments like Bentley's spread as white evangelicals seemed to drop black interests from their agenda. A 1975 conference organized to address race garnered a small crowd and only a few big-name leaders. Jim Wallis's publication, the *Post-American* (which would later become *Sojourners*), pared back its coverage of race issues. Meetings between editors at the *Post-American* and NBEA leaders grew confrontational and drove a deeper wedge between the races. Workshop organizers tried forming a center for the study of racism, but it flopped. They also tried reserving spots for blacks on the workshop planning committee, but couldn't find enough leaders to serve. Racial conflicts intensified and even went public. Perkins and Tom Skinner, a founding member of NBEA, openly attacked Gordon-Conwell Theological Seminary, calling it the "biggest rip-off in evangelical history" for abandoning founder A. J. Gordon's mission to train urban blacks.[25]

By the end of the 1970s, black evangelicals retreated from the progressive white evangelical movement, instead moving toward a more rigorous black theology that forged a stronger sense of black identity and self-acceptance among their own congregations. Swartz writes that the emphasis on black identity deepened the divisions among progressive evangelicals.[26] Others argue that the white evangelical blind spot to the concerns of black leaders played a part in fueling the increasingly bitter clash. Wherever the blame lay, segregated congregations and the divided leadership thwarted the momentum of the progressive evangelical movement, clearing the way for the newly mobilized Religious Right to steal the spotlight.

QUESTIONS

One decade later, in the late 1980s, the Religious Right had effectively sidelined progressive evangelicals from the national conversation. This was evident in the pro-life demonstrations swarming college campuses and in the new, rigorous model of evangelical faith so many young people began following. For Lisa, that meant mastering the motions of conservative white evangelicalism. She faithfully supplied her chants to the pro-life rallies and heckled pro-choice demonstrators when they marched through campus.

She could recite the "Four Spiritual Laws," an evangelistic tool developed by Campus Crusade founder Bill Bright. The laws, printed on pocket-sized tracts, explain the faith's core principles and the path to salvation: Law one, God loves you and offers a wonderful plan for your life. Law two, man is sinful and separated from God. Therefore, he cannot know and experience God's love and plan for his life. Law three, Jesus Christ is God's only provision for man's sin. Through Him you can know and experience God's love and plan for your life. Law four, we must individually receive Jesus Christ as Savior and Lord; then we can know and experience God's love and plan for our lives.

Meanwhile, personal piety was imperative; Lisa worked hard to eradicate sin from her life. She devoted most of her spare time to the evangelical cause, attending every club meeting, retreat, and leadership conference that she could. The summer after her freshman year she went on a mission trip where, armed with a gold booklet outlining the Four Spiritual Laws, she approached strangers on the boardwalk in Wildwood, NJ; told them about salvation through Christ; and with many, led them in a prayer of repentance.[27]

But toward the end of college, Lisa began to feel a gnawing unease. She had a growing interest in racial issues, but often squashed those inclinations for the comfort of those around her. When she and her friends watched *Glory*, the 1989 movie about the first black unit of the Union army in the Civil War, Lisa felt a mix of strong emotions. The movie spoke to her; her great-great-grandfather, after all, had fought in the Civil War. "It was personal for me," she said. She wanted to process her feelings aloud but she knew she was alone. "I realized I couldn't necessarily share this with my friends. I had to exclude part of myself to be accepted by the group."

Moments like these prompted bigger questions about the relationship between faith and racial identity. What did it mean to be a black woman of faith? Did it even matter? And if it did, what should she do about that? Who could serve as her role model? It also raised uncomfortable questions about the true essence of Christianity. Was it all about conversion, personal piety, and Republican values? She wasn't sure anymore.

Not until her final year of college did these questions escalate to what Lisa would describe as a breakthrough, when she awoke to the fact that she had been suffocating herself for years.

JOHN PERKINS

Lisa had not yet heard of John Perkins, a man whose story would inspire her own journey. Perkins is one of the few prominent black evangelical leaders who have been able to cross the racial divide. He and a handful of contemporaries spent the decades following the civil rights movement developing a theology of racial reconciliation rooted in combining faith with racial identity and life experiences.

Perkins grew up in rural Mississippi in the 1930s and 1940s.[28] In his autobiography, *Let Justice Roll Down*, and in his book *With Justice for All: A Strategy for Community Development*, Perkins unravels the details of his deeply impoverished, hardscrabble childhood. His mother died when he was seven months old. His father left shortly after. His grandmother raised him and his brother, Clyde. White folks paid them a pittance to work as sharecroppers, and the three lived on a plantation in a crowded three-room shack with about a dozen other relatives. Local whites weren't wealthy, and felt the best way to preserve their modest status was by "keeping the blacks in line."[29]

As a teenager, John witnessed tragedy and injustice. His brother, Clyde, was shot by a deputy marshal while Clyde and his girlfriend waited at the black entrance of a cinema. Clyde bled in John's arms as the two rode to the hospital. He died soon after. There was no official inquiry into the incident. White folks "took it for granted that whites in authority were always justified no matter what they did," John writes. Most black folks were silent too. "They were practical enough to know where the power lay." At age sixteen, John boarded a train heading west for California. He wanted a new life. He seemed to be leaving Mississippi for good.

It was in California that John encountered real opportunities. He got good work making cast-iron pipes at a foundry, climbed the ranks, started a family and, years later, found faith. It was his faith that ultimately brought him back to Mississippi after he had been away for fifteen years. His goal: to forge reconciliation between the black and white communities using biblical principles.

John was part of a larger contingent of rising black leaders forming an evangelical movement called "racial reconciliation." His contemporaries were Tom Skinner, who grew up in impoverished Harlem and went on to become a traveling evangelist focused on teaching reconciliation to youth, and Samuel Hines. Hines, a Jamaican who rebelled at a young age against his strict religious upbringing, later became a minister and relocated to Washington, DC, where he practiced reconciliation. William Pannell, who was raised by a white Plymouth Brethren family in suburban Detroit, experienced intimacy within white evangelical culture but also struggled with being "a colored stranger" in his community. Among white evangelicals, he was both an insider and a critic, and he brought that perspective to the reconciliation movement. Other significant leaders included men like James Earl Massey and E. V. Hill.

Together, these leaders—all black, evangelical, connected to white evangelicals, and influenced by Martin Luther King Jr.—helped shape the theology of reconciliation, which asserts that the central message of the gospel is the reconciliation of human beings to God and to each other. John Perkins framed the practical application of reconciliation through the "three R's of community development," which include relocation to places of need, reconciliation with God and neighbors across barriers like race, and redistribution of resources to help people break the cycle of inequality. As George Yancey explains in a 1998 paper, this cohort of leaders outlined four key steps to racial reconciliation: First, people of different races need to develop primary relationships with each other. Second, they must acknowledge the ways social structures cause inequality. Third, because most of the people who set up these social structures and benefited from them were white people, they need to repent of their personal, historical, and social sins. And last, it's key for African Americans to forgive repenting white people individually and corporately, and repent of their own hatred toward white people and society.[30]

The movement had some white supporters among progressive evangelicals early in the 1970s, but their numbers were uneven and ultimately the audience was limited. In the late 1980s and 1990s, however, the movement experienced a resurgence as new leaders of varied racial backgrounds joined the fold. Mainstream evangelical groups embraced conversations about racial reconciliation. The Christian publishing industry released a succession of books and study guides. Racial reconciliation conferences attracted a new generation. Sermons addressed the subject and leaders issued formal apologies. In 1995, Southern Baptists publicly requested forgiveness for their historic defense of slavery and their continued racial sin. Billy Graham wrote that racial conflict "threatens the very foundation of modern society."[31] In 1997, the *Wall Street Journal* called evangelicals, "the most energetic element of society addressing racial divisions."[32]

BREAKTHROUGH

In the late 1980s, around the same time the initiatives of black evangelicals began making modest headway, Lisa was wrapping up her junior year at Rutgers. She learned about a new summer project Campus Crusade had been developing: an urban mission aimed at immersing students in the world of the poor. The same group that had sent her to the front lines to protest abortion rights had also decided to embed students in environments where they might learn more about social justice, a model crafted by John Perkins that today represents the heart of the reconciliation movement within the evangelical world. Unintentionally, the agendas of the Religious Right and the progressive evangelical movement were beginning to merge. And for the first time in Lisa's life, the message of black progressive evangelicals had reached her.

In New York City, Lisa volunteered at the Love Kitchen, the soup kitchen of the Times Square Church. On her first day, while walking up and down Eighth Avenue giving boxed lunches to homeless people, Lisa met Johnny, a homeless veteran who lived in a doorway across the street. He had never made it into the Love Kitchen before because he frequently soiled himself and was too weak to climb the stairs. Lisa began visiting him daily in his nook, listening to his stories about war, his family, and his life before becoming, as he put it, "a wino." Johnny was black and had "the biggest eyes and biggest tears," Lisa recalled. They laughed a lot; there was something so familiar about Johnny.

"It felt like coming home," she said. For so long she had been a foreigner adapting to the customs of white evangelical culture; but with

Johnny it was as if they spoke each other's native tongue. Even though they came from different economic worlds, they got each other. Lisa felt no need to hide any part of herself or filter her behavior. There was a shared sense of humor, a natural conversational rhythm, and an immediate familiarity. "I felt like I was talking to my grandpop."

Next, her team moved on to an at-risk youth camp, Camp Comanche, which served mostly African American kids. Lisa was a camp counselor to a tent of twelve- to fourteen-year-old girls from the Bronx and Bedford-Stuyvesant. Over campfire songs, swimming lessons, and stargazing, Lisa was reminded of her childhood friends from Philadelphia. "There was something that was just free that wasn't in the community I was part of" back at Rutgers.

"Those kids could have been my kids," Lisa told me. "Or they could have been my brothers or sisters. I just fell in love with those kids. I had an immersion experience among my own people that I had not been able to have since we moved from Philadelphia to Cape May. That summer was when I was reintroduced to myself as a black person and also when I began to see myself through the eyes of God, as someone made in the image of God whom God loves. God loves these people and therefore God loves me as a black person."

All the while, Lisa and her fellow participants, about thirty students—mostly white—from other Campus Crusade chapters, were reading Perkins's *With Justice for All*. As a group, they never explicitly discussed the racial themes of the book, but they did walk away with such "a strong sense . . . that God loves the city and God loves poor people" that in the years that followed, many participants devoted their lives to urban ministry.

For Lisa, the Perkins book opened her eyes to the ways racism and systemic injustice afflicted African Americans. His writing offered the historic and theological education she had been missing in her years in white evangelicalism, and his knowledge, paired with her time with Johnny and the camp kids, unlocked a part of her faith that helped her see the beauty and worth of her people and even herself.

Once the theology and ministry of progressive black evangelical forefathers had reached Lisa, it sparked an awakening within. Very quickly, Lisa discovered that beyond her world of starched pants and neutral tones, a complicated, electric world was beckoning her to see faith through a different lens.

Lisa sensed a tectonic shift inside herself, a breakthrough that would change her forever. She felt fired up but also petrified: how would this new Lisa survive senior year amid her all-white community back at Rutgers?

TWO

Good Christian Girls

JENNIFER

One Sunday morning in the summer of 2008, Jennifer Crumpton, thirty-five, walked into a cavernous megachurch auditorium in Birmingham, Alabama. She sat down among the cascading stadium seats that pointed toward one focal point, a young male pastor with buzz-cut blond hair and a chiseled jawline, standing on the stage, flanked by Jumbotrons and washed in stage lights.

Jennifer had come to this Southern Baptist church to learn more about this pastor, David Platt, who at twenty-nine was shaking up the evangelical world. His sermons criticized consumer Christianity and megachurch materialism. He encouraged his mostly white, wealthy congregation to pursue downward mobility and to live off what they needed while giving the rest away. This Southern Baptist wunderkind led a congregation of more than four thousand members, had a *New York Times* best-selling book, and had practically been anointed as a rising leader of the next evangelical generation. Impressed that Southern Baptists held someone young and antimaterialistic with such esteem, Jennifer began to see Platt as "a sign of hope" that the staunchly conservative denomination was turning a corner. Sitting in her cushioned seat, she watched the lights train on Platt's youthful figure, and eagerly awaited his message.

Jennifer had visited Platt's church not only to observe this rising-star pastor, but also to hear from God. Up to this point, Jennifer's adult life had taken many abrupt twists and turns: though an Alabama native, she had left at age thirty to escape the sexism of her Southern Baptist upbringing and to build a new life for herself in New York City. Of course, there she found another variation of misogyny. In Alabama, society prized an unwed woman's virginity and a married woman's home-making skills; in New York, she met a string of men who valued women for their sexual availability and not much more.

For years Jennifer struggled to unlearn the unhealthy gender expectations foisted upon her. In the process, she emerged a changed woman. She read feminist books. She left unhealthy relationships. She processed her internalized sexism with her closest friends. By her mid-thirties, Jennifer had lost her faith and regained it again. She had gotten married and divorced. As an advertising executive, she had climbed the cut-throat ranks of her industry, but woke up thirteen years into her career unhappy with the work and ready for a drastic change.

The day she walked into Platt's church, Jennifer's life was already veering in a new direction. She had recently left advertising to enroll in seminary. She had been accepted to Union Theological Seminary in Manhattan, but beyond knowing the basic outline of the curriculum, she had no idea what to expect of this experience and what it meant for her future. Before school began, she pulled herself from the throbbing crowds of Manhattan for a brief respite in her hometown, a suburb of Birmingham. She wanted to relax with family and old friends and take in the familiar sights of the wide-bending streets and canopies of dogwood trees. Here she would reflect on her seminary goals and listen for God's guidance on her future. Where would seminary take her? To a pulpit of her own as a church pastor? To become head of a Christian nonprofit? Would she forge a ministry of her own? She envisioned herself doing something rewarding and profoundly meaningful. The possibilities excited her.

During the service at Platt's megachurch, Jennifer listened to the thousands of voices lifted in worship and sang along. She looked around at the audience. They were young and old, men and women, dressed impeccably in their business casual attire. When Platt began speaking, she straightened in her seat; she had been waiting for this moment. Would God speak to her through Platt?

Standing at the podium, Platt told his listeners that the church was nominating deacons and elders that day. Jennifer expected this to be a brief announcement before he moved on to the meatier parts of the service. Instead, Platt began sermonizing about why women could not be nominated to these positions. He cited Bible verses from 1 Timothy 3:1–13, which details the qualifications required for church overseers and deacons. An example of the text: "A deacon must be faithful to his wife and must manage his children and his household well." Platt argued that based on the pronouns used and the social position of women in biblical times, God barred women from leadership. Jennifer listened, waiting for the punch line, but none came. *Is he serious?* she thought. And then a strange series of emotions tumbled like dominos inside of her. First amusement, then confusion, then shock and discouragement, followed by so many questions.

Platt's message plunged Jennifer back into the patriarchal Southern Baptist world of her youth. She had spent her whole life trying to unlearn the message that women ranked lower than men in intellect, value, and leadership abilities. She had hoped that her generational leaders—leaders like Platt—were slowly upending those traditional ideas and expanding the church's vision of who belonged in leadership. Jennifer had gone to Platt's church hoping to hear from God, hoping to be filled with inspiration as she began seminary training to become a faith leader herself. Instead, Platt's message served a devastating blow. It reinforced all the invalidating, sexist messages she had worked to silence. For a moment she wondered, was there anything for her on the other side of seminary? If women weren't allowed to lead, how could she find a place to use her talents and fulfill her dreams?

For one long moment, Jennifer had no answers to her questions. She did not know that very soon she would find the answers on her own. She did not know that in a few short years she would forge an entire ministry around those answers. She did not know that her ministry would add momentum to the growing push for gender equality in the church. She did not know because in that moment, with the weight of Platt's words on her shoulders, the entrenched sexist values of her past threatened to overpower her.

SHE MUST BE QUIET

I do not permit a woman to teach or to assume
authority over a man; she must be quiet.
1 Timothy 2:12

Conservative evangelicals have long restricted the roles of women. In the nineteenth century, their efforts increased in reaction to the suffrage and gender equality efforts of first-wave feminists. In the twentieth century, their fight against feminism reached a fevered pitch in the wake of second-wave feminism and the sexual revolution of the 1960s. Harold Lindsell, an editor of *Christianity Today,* the flagship conservative evangelical magazine, and former president of the Evangelical Theological Society, concluded that "the world is in the process of committing suicide."[1] Lindsell, a bespectacled professor and staunch champion for biblical inerrancy, argued that the country was revolting against God's natural order. "We have fornication, adultery and lesbianism, homosexuality, wife-swapping, rape, sodomy, incest. . . . Society is becoming unglued."[2]

Leaders like Lindsell worked to establish a theology rooted in assumptions of female subordination and male authority. Lindsell pointed to a departure from biblical inerrancy as the root cause of heresy and moral decay.[3] By extension, conservative evangelicals equated a belief in biblical inerrancy to orthodox thinking, and used this to advance strict gender boundaries: the apostle Paul commanded that women not hold authority over men, therefore obedience to scripture can result only in male authority and female submission. Conservatives argued that because God ordained male leadership and female subordination, any departure from these views assaulted God's creation.

Many evangelicals disagreed with this theological approach. Moderate believers leaned toward more allegorical readings of the Bible and preferred to interpret texts in their historical and cultural contexts, often leading to more egalitarian beliefs. But Lindsell and other conservative leaders rebuked these Christians and warned that departing from inerrancy destroyed faith. While some conservatives conceded that women deserved job equality in the workforce and were allowed to lead, for example, the music or children's ministry, their unbending belief in female submission to men would not allow for women's ordination. "I believe there are many opportunities for women to be engaged in ministry and serving the Lord," said Morris Chapman, a Southern Baptist leader. "It's simply that I believe the Bible teaches that . . . the role of pastor in the church [is] to be a male."[4]

Conservative evangelicals codified these beliefs in a concept called "complementarianism," which asserts that men and women have different but complementary roles in the home, church, and society, with men leading and women following. They buttressed their ideology with religious authority, using theology to argue that God himself restricted women's roles to motherhood and homemaking. In 1970 Billy Graham told the readers of *Ladies' Home Journal* that they belonged in the home: "Wife, mother, homemaker—this is the appointed destiny of real womanhood."[5]

This theological line grew more rigid over the course of the 1970s, especially since the civil rights movement had made theological arguments for racial segregation taboo. While toning down calls for racial separation, evangelicals campaigned more loudly against the threat to gender order. They coalesced around the launch of the Religious Right, fueling a "family values" campaign that quickly spread to local legislatures and congregations.

Strikingly, the complementarian model flourished largely because women emerged as its most vocal advocates. Dorothy Patterson, wife of Paige Patterson, president of Southwestern Baptist Theological Seminary, emerged as a leading promoter of this theology, traveling the country and addressing female-only audiences. Though she assumed a prominent place in the evangelical world, especially among Southern

Baptists, and taught as a theology professor, she identified first as a "homemaker." Sandra Foh argued in her 1979 book *Women and the Word of God* that evangelical egalitarians had rejected the Bible. "Biblical feminists," she wrote, "do not believe that God has given us his word true and trustworthy." Antifeminist Mary Pride insisted that wifely homemaking was core to female identity, and violating their God-ordained gender role was a perversion.[6] One of the most controversial figures of the era, a Catholic named Phyllis Schlafly, mobilized women across the country to campaign against the Equal Rights Amendment. By Schlafly's logic, the amendment would dismantle the traditional family and thereby strip women of their rights as homemakers and restrict motherhood. This increasingly vocal group of women argued that feminists were destroying the very essence of womanhood.

I remember learning about complementarian theology when I joined InterVarsity Christian Fellowship, despite the fact that InterVarsity stands in stark contrast to other student ministries for its decisive support of women in leadership. But conservative complementarian culture infected even an organization that purported to be egalitarian. At InterVarsity, nobody I knew openly identified as "feminist." When I declared myself a feminist to a close friend, she insisted that it was only proper to be a "*Christian* feminist," the kind that celebrates strong women but is actively antiabortion. In a female-only small group, we studied passages of the Bible about wifely obedience. On the industrial blue carpet of our dorm room, we sat amid Bibles and boxes of candy. I pointed to the other verses that spoke of *mutual* submission between wives and husbands. But my bright, funny, independent college girlfriends insisted that, as one of them put it, a wife could be sassy, argumentative, and brilliant, but at the end of the day she should let her husband have the final word.

I was shocked when most of the women in the circle agreed with her. I grew up in an egalitarian household and, as a young girl, I loved seeing my power-suited mother come home from her accounting job with stories from the office. She and my father, a civil engineer who also worked all day, kept the household humming along by sharing cooking and cleaning duties—and they still found the time to help me with homework at night. I'm grateful for the example my parents set. To me, their marriage was a model of partnership and balance, and I couldn't imagine why my female Christian friends couldn't see the benefits of sharing authority and support in a relationship.

Many male evangelical peers reinforced the complementarian message, countering my objections with gentle observations about how as the head of the household, the husband's role was less about dominance and more about being a source of nourishment, wisdom, and leadership.

I found other women in the group who, like me, identified as egalitarian. We laughed at the way more conservative women said the top trait they sought in a man was protection. "Protection from what?" one friend asked. "Bears?" Other egalitarians were more diplomatic, insisting we give equal weight to the complementarian model.

To me, that system felt oppressive and I wished someone would call it out as such. Instead, so many of the smart women around me were preparing themselves for subservience. During my senior year, the book that made its rounds at my fellowship was *Every Man's Battle,* a self-help book that Christian men used to win "the war on sexual temptation." It included special sections for wives reading along, encouraging modest dressing—and sexual availability and hotness. Advice included: "When . . . his hunger for you escalates, help him without complaint," and since men desire sexual release every forty-eight to seventy-two hours, the authors say, "Give him release." One wife said in an interview, "I used to think that Victoria's Secret was a store for sleazy women. My husband helped me understand that my wearing 'intimate apparel' was a big plus for him. I think Christian women need to feel freer to use whatever turns their man on." But this was quickly followed by a warning from the authors: "At the same time, wives have to be careful of how their appearance can turn on other men. The Bible instructs women to dress modestly, but many women tend to take such verses lightly." The condescending message bothered me, especially the unspoken, but underlying implication throughout the book that women's immodesty was to blame for so much male sexual sin. I criticized the book, but felt alone and "unchristian" in my opinion. I tried to persuade others to consider my point of view, but they would just smile and change the subject.[7]

THE MEN, THE MEN, THE MEN

As the Christian Right sought to restore "traditional gender roles" in every facet of church and family life during the 1970s and 1980s, Jennifer was part of the first generation raised to embody all of these expectations.

Jennifer grew up in a white, lower middle-class Birmingham suburb. Families lived in bungalows or split-level homes with big yards. Jennifer's rare occasions of rebellion looked more like idyllic Hallmark moments: summer days jumping into the local creek with her best friend, against her parents' wishes.

During childhood, before her culture's loaded expectations of women had infiltrated her consciousness, she oozed with confidence, in both her body and her brain. She learned ballet and loved the agency she felt over her body and the way she could use it for artistic expression. She spent her free time romping around the woods, chasing butterflies, delighting at the texture of strange bugs and playing with neighborhood cats. She felt limitless. She understood that she was a girl, but saw no reason why she couldn't be a boy. She didn't understand the difference. "I thought I could do anything," she recalled. "I thought I was just as smart as anybody. I remember feeling this vividly. I didn't have any idea about gender. At some point, that changed drastically."

Once she hit puberty, the expectations of her Southern Baptist culture were thrust upon her. She slowly internalized the patriarchal message of the Christian Right, limiting her imagination to her future roles of wife and mother, and possibly teacher or administrator if she got a job. Year by year, Jennifer grew more anxious, wanting to do everything right. She read her Bible nightly, spoke respectfully to adults, and coordinated cross and fish necklaces with her modest sundresses every Sunday.

Jennifer's family was an icon of suburban family life—a mother, a father, and three young daughters driving to church in a powder-blue station wagon. Later, her family stopped attending church because life for her parents had gotten so busy (two jobs, three kids) that they needed to rest on Sunday. But Jennifer continued all by herself. She hung on every word the pastor spoke. He wore polished suits and had "a commanding presence," pacing the platform and speaking without notes. While people rarely spoke explicitly about "the role of women," Jennifer understood what was expected of her just by looking around. Every leader at church was a man because, as they saw things, God designed men for authority and women for service as the "help meet," or assistant, just as God had instructed in Genesis, starting with Eve.

At home, Jennifer saw that men ruled the house. Her father controlled her mother. "He told her when she could come and go. He made all the decisions." Jennifer grew up internalizing her parents' power imbalance and understood relationships only in the context of tension. At holidays, the women cooked all day, sweating in the kitchen, whipping up multicourse meals, as the men relaxed in the next room, watching sports and talking. After the women finished cooking and presenting the meal, Jennifer's grandmother would instinctively say, "Let the men get their plates first." When the men finished eating, they would wander back into the living room, leaving their dishes behind for the women to clean up. A similar scenario played out during regular dinners at home, Jennifer added. "My dad would just waltz in, sit down, and eat." When he finished eating, "he would just leave his plate."

In a million other unstated ways in the home, in church, and in the larger culture, a clear message came through and coalesced in Jennifer's mind. "The man was always the most important person. You didn't do anything to mess up whatever the men wanted to have going on. If the men were watching sports, you were quiet. If the men were hungry, they went first. The men, the men, the men. Men clearly had some inexplicable preordained something that made them more important all the time." Men managed the family finances, making major decisions about the family's future. Men spoke to other men and boys about serious matters, such as careers, current events, and big life decisions. Throughout Jennifer's life, even after she conquered the competitive advertising world, her father, a businessman who sold furniture, never broached the subject of her career, even though he did so with her brothers-in-law. There was an unspoken assumption that when it came to conversations, women merely gossiped; they were not intellectual equals to men.

It was also assumed that men were right all of the time. Jennifer didn't question that. If a man made a decision about anything—whether it was determining a biblical belief or choosing where the family would eat that night—a woman should agree. Jennifer focused on playing this part perfectly. "You just thought, this was the world's order. The men were in charge."

EVANGELICAL FEMINISTS

Beyond Jennifer's world, a new evangelical feminist movement had been emerging. It sprang to life over the course of her childhood, challenging gender norms and expanding the vision of womanhood.

One key moment in the movement came in October 1969, when Letha Scanzoni, a Christian feminist writer, sat down at her typewriter. A diminutive thirty-four-year-old, with short brown curls and an easy smile, Letha identified with the struggles of many women her age as she juggled the responsibilities of marriage and children with forging a career. For years she had dreamed about writing a book on women's liberation for an evangelical audience, but it wasn't until this fateful October day that she took the first step in doing so. Over the years, Letha had gotten to know an editor at *Eternity* magazine named Nancy Hardesty. Nancy was plucky, in her late twenties, and had a ready sense of humor. And she wasn't afraid to wear her heart on her sleeve. She had responded positively to Letha's earlier writings about equal-partner marriage, occasionally sending her quick notes about related books and articles. Letha, sensing she had found a "sister Christian feminist," proposed in a typed letter to Nancy that they cowrite this Christian feminist book. Letha predicted that such a project would catapult them into dangerous territory, and imagined their shared values, along with their different perspectives (Letha as a married woman, Nancy as a single woman), would make them good battle partners.

"The men and women who have the strongest opinions and seem most eager to express them are those who have rigid traditional ideas which really restrict women—and they're quick to cite Scripture to back them up," Letha tapped on her typewriter in her letter to Nancy.[8] "Many women in Christian circles would be afraid to voice their disagreements with traditional views, and many others seem perfectly content with things as they are. This is changing, however, among younger evangelicals—particularly on college campuses; and I feel the projected book could be of real help to many of these (both men and women)."

Letha signed her letter, dropped it in the mailbox, and waited.

One week later, Nancy wrote back, offering a heartfelt account of her life situation and her hesitations about what she could contribute to the book. Nancy jokingly described herself as an "old maid school teacher," having recently left her editorial job for a teaching position at Trinity College in Deerfield, Illinois (now Trinity International University). She wrote about the practical and emotional struggles of single life, especially as a woman in evangelical culture. She felt bitter at times. She wrestled against the Christian myth that "one is most truly human in a marriage relationship," and felt that "if you buy this and then don't get married, you have a very difficult time justifying your own continued existence."

From there, the two began to regularly correspond, swapping life updates and hammering out the details of a book that would become *All We're Meant to Be*, which, through scholarly analysis, argues that a contextualized reading of the Bible dismantled hierarchy and polarizing gender roles. In addition to dispelling the myth that God is male (pointing to the biblical images of God as a nursing mother, "baker woman, mother hen, homemaker, Dame Wisdom, midwife, female pelican, and she-bear"), the authors map out a theologically rigorous case for gender equality in all realms, including marriage, the church, and throughout society.[9] They condemn traditional arguments that support female subordination. For example, theologians have long insisted that the biblical assignment to males of the Greek word for "head," *kephale*, supports gender hierarchy.[10] Hardesty and Scanzoni call this "the most blatant example of . . . (the) perversion of God's word," arguing instead that Paul's bodily metaphor points to a message of marital unity.[11] "His point is a simple one: united head and body, we live; severed head from body, we die," they write. The two felt proud of their radical tome, but for years, sensing there was no audience for this, publishers rejected it.

Despite this setback, Letha and Nancy found other forums for their message. Letha's magazine articles earned her invitations to speak to crowded lecture halls at Christian colleges across the country.

In 1973, Nancy was among a small handful of women invited to the historic Thanksgiving Workshop in Chicago, the same group that drew together Ron Sider (the meeting organizer), Jim Wallis, John Perkins, and other progressive evangelicals. Nancy quickly noticed that the convening committee was all male, and that the statement of faith they had drafted, the Chicago Declaration, addressed issues of racism, economic injustice, and militarism, "but [made] no mention of women at all," she recalled later in a 2004 speech.[12]

The all-male committee had planned to make revisions to the declaration, so Nancy raised her hand and asked that they include a statement about women. A member of the committee whispered to Nancy from across the table, "Give me something to add to the statement and I'll try to get it in." So Nancy pulled out a piece of scrap paper and scribbled, "We acknowledge that we have encouraged men to prideful domination and women to passive irresponsibility. So we call both men and women to mutual submission and active discipleship."

After some debate, a modified version of Nancy's statement made it into the final draft of the Chicago Declaration. "Ron Sider later told me that when Billy Graham was shown the statement, he pointed to those sentences as the reason why he would not sign it," recalled Nancy. Still, some Thanksgiving Workshop leaders attempted to include feminist concerns in their agenda. Sider encouraged husbands and wives to "foster mutuality in child care tasks."[13]

One year later, at the 1974 Thanksgiving Workshop, the attendees had diversified somewhat. "It was clear that they intended to widen the group only slightly," recalled Nancy, "and women and blacks would have limited quotas." As part of the workshop, attendees gathered in smaller "caucuses" to tackle the various priorities of the Chicago Declaration. A group of women, including Nancy and others she had personally invited, began discussing their goals for advancing women's rights in the church and society. The Evangelical Women's Caucus was born.

There was immediate energy behind this small group of female evangelical leaders. They had found their kindred spirits, other women who had felt too Christian among secular feminists and too feminist among Christians. Their common ground made agenda crafting easy. They wanted the church to embrace gender-inclusive language and an egalitarian marriage model. And in a bold move, they worked to garner support for the Equal Rights Amendment.

Enthusiasm for feminism was building in the greater evangelical world too. That same year, an editorial published in *Christianity Today* supported the Equal Rights Amendment, and a rough survey showed that Christians favored the amendment by a three-to-one margin.[14] Also that year, Letha and Nancy's book *All We're Meant to Be* finally saw the light of day. It was published by Word Books and became an instant hit. It won *Eternity* magazine's Book of the Year award. It flew off the shelves of Christian bookstores. Decades later *Christianity Today* would list it as one of the "Top 50 Books that Have Shaped Evangelicals," and historians heralded it as "the most influential work in helping launch the evangelical feminist movement."[15]

By harnessing a deep scholarly reading of the scripture, the authors gained credibility among evangelicals. They argued that the gospel of Christ dismantled sinful social systems like patriarchy, equalizing all people, as revealed in Galatians 3:28: "There is neither Jew nor Gentile, neither slave nor free, nor is there male and female, for you are all one in Christ Jesus." Their women's liberation did not stem from the feminist movement, they argued, rather it blossomed out of the gospel message itself. Patriarchy, they insisted, emerged from a fundamental misinterpretation of scripture. Yes, the cherry-picked verses of traditionalists appear to justify gender hierarchy, but Letha and Nancy held that "any teaching in regard to women must square with the basic theological thrust of the Bible." And that basic thrust, they concluded, was equality.

Conservatives fiercely criticized Nancy and Letha's theological approach. Complementarians favored an inerrant, literal interpretation of scripture, and saw Nancy and Letha's analysis as a dangerous departure from that tradition. Very quickly, a splintering occurred between complementarian literalists and egalitarians, who read the Bible in its historical context.

The hottest point of contention was egalitarians' support for women's ordination. Even left-leaning evangelical leaders split over this issue. Among the Thanksgiving Workshop delegates—those forging the broader progressive evangelical movement—many found women's ordination at odds with the Bible. This alienated the female participants from the workshop. Eventually, emboldened by their growing network, the EWC became an independent institution, with its own conferences, leadership structure, publications, and local chapters.

Much like the black evangelicals who departed, feminist evangelicals forged their own movement apart from the progressive evangelical leaders of the Thanksgiving Workshop. This granted the group flexibility to wrestle openly with the issues that concerned its members the most. Though the group didn't take an official stand on reproductive rights, many of its leaders spoke and wrote openly about their pro-choice convictions. But this was a time when "evangelicals were open to various views on abortion," Scanzoni explained, which is why the group encouraged women to speak their minds but also remained sensitive to the varied opinions within its constituency.

Nancy and Letha breathlessly watched a movement take shape as evangelical feminists publicly tackled a range of women's issues. Leaders and followers began to write articles to educate the evangelical masses about the Equal Rights Amendment. They mobilized others to lobby for the ERA. The EWC leaders lobbied legislators, gave speeches at the National Organization for Women rallies, and distributed to evangelicals buttons and bumper stickers that read "People of Faith for ERA." Some openly supported *Roe v. Wade*. Meanwhile, egalitarian principles gained momentum. In the mid-1980s more evangelicals began advocating for women's ordination. Even the conservative Southern Baptist denomination saw a twentyfold jump in its ordained female pastors from 1974 to 1983.[16]

In the years after publishing *All We're Meant to Be*, Nancy and Letha received an outpouring of praise from readers. "We were finding a deep hunger out there," Scanzoni told me, reflecting on that era decades later. In "letter after letter," evangelical women confessed that, for so long, they had felt alone in their feminist inclinations. They celebrated the liberation the book had revealed and shared their resolve to attend college, to become pastors, to pursue their dreams. The EWC helped launch a feminist publication called *Daughters of Sarah*, which grew over the years to a circulation of ten thousand.[17] EWC began holding annual conferences that also flourished over time. By 1978 they had roughly a thousand attendees. Scanzoni recalled the buzz in the conference halls as women expressed astonishment that there were others like them. The evangelical feminist movement felt like an unstoppable train. Where would this movement go? How far would its influence spread? The possibilities seemed endless.

PURITY

Despite this energetic burst of evangelical feminist activity, the movement never did reach Jennifer during her girlhood. Instead, she spent her formative years molding herself in the image of conservative biblical womanhood.

Nowhere was this more challenging than in the realm of dating. As Jennifer blossomed into a young woman, she felt herself wading into tricky territory. There were two important rules for women, and they seemed to be contradictory: one, that responsibility rested with the woman in guarding her virginity and stopping boys from escalating intimacy; and two, that the woman should submit to the man in a relationship.

These values were promoted most vigorously by the True Love Waits movement, launched in 1993. Hundreds of thousands of Christian youths gathered at conferences where they would pledge to remain virgins until their wedding night. This campaign came after Jennifer's teen years, so Jennifer never signed a pledge card, but it systematized the exact message Jennifer had grown up with in Southern Baptist Alabama.

Sex was the one area where gender roles were explicitly discussed. The lessons from youth group and her mother made the takeaways very clear: "Do. Not. Have. Sex." And, "As the female, you are responsible" for keeping relationships chaste. If a couple crossed the line and had sex, "Boys will be boys, but the female was a slut."

In high school Jennifer and her friends dated casually. "It was very innocent," she recalled. Before class a girlfriend might declare that she was "going" with one boy. The couple might share a pizza or a few sweaty-palmed walks between lockers before the relationship faded away. Occasionally there'd be a kiss, or the heat would turn up at a house party where a couple might be found making out in the corner by the coat rack. But it was universally understood among her friends that boys and girls alike were saving sex for marriage.

This sentiment held true even in college. If the conversation ever veered toward the subject of Jesus's second coming, college girls would sigh and say, "I hope Jesus doesn't come back before I get married and get to have sex!"

When rumors about peers having sex swirled, Jennifer's friends would cluck their tongues and lament the lack of female restraint. It was always the woman's fault. Even if she said no to the advances of her boyfriend and he had his way with her anyway, she needed to examine the actions she took that led him to stumble. Was her neckline too revealing? Did she send confusing signals? "Girls just test fate if they cuddle with boys or make out with boys," was the prevailing sentiment.

And while women were responsible for a relationship's purity, they were also taught to follow men, not to lead. The cognitive dissonance was dizzying for Jennifer—take charge but also be subservient. That meant Jennifer could never ask a boy out on a date. "The man approaches you," she learned. She needed to wait passively for one to pursue her. She might tell her girlfriends about a crush, and hope that he'd come around to asking her out. But she could not make the first move—that would make her a promiscuous girl in the eyes of others.

"I never proactively imagined what it is that I wanted," she added. "She had no checklist of traits, no image of an 'ideal boyfriend.' She had no choice in the matter. "It was never on my terms." Her role was clear. Don't speak unless spoken to. Follow his lead.

As Jennifer grew older and began to date more, she struggled under the weight of these expectations. This model did not seem to produce healthy relationships. She constantly felt friction with whomever she was with, and anger would brew beneath the surface as she felt powerless in every partnership. For example, she waited for the guy to define the relationship; she never expressed if she wanted the relationship to advance to the next level of commitment or if she wanted it to slow down. "I felt easily embarrassed about my thoughts and opinions," she recalled. "I didn't speak up about things." So if a boyfriend said or did something that hurt her feelings, she'd stay quiet and simply bottle those emotions within. She didn't even have the confidence to express what she'd want to do on a date. "I had no sense that my opinion mattered at all."

Later, many years into adulthood, Jennifer realized that she did, in fact, have beliefs and opinions and preferences. As a result, the unspoken rule that she subordinate herself to men became more difficult to accept. But instead of questioning or rejecting this value, she thought she'd fare better if she tried *harder* to embrace it. She once sent a boyfriend an enthusiastic e-mail that read something like, "I totally get the concept of submission. You're so wonderful!" Jennifer was striving to be the most godly Christian woman she could be. Also, "somehow I thought it just meant he would treat me really well."

Of course, her efforts did not result in better treatment or healthier relationships. She found herself routinely unhappy, even with the most "ideal" Christian boyfriends. This pattern continued well into adulthood. After all, there didn't seem to be any other way.

THREE

Safety in the Closet

WILL

In the spring of 2011, Will Haggerty, a college sophomore, sat on the grass quietly looking at his girlfriend, Heather.[1] From a distance they looked like a couple sitting in a sun-splashed California park, speechless and dumbstruck by love. But up close, there was anguish in their eyes.

They had come to this park for a heart-to-heart. Their relationship had stalled and Heather could sense that Will was hiding something. *Was there another woman?* Will shook his head. He did have a secret, but by his estimation, it was worse than what Heather had suspected.

Will was gay.

After dating Heather for several months, Will had grown to love her, even if he felt no sexual attraction to her. He hated that he was causing her pain. In that moment he knew he had to come clean.

He tried to speak, but the words got caught in his throat. He had so many fears. His mind raced as he thought about the consequences of coming out. Will and Heather attended a conservative evangelical college, Biola University, where homophobic comments raised few eyebrows and school policy deemed "homosexual behavior" as grounds for dismissal. To Will, the closet felt like the only safe place. Coming out could spell social suicide, scrutiny from the administration, and possible expulsion. Will looked at Heather, who was waiting for an answer. His heart thumped in his chest. And then finally, the words came out.

Growing up, Will learned early on that homosexuality was not just a sin, but the worst sin out there. Nonetheless, he loved his conservative evangelical upbringing. Will was homeschooled, which meant he and his two siblings spent every day under the gentle guidance of their mother. As Will described it, Mrs. Haggerty was an easygoing teacher whose lessons seamlessly wove in conservative values and Christian faith. Her home, nestled in Los Angeles County, was a safe haven, guarding Will and his siblings from the decadent liberalism around them. They played with a carefully curated group of friends, equally sheltered kids from church or from the homeschool community. Together, they were raised on a diet of *Anne of Green Gables*, regular church outings, and Bible lessons.

Unlike most teenagers, Will didn't bristle at his mother's constant presence. "My mom was and is the biggest influence in my life." He told her everything.

But one afternoon, as Will and his mother were watching *The Ellen DeGeneres Show*, something changed. Ellen had dropped her playful banter to implore her viewers to vote against Proposition 8, a ballot measure that would nullify same-sex marriages in California. Scores of religious conservatives supported the measure, viewing gay marriage as an attack on the traditional family. Will grew up listening to pastors call gay people abominable. They'd use a falsetto and limp wrist for a convenient punch line. That's why, as a boy, when Will realized he was attracted to other boys, this scorn planted in him a terrible seed of self-hatred.

So when Ellen made her plea on television, Will felt his stomach flip. He shot a sideways glance at his mother. *Can she tell I'm gay?*

Mrs. Haggerty sighed. "Why do gay people have to always force their agenda on others?"

"She doesn't do it that much," Will offered cautiously. But Mrs. Haggerty had already launched into a rebuke about the depravity of "the homosexual lifestyle."

Will listened quietly, the words landing like rocks on his heart.

As high school dragged on, Will's self-hatred mushroomed under the onslaught of adolescence and his unmistakable same-sex attraction. He'd catch his reflection in the mirror and see gangly limbs strung together, gleaming braces, and dorky glasses. Behind all that, he harbored an unfading attraction to boys. Despite being the popular, funny guy who played the stand-up bass in the church worship band, Will felt alone. He prayed that God would make him straight. But it seemed like God wasn't listening. Sometimes Will considered killing himself. "There was no reason for me to live because I felt worthless. I dreaded the day someone would find out."

By college application time, Will knew he wanted a few things: a Christian education, Christian nonprofit business classes, and ex-gay therapy. He didn't know much about the last thing, but if it could make him straight, he wanted to learn more. The college that seemed a perfect fit was Biola University, a nearby conservative Christian college that Will's older brother had attended and praised. Among evangelicals, the school is considered prestigious, and because its honors program is tailored for homeschooled kids, Will eagerly applied.

When Will entered Biola, he signed the Biola contract pledging to abide by the school's sixty-two-page "Community Standards" handbook, which forbade what the school then referred to as "homosexual behavior."

Hundreds of Christian colleges have similar policies, as do conservative evangelical parachurch ministries, churches, and charities.[2] Across these organizations, queer Christians risk expulsion or job loss if they are outed or even just hold LGBTQ-affirming views. At one prominent Christian college a lesbian professor, who asked to remain anonymous, told me that coming up in this system forced her to remain closeted her whole life. Now, middle-aged and never having loved, she wonders if it's too late. And even though her school is on the progressive end of the evangelical spectrum (it sanctioned a gay-straight alliance), its exclusion of sexual orientation in its nondiscrimination hiring policy sends a mixed message to queer students: "You can come here. There's a safe place for you. But we won't be giving you role models in faculty." Christian college faculty members who do come out have been swiftly punished. In 2013, when a professor came out as transgender at Azusa Pacific University, an evangelical college in the Los Angeles area, he was promptly dismissed despite fifteen years of service and the praise of his students.[3]

These policies are too vague, complain Will and other queer students at Christian schools. *What exactly is punishable? Dating even if there's no sex? Simply being openly gay? Disagreeing with the school's position?* In the swirl of uncertainty, the closet can feel like the most secure place.

Freshman year, Will resolved to reinvent himself by banishing his same-sex attraction and living like a straight guy; it was his only shot at a normal life. Now that he was eighteen, Will's body had filled out. He had lost the glasses and braces, revealing an attractive college kid with a crop of boy-band curly hair and bedroom eyes. Much to the envy of other guys, Will flirted with the many college girls who adored him, which fueled his confidence.

Will played up his ladies' man persona. It guarded him against the pain of antigay chapel sermons that left him feeling "like a joke, or the dirtiest person there." It protected him from his male friends' taunting language over games of *Halo*: "Faggot." "Queer." "I'm going to rape your ass!" And as his research on ex-gay cures revealed an empty, deeply flawed form of therapy, his rapport with women seemed to be the only thing helping him pass. When he found out that Heather, his effortlessly gorgeous classmate, liked him, he began to date her. *This is my ticket*, he thought. Visions of the life he always wanted flashed in his mind: the beautiful wife, the chubby babies, a sun-dappled home with a lawn.

But when Heather confronted him that day in the park, Will knew the jig was up. She sensed he had been distant and wanted to know why. The words "I'm gay" finally tumbled out, and they cried together.

Will apologized for lying. He offered to stay with her if she wanted—anything to make things right. But nights later, after Will walked Heather to her car, she turned to him in the darkened parking lot and said it was over.

Will cried in the shower that night. The next morning, he vowed to get her back and sent a series of pleading letters. The two went back and forth, Will making a case for spending a lifetime together ("a lot of blessings can be found in this struggle," he wrote), Heather suggesting an ex-gay support group. It was a raw deal for both sides, and they never did get back together. But Heather honored Will's request to keep his sexuality under wraps. Her silence led to all sorts of wild assumptions. Through the rumor mill, Will heard that her parents thought he had raped her. Some peers wondered if Will was an alcoholic or a drug dealer. Will didn't quash the rumors. They were nowhere near as bad as the truth.

PRIVATE IS DIFFERENT

For outsiders to evangelical culture, it can seem absurd that a school can hire, fire, admit, and expel based on sexual orientation and not be in violation of nondiscrimination policies.[4] But as *private, religious, educational* institutions, Christian schools are within their legal rights to pick and choose whom they let in and kick out. And in the wake of the Supreme Court's *Hobby Lobby* ruling, more institutions are demanding religious exemptions from laws and asserting that their discriminatory practices count as protected religious expression. They also point to their disassociation from government funding as a reason why their schools are not beholden to state or local policies regarding sexual orientation.

It is this last point that some LGBTQ advocates are trying to dismantle (after all, federal or state funding touches most schools through grants or other programs), though so far they've not made significant progress. In a recent case against California Baptist University's exclusion of a transgender student, the student's lawyer argued that because 1) the school participates in a tax-exempt bond-financing program; 2) the school "competes in the public market place to attract students regardless of their religious affiliation"; and 3) the school has no policy prohibiting transgender students, it was beholden to the state's Unruh Civil Rights Act, which bans businesses from gender identity discrimination.[5]

In 2014, a California judge found that Cal Baptist acted within its rights: it was not a business establishment and was therefore not subject to Unruh regulations. The judge did, however, rule in the student's favor on her third claim, that the school's decision to exclude her from parts of the school open to the public had violated Unruh.

TASHA

When Tasha Magness signed the Biola contract, she knew she was gay, but assumed she could stay in the closet until graduation. She had come to terms with her sexuality in high school, and as a homeschooled kid she already had a few closeted years under her belt. What was four more?

But as soon as she settled into her seat at honors freshman orientation, she realized the folly of her plan. The honors program director explained, as she recalled, "how the role of the program was to teach people to defend Western Christianity against liberalism." Liberalism, of course, included gay marriage. Tasha left orientation feeling tired and dejected. *What the heck was I thinking going to this school?* she asked herself as she walked across the leafy campus.

Her thoughts were interrupted when the orientation director caught her eye and flashed a smile. "Keep going, culture warrior!" he shouted enthusiastically. Tasha forced a smile and trudged home, praying for things to improve. But from that moment on, the anthem of the culture war would play out in every corner of her Biola life, from chapel services that called same-sex relationships "illegitimate," to professors scorning the "homosexual lifestyle," to homophobic comments made by her peers.

And who was the enemy? She was. She had not anticipated this. After all, on paper, Tasha was a born-and-bred Biola girl. She grew up in La Habra, a neighboring suburb, and attended Biola Star, a biweekly program aimed at junior high and high school homeschool students. Her circle of friends: all Biola Star students. Her church frequently partnered with Biola groups on projects. Her pastor taught at Biola. And toward the end of high school, Tasha and her friends were giddy about Biola's honors program. Tasha's parents expected her to attend a Christian university (it's all they would likely fund), so Biola seemed like the perfect fit.

Up until freshman orientation, Tasha loved the culture she grew up in.

"I had an amazing homeschool experience," she said, recalling her tight-knit group of friends and their innocent adventures hiking or guzzling energy drinks at homeschool prom. "You create a second family for yourself. You do your entire life with them."

She fit in with her group, but on her own, she couldn't shake the feeling that she was different. She couldn't put her finger on why exactly, but she knew there was something wrong with the smile that crept across her face when she told her parents about a cute female friend, or the way she'd duck out early from dates with her high school boyfriend to secretly watch episodes of *The L Word*. On a family trip to Seattle she thought to herself, *I bet there are lesbians in Seattle!* Her train of thought halted. *Why would I want to see lesbians?* Then everything clicked. *Oh, I'm a lesbian.*

While the years that followed had an undercurrent of shame, more than that, Tasha felt compelled to understand her sexuality and the theological arguments for and against same-sex relationships. She devoured books and articles obsessively, mapping the arguments in her head. In the end, she accepted her sexuality and felt confident defending it to any Christian who asked.

But Tasha had no intention of coming out until after college. She told only two friends, who accepted her, but beyond that she told no one else. She was still a teenager, well aware of the social structures of her community; she didn't feel equipped to become an outcast with a dismantled life. In the meantime, she would stay in the closet. When peers said "fag," she cringed, but didn't make a big thing of it. When her mother assured Tasha and her sisters that she didn't hate gay people—she simply believed they could live great lives as single celibates—Tasha didn't object. Even that one time, when they saw two women holding hands, Tasha let it slide when her mother called their affection "gross."

But inside, Tasha remembered, "it destroyed me."

The dissonance especially clawed at her faith. Before questions of her sexuality arose, Tasha felt intimately in tune with her relationship with God. She identified as a Christian as early as the first grade, when, after hearing a teacher speak about Jesus, she went home, walked around her backyard, and felt a stirring of something new inside her. With time, she applied the tenets of her evangelical faith with fervor. She spent her summers on mission trips in Mexico and Costa Rica, and on the beaches of Southern California.

"If you died today, do you know where you'd go?" she would ask people on her beach missions. She was relentless, speaking to hundreds of strangers over the course of a few trips. Tasha applied this diligence to every corner of her faith. She became obsessive. When the Bible commanded her to "pray without ceasing," she tried to do this literally, maintaining a running conversation with God in her mind. After questions of her sexuality arose, she prayed constantly for change.

Only later would Tasha understand her behavior through a diagnosis of obsessive-compulsive disorder. Only later would her panic attacks grow so acute that her body could barely function.

But in the heat of her all-consuming youthful faith, Tasha felt a deep call to become a missionary, go to destitute places, suffer, and die a martyr. It all fit together with her sexuality, she explained: as a Christian lesbian, she would have to stay single. And in the American church, women lacked agency; as Tasha put it, if they "really wanted to do something kick-ass, they'd have to leave the country." She accepted this as her fate and applied to Biola as an intercultural studies major.

Then the reality of her decision hit her—she had signed up for an impossible task. Just a few weeks into her freshman year, she met a girl.

THE DURABLE MYTH

For decades Christian private schools have defended their right to kick out groups or ban certain behavior—like interracial dating—because of their biblical beliefs. In the 1970s, Christian schools with racially discriminatory policies fought the government's attempts to enforce terms of the Civil Rights Act of 1964, saying these moves attacked their religious freedom. The battle between private schools and the government played out in a series of landmark court cases. In 1971, a district court ruled in *Green v. Connally* that these private schools were not entitled to federal tax exemptions, as their racial discrimination violated federal public policy and disqualified them from being considered "charitable institutions."[6] The IRS began inquiring about the racial policies at Christian schools, raising the ire of Christian leaders. Then the IRS targeted Bob Jones University for its racially discriminatory policies. The Greenville, South Carolina–based college was reluctant to admit black students. In 1971 it began accepting black students, but only if they were married, because the school feared interracial dating. In 1975 it lifted the "married only" admittance policy, but maintained a policy—based on sincerely held biblical beliefs—that banned interracial dating (this policy was not lifted until 2000). The school not only threatened to expel students engaged in interracial dating and marriage, it also levied that same threat on students who advocated for interracial marriage, associated with groups that advocated interracial marriage, or who espoused, promoted, or encouraged others "to violate the university's dating rules and regulations."[7] The language is hauntingly familiar.

After the IRS attempted to revoke its tax-exempt status, the school fought back, taking its appeal all the way to the Supreme Court, which eventually ruled in favor of the IRS. This fight sent shock waves across the white evangelical community and served as a critical galvanizing force for the Religious Right. According to historians and Religious Right leaders themselves, *this* was the beginning of the culture wars.

This may come as a surprise, as the dominant narrative suggests that conservative evangelicals mobilized to fight abortion. In his 2005 book *Building Dynamic Faith*, Jerry Falwell insists that the moment that propelled him to organize his Religious Right powerhouse, the Moral Majority (founded in 1979), came January 23, 1973, while he was reading the *Lynchburg News*. He recalls sitting there "staring at the *Roe v. Wade* story" and realizing his mission was to organize evangelicals to combat this Supreme Court decision.[8] This is the unquestioned narrative understood by many religious and nonreligious Americans alike. But it simply isn't true. Falwell and other Religious Right leaders have rewritten this part of history. In the words of historian Randall Balmer, the Religious Right's abortion-origin story has become "one of the most durable myths" of the movement.[9]

The historical facts point to a very different version of events. Yes, conservative evangelicals rejected the feminist movement for years, dismissing the demands for female liberation as rooted in boredom, envy, and prideful disobedience. But it is not true that an antiabortion ethos (which they like to ironically call "new abolitionism") launched the Religious Right.

Balmer, an evangelical and religious historian at Dartmouth College, uncovered this in 1990 when he sat in on a meeting with key figures of the Christian Right, including Religious Right architect Paul Weyrich, Jerry Falwell sidekick Edward Dobson, and leaders from the Christian Coalition, Focus on the Family, the American Family Association, and the Southern Baptist Convention.

The moment that startled Balmer was Weyrich's admission that race, not abortion, launched the conservative Christian political movement. Balmer writes,

> Let's remember, [Weyrich] said animatedly, that the Religious Right did not come together in response to the Roe decision. No, Weyrich insisted, what got us going as a political movement was the attempt on the part of the Internal Revenue Service (IRS) to rescind the tax-exempt status of Bob Jones University because of its racially discriminatory policies. . . .
>
> Initially, I found Weyrich's admission jarring. He declared, in effect, that the origins of the Religious Right lay in *Green v. Connally* rather than *Roe v. Wade*. I quickly concluded, however, that his story made a great deal of sense. When I was growing up within the evangelical subculture, there was an unmistakably defensive cast to evangelicalism. I recall many presidents of colleges or Bible institutes coming through our churches to recruit students and to raise money. One of their recurrent themes was, We don't accept federal money, so the government can't tell us how to run our shop—whom to hire or fire or what kind of rules to live by. The IRS attempt to deny tax-exempt status to segregated private schools, then, represented an assault on the evangelical subculture, something that raised an alarm among many evangelical leaders, who mobilized against it.[10]

In 1983 the Supreme Court ruled in favor of the IRS. The majority opinion stated that First Amendment religion clauses did not forbid the IRS to revoke the school's tax-exempt status based on school practices that were contrary to public policy.

Today, especially after the Supreme Court legalized same-sex marriage, evangelical leaders worry that a similar pattern will play out with gay rights: institutionalized discrimination against gays and lesbians could lead to the same tax, or other funding, consequences for churches, Christian charities, and other organizations.[11] They say that LGBTQ equality threatens their religious freedom, but for many, what's at peril is not religious freedom but their ability to discriminate while receiving government support.

The culture war against sexual minorities began to flourish around the same time Will and Tasha were born, in the early 1990s. This occurred after the evangelical fight against divorce fell off in the 1970s and inroads against legalized abortion in the 1980s were stymied by the election of Bill Clinton. Randall Balmer puts it this way: the Religious Right needed a new enemy.

Very quickly, the widespread condemnation of gay people became integral to the fabric of conservative Christian faith and its institutions. Pastors jabbed their fingers at the Bible verses in Leviticus, Deuteronomy, Romans, 1 Corinthians, and 1 Timothy, reminding their congregations that those who gave in to same-sex attraction were "unnatural," "lawless and disobedient," "unholy and profane," had committed "an abomination," "shall be put to death," and "shall not inherit the kingdom of God."

Will and Tasha grew up internalizing this message and loathing the desires blossoming within them. I was a teenager in the 1990s, exploring my nascent faith at a Chinese immigrant church in the Chicago suburbs. We were an apolitical congregation; our biggest controversies revolved around whether or not we should allow drums during worship. But even there, where the pastor didn't preach about homosexuality, I found James Dobson's weekly newsletter tucked between the pages of the church bulletin. One Sunday, I read Dobson's polemic against "the homosexual agenda." I still remember the grainy photographs of gay-rights picketers, and Dobson's panicked tone as he explained the plot to destroy the American family. And another time, at a sleepover, I listened to a church friend explain how being gay was the worst sin. At school, I had heard the mean kids use "gay" as an insult but I didn't understand why my nice church friend would speak derisively about homosexuality. "What's wrong with being gay?" I asked. She gave me a look like I should have known better. I interpreted that conversation the way I interpreted a lot of unfamiliar Christian ideas: I was the convert from the atheist family; there was so much about faith that I did not know.

In the 2003 book *The Homosexual Agenda*, authors Craig Osten and Alan Sears write apocalyptically about what they consider the areas of American life most vulnerable to the "attack of the gays": media ("Hilary Swank won Best Actress for *Boys Don't Cry*, in which she played a transgendered person, a girl who dresses up as a boy and is eventually murdered in a so-called hate crime"); public schools (an "alarming front" soon to infect our children with STDs and sexual confusion); the workplace (where gay-rights opponents will face "intimidation"); and marriage laws that give way to no-fault divorce states and to gay marriage, "cheapening" marriage.[12]

To battle this alleged affront on family values, leading Christian Right activists doubled down on efforts to eliminate legal protections for LGBTQ people. In 1992, Dobson and other leaders gathered widespread support for the successful passage of Amendment 2 in Colorado, which reversed state and local statutes that outlawed discrimination against sexual minorities and prevented any future protective laws.[13] (The Supreme Court overturned Amendment 2 four years later.)

In the run-up to the 2004 election, the Christian Right fought back against the slew of recent gay rights victories in Hawaii, Massachusetts, Vermont, and Texas. In the 2003 case *Lawrence v. Texas*, the Supreme Court struck down a Texas law that criminalized gay sex, and it deemed the sodomy laws in thirteen other states unconstitutional. Inflamed by this decision, the Family Research Council and Focus on the Family jointly filed an amicus brief arguing that states should be allowed to criminally prosecute "sexual acts outside of marriage" but may also "reasonably decide to leave all these opposite-sex relationships undisturbed by the criminal law." In other words, criminalize sex outside of marriage, but only for the gays.[14]

This message made its way to congregations from coast to coast, with preachers poised on pulpits condemning what became known as "the homosexual lifestyle." As congregations recoiled, the Christian Right realized that it could turn this political issue to its advantage.

Marriage amendment proposals appeared on the ballot in eleven states in the 2004 election, a move many political analysts said drew evangelical voters and gave President Bush a critical edge. As the *New York Times* reported, political scientist John Green estimated there was a resulting uptick in turnout of as much as 3 or 4 percent, which may have tipped the election in Bush's favor.[15]

What made homosexuality such an effective issue for mobilizing evangelicals? Balmer attributes it to the convenient "ruse of selective literalism." It's the classic fundamentalist paradigm, Balmer explains: "They construct strict delineations between right and wrong—careful, of course, to place themselves on the right side of whatever lines they draw."[16] Protesting divorce fell out of fashion as divorce rates among Christians matched everyone else's. But homosexuality seemed safely outside the church. For surely no one in the church could be gay.

A PARTIAL COMING OUT

Shortly after Will and Heather broke up, Will returned home for spring break only to be clobbered with questions from his father. *What did Will do to mess this up? Did he cheat? What happened?* Will muttered indecipherably and retreated to his room, where he hid for most of his vacation.

Later, Mrs. Haggerty walked by Will's open door and poked her head in, hoping to comfort her son.

"Was it her family?" she asked quietly, referring to Heather's super-strict family.

"No, it wasn't her family," Will said. Then he gave her an imploring look. "Don't you know?"

Mrs. Haggerty saw the anguish in her son's face and her eyes filled with tears.

"No, what is it?"

As Will searched his mother's eyes for recognition of his sexuality and saw none, he began to cry too.

"We broke up because I'm gay," Will said at last, and his mom rushed to his bedside.

The next moments were a collision of tears and questions and hurt. His mom insisted that Will was not gay. These feelings were not his own. They were lies from Satan. They were lies from bad friends who had convinced him he was gay. They were lies from our broken world.

Her words crushed Will, so he responded sharply, angrily. He hurled a pen across the room, recoiled into the fetal position, and refused to speak to his mother. She left in tears.

Later that day, when Will came out to his brother while explaining why their mother was so upset, his brother gave him a confused look.

"What do you mean you're *gay?*"

"What do you mean, 'What do you mean you're gay?'" Will shot back.

"Well, I don't know if you mean, like, you're *gay* gay or you're gay as in you're stupid."

Will's coming-out had not gone as he had hoped. He decided not to tell his dad. Instead, he stayed quiet. Then he returned to school even more brokenhearted than when spring break began, when he had the weight of the breakup and terrible rumors on his shoulders. Now, it felt like he had lost his closest confidante, his mother.

When the school year ended, Will had no idea how he'd survive a summer at home. Will typically enjoyed standing at his mother's elbow, learning how to cook a new dish or sew or crochet, but his sexuality had made everything strained and awkward. Will often reassured his mother that he knew being openly gay was a sin. Then he'd retreat to his room and pray desperately, *God, please take this away.*

It was a dark summer. Will watched online videos of ex-gay speakers who spoke about their journeys out of homosexuality and into satisfying marriages with women. "I'm living a life I never thought I could have," beamed one ex-gay preacher. But their stories of child molestation, abandonment, years of promiscuity, rebellion against God, and ex-gay revelations didn't resonate with Will. He was a good kid who loved his family and his church, but simply could not alter his sexuality.

To a large degree, Will had come to accept the fact that he would never change. But as someone who took the Bible seriously, it seemed clear that he could never love another man and still have God's blessing. When he thought about his future, it dawned on him—as a gay Christian, he would have to stay celibate for life.

"You know when you are in such a sad and lonely place that you go to Google's search engine to ask your deepest, darkest questions?" That's how Will would later explain that period of his life. That summer, Will opened a browser and typed, "Can I be gay and Christian?" The search results loaded. At the top of the page was a link to a group called the Gay Christian Network.

The website changed his life. Will found a vast online community of LGBTQ Christians asking the exact same questions he had been asking all these years. *Are these feelings sinful? Does God bless same-sex relationships? Does the Bible say I should remain celibate?*

Will spent hours reading the discussion boards, engrossed by the debate unfolding on the pages before him. Among this new community, Will discovered two startling facts. The first was that among these Christians, there existed a vast diversity of opinions. The second was that these LGBTQ Christians had adopted a unique language to explain themselves: as they described it, there were roughly three schools of Christian thought, "Side A," "Side B," and "Side X." Will learned that Side A Christians believe that God affirms same-sex relationships and marriage. In other words, same-sex behavior is not a sin. Side B folks believe that having same-sex attraction is not inherently wrong, but that acting on it is sinful. Therefore, gay and lesbian Christians were called by God to remain celibate. Side X supporters, or ex-gay Christians, believe same-sex attraction *and* activity are sinful and that Jesus and therapy can reorient a person toward heterosexuality.

This language was new to Will. Never in his life had he come across a Christian opinion in support of same-sex relationships. So when he read a meticulously thought-out, theologically supported Side A essay by the site's founder, Justin Lee, Will was floored. In Justin's childhood story, Will saw a reflection of his own life: a committed Christian from a loving conservative home battles same-sex attraction and self-doubt.

And in Justin's adult life, Will felt absolute soaring hope: Justin is an openly gay Christian who runs a nonprofit ministry. Like Will, Justin holds fairly conservative theological views. "I believe that the Bible is morally authoritative, that sex is for marriage, and that promiscuity is harmful to everyone involved," Justin writes in his Side A essay.

"It was, like, the most convincing thing that I had ever read as an argument for monogamous same-sex relationships being blessed by God," Will said. But before it liberated him, it broke him down. Well before he knew the language, Will had been Side X, trying his best to become straight. But after he broke up with Heather, he slowly inched toward a Side B perspective. He was confident that he couldn't change his sexuality. But he was also sure that the Bible would not condone same-sex relationships. And now he was confronting an argument that said God *blessed* same-sex relationships; it made his mind spin.

"It kind of threw me into Identity Crisis 2.0." The Gay Christian Network cast his old worldview under a shadow of doubt. "I was a wreck. I didn't know anything."

When he explained this to his mother, she amped up the pressure for ex-gay therapy. Will declined. She urged Will to meet with an influential couple in the church—a gay man married to a lesbian woman. The two had adopted children and served as a model for a healthy Christian choice for those with same-sex attraction. Maybe this option would have appealed to Will earlier, but after reading Justin Lee's Side A argument he was a changed man. His gut told him that this setup would only send him on a dark path of unhappiness and dissatisfaction. He just knew, "That's not what I want for my life."

When Will returned to school that fall, a random room assignment put him together with a staunchly conservative roommate who spent his time launching arguments in Christian chat rooms and in the comments section of articles and Facebook posts. Will found this roommate's patriarchal opinions confrontational; it put him on edge constantly. Every day Will worried that his roommate would find out he was gay. *If he does*, Will thought, *my life will be over.*

"One of the darkest points was not feeling like I had any place to go," Will recalled. The stress got so bad, sometimes Will would just cry in bed, hoping that his roommate would not return. As first semester came to a close, Will began to look into other housing options. He had to get out.

FEAR AND LOATHING

When out reporting, I spent a lot of time trying to understand why evangelicals were so concerned about homosexuality. In their explanations, most turned to familiar arguments about theology, religious freedom, nurture versus nature, and definitions of acceptable moral behavior. Some also lamented the church's mishandling of the issue. But even the compassionate people ignored perhaps the most consequential problem at the heart of this issue: the fact that today's queer Christians face alarming mental health risks, especially *because* of their nonaffirming Christian communities.

This was a common, glaring omission in my interviews with evangelicals, both conservative and progressive. While the broader LGBTQ community has advanced equality, devout queer believers live their lives in the crossfire of the culture war, exposing them to unique and grave psychological vulnerabilities, as evidenced by a battery of studies. Already, lesbian, gay, and bisexual youths are four times more likely to attempt suicide than their straight peers, according to a CDC report that examined those populations.[17] Meanwhile, suicide figures among transgender people are particularly alarming, with 57 percent of those who face family rejection attempting suicide and over 50 percent of those who face discrimination at school attempting suicide, according to a 2014 report by researchers from the American Foundation for Suicide Prevention and the Williams Institute at the University of California, Los Angeles, School of Law who analyzed results from the National Transgender Discrimination Survey.[18] On top of all this, sexual minorities are more susceptible to a litany of other mental health risks. And rejection by one's religious community makes matters significantly worse.

"If you see that the only Christian sexual ethic excludes who you are, there's a part of you that internalizes that self-hate," explained Yolanda Turner, professor of psychology at Eastern University, an evangelical Christian college outside of Philadelphia. In addition to specializing in the psychological intersection of faith and sexuality, Turner advises Eastern's gay-straight alliance. "It's hard enough for kids who are in their twenties who have been taught that they're full of sin to love themselves anyway," Turner told me in an interview. "But to also hear that the core of who you are is unacceptable to God is really shaming, and so the internalized loathing is compounded by the fact that God thinks that too. It's a whole other layer of psychological injury."

Despite the long history of research that shows that coming out of the closet boosts psychological health, these gains are mostly negated for LGBTQ people in nonwelcoming communities, according to a 2011 study.[19] University of Rochester psychologist Richard Ryan, one of the study's authors, found that the perks of coming out—"fewer symptoms of depression, less anxiety, more self-esteem, less anger, and other negative emotions"—didn't play out for people in an environment that stigmatized sexual minorities. Instead, "people feel pressure toward a specified outcome—they are pressured to be how others want them to be."

When I read this line in the study, I thought of Will and how he didn't simply tell Heather he was gay; he crafted a plan for their future in which he lived like the straight guy everyone expected him to be. And after they broke up, he stayed vigilantly closeted at Biola. Indeed, Ryan's study shows that respondents were far more closeted "in environments they rated as controlling and judgmental," stated a press release highlighting the study's findings. "They kept their sexual orientation hidden the most in religious communities (69 percent)."[20] The study underscores that the chief determinant of outness was not the individual's age, gender, orientation, or any other factor—it was ultimately the person's environment. In other words, when there's a barrier to being out, it's not the individual that needs to be fixed, it's the environment.

Many LGBTQ Christians face institutional as well as personal discrimination in their schools or churches (and sometimes even within their own families), so they withdraw to protect themselves. In discriminatory environments, they cannot come out. And staying closeted can lead to increased anxiety and burnout, as well as higher levels of cortisol, a stress hormone, as evidenced in many studies, including a 2013 study published by the American Psychosomatic Society.[21]

The authors, researchers from McGill University and the University of Montreal, argue for "established social policies that facilitate" the coming-out process. After all, plenty of other studies have shown how American lesbians, gays, and bisexuals with fewer legal protections, such as living in states without policies that ensure their safety, experience dramatically higher rates of mental illness.[22] According to a 2012 study, twelve months after Massachusetts legalized gay marriage, medical and mental health care visits among gay men sharply declined.[23]

Altogether, research points to two key elements for positive mental health among sexual minorities: coming out and doing so in an environment with policies and attitudes that affirm those who come out. None of this may be surprising to those aware of the heartbreaking LGBTQ suicide and mental health statistics. But those who often seem the least aware are the very people supporting policies that inflame this problem.

If religious communities magnify mental health problems for sexual minorities, what exactly does that look like and what can be done? Josh Wolff, PhD, a faculty member at Adler University, has been exploring that question for years. His quest began in March 2009 when he spoke to a troubled adolescent boy who had tried killing himself by swallowing a bottle of medicine. The boy was reluctant to offer details, but with time, he told Josh that he was gay and had faced relentless bullying and tormenting from his classmates. His school had done little to help. *This wasn't a life worth living*, the boy concluded. The boy's despair sounded so familiar—it reminded Josh of his own years of anguish.

Josh grew up in a conservative evangelical community in Wisconsin and he knew early on that he was gay. For a while, he truly believed he could turn himself straight. When he entered Biola University as a graduate student of clinical psychology, he listened to a series of speakers testify to the reorienting power of reparative therapy. It was a "very isolating and very lonely" time for him. A professor referred Josh to a psychologist who impressed him with stories of past clients who had forged new attractions to the opposite sex. But after spending a year and a half and roughly five thousand dollars in therapy, Josh had begun to doubt the claims that he could change his sexual orientation. He ended therapy; it hadn't budged him an inch. And he was beginning to fall for his first love. Theirs was "a long-term emotional relationship, and that really challenged a stigma I had of what being gay meant," Josh recalled, explaining that a lot of evangelical literature perpetuates the idea that gay people are promiscuous and unable to form long-term relationships. "I started to question that because I was having these feelings for this guy that were really . . ." Josh's voice trailed off. "I loved him." Josh eventually banished the self-loathing thoughts and has found happiness on his own.

After that meeting with the adolescent boy who was suicidal, a flood of memories rushed back to Josh and he realized he needed to dig deeper into this issue. The stakes for these young sexual minorities, especially those in Christian colleges, were dangerously high. Their lives were at risk, and he wanted to do something to help them. He moved away from individual medical treatment to focus on researching the wider public health implications of LGBTQ youth in religious climates.

In one study, Josh and his coauthors analyzed data collected from 31,852 Oregon teens to assess the impact of affirming and nonaffirming religious communities on lesbian, gay, and bisexual youths.[24]

"What we found was that the more supportive a church was for gay youth, the less likely they were to engage in high-risk behaviors including alcohol abuse, as well as fewer sexual partners in adolescence," Josh told me in an interview. "And the opposite was also true—for gay youths who lived in an environment where the church was officially on record as being unsupportive of gay rights, or their official position was that this is a sin and was against God. We found that those gay youths had higher rates of alcohol abuse as well as had more sexual partners."

In a later study, which compared sexual and gender minority students and alumni of faith-based (and mostly Christian), nonaffirming colleges with a national sample of college students (mostly nonreligious), Josh found that the Christian college sample (students like Will and Tasha) faced a higher degree of suicidal thoughts, family distress, eating disorders, and body image concerns.[25] Comparing the Christian college sample to the broader adult community, Josh found his sample had "a greater internalized homo-negativity—sort of this view that there was something lesser about being gay or something deeply negative about being gay," as well as higher difficulty with coming out, which correlated with overall emotional stress. The study also revealed that one in five participants said that "a mental health professional had attempted to change their sexual orientation."

Josh has presented these findings, which are in the process of being published, to Biola faculty and staff, as well as to two of the American Psychological Association's annual conventions, where standing-room-only audiences (which included students and professors from conservative religious schools) listened in. Josh's hope is that this empirical evidence will foster dialogue and motivate administrators to make concrete changes for the benefit of sexual minorities on campus.

DOUBLE LIFE

The panic attacks were so frequent that Tasha quickly learned to recognize the telltale signs. The sweat. The shaky hands. The slamming of her heart against her chest. Sometimes there was an urge to vomit, sometimes an urge to leave the room. Always, the "gay issue," a frequent topic at Biola, triggered the panic.

It's hard to imagine Tasha on edge. Today she looks like a confident college student poised to succeed at whatever she does. She has the breezy manner of a native Californian, long brown hair that's usually swept up in a ponytail, and a hopeful, if sometimes mischievous, baby face. In her brisk conversational style, she comes across as fiercely intelligent, driven, and compassionate.

But when she was a freshman, the culture shock of Biola sent her into isolation and changed her personality. She feared being found out, so she distanced herself from her peers. When conversations turned to relationships, she'd talk casually about guys she dated in high school. But she was just treading water. These would never be true friends because she could never be her true self. She couldn't talk about the girl who broke her heart in high school. She couldn't talk about the girl she had recently begun dating. Instead she lied, calling Nicole "Nick," and prayed no one would ask to see "Nick's" picture.

But this wasn't enough to stave off the panic attacks. Everywhere she turned, the culture taunted her, telling her it was only a matter of time before she would be exposed. Early in her freshman year, she rounded a corner and saw a large sign encouraging students to talk about homosexuality. But the tone "was so ominous." In the library she overheard one student say to another, "Did you know she came out as *a lesbian?*" Tasha noted their looks of disgust. Professors spoke out against gay marriage. Prayer requests were raised over people who "struggled" with same-sex attraction. Once, when strolling through campus, Tasha heard someone yell, "Yo, dyke!" She ignored the call, until she realized it was a friend of hers. *Does she know?* Tasha wondered frantically. The friend caught up to Tasha and laughed. "You're dressing like such a lesbian these days!"

Tasha spent her freshman year buried in schoolwork, keeping a low profile and working through her anxiety with a sympathetic school counselor. But sophomore year, she started dating another Biola student and the stress of their secret made her more unhinged. The two would go to great lengths to hide their relationship, scheduling their dates at restaurants far from campus, lying to everyone they knew, propping up an impossible best-friends facade. Once, in the honors office where Tasha worked, her girlfriend brought her coffee and instinctively leaned in for a kiss just as Tasha's boss walked in the room. Hearts racing, they collected themselves. Moments later Tasha downloaded applications to transfer schools.

"I really couldn't care less about Biola at that point," she recalled. She was halfway through her sophomore year and could no longer manage the stress the school provoked. "I was just ready to leave."

That January, Tasha applied to a few nearby colleges. Soon Biola would be nothing more than a sad blip in her past. She was done with this place.

Then, a few weeks later, she met Will.

PART 2

Skeptics

FOUR

Racial Awakenings

CAST OUT

In the fall of 1989, Lisa Sharon Harper returned to Rutgers University for her senior year of college. The campus felt warmly familiar: the ebb and flow of students walking along the tree-lined walkways, the welcome-back festivities, the fire-truck red Rutgers sweatshirts dotting the cafeteria. But for Lisa, one thing was very different. Returning to campus on the heels of her summer urban project in New York City, she ushered in this new school year as a transformed woman.

As Lisa bounced between classes and meals and Campus Crusade meetings, memories of the summer flashed into her mind. She thought about the Love Kitchen. She thought about Johnny and the laughs they shared in his midtown Manhattan doorway. She thought about the adolescent girls at Camp Comanche, smiling at fun memories of discussing black hairstyles and enjoying the familiar banter reminiscent of her Philadelphia childhood. The experience transformed Lisa's faith, instilling in her a deep desire for justice and a new sense of self.

But these revelations existed within Lisa alone; her white evangelical community had not changed. When she returned to Campus Crusade, she experienced a sort of reverse culture shock. She tried to open up about the lessons she had learned over the summer, but those around her didn't share her concerns. They were obsessed with protesting abortion;

she cared more about homeless men and women, many of them black, whom she suddenly noticed all around.

Lisa joined a campus group devoted to helping local homeless people. The group, RU with the Homeless, opened a shelter close to campus, and members like Lisa took turns spending the night and helping out. Lisa was also the worship team leader at Campus Crusade, and she enlisted her musical friends to help her lead singing at the homeless shelter one Sunday night each month. Meanwhile, Lisa's mother had called with the news that Johnny, Lisa's childhood hairdresser who was gay, had died of AIDS. When the traveling AIDS Memorial Quilt arrived at Rutgers, Lisa paced along the rows of colorful fabric memorials weeping, looking for Johnny's name. Losing him and seeing the magnitude of the disease's impact unfurled in the extensive quilt "brought the experience of AIDS down to the human level." It also underscored the humanity of the gay community, which had been vilified by evangelical leaders, she said. "It was an injustice. Specifically, the injustice was that we did nothing for so long and because we did nothing for so long so many people had died. And the reason we did nothing for so long was because these people were not important enough for us to take action."

Lisa's transformation began to drive a wedge between her and some within her fellowship. She was no longer a reliable backer of their efforts, such as antiabortion rallies. She attended demonstrations to raise awareness about homelessness and to protest tuition hikes that would edge out poor students. She gained confidence and became a leader forging initiatives of her own. Some people took issue with that.

While Lisa's worship team friends responded happily to her invitation to serve at the homeless shelter, when Lisa tried recruiting the broader Campus Crusade community, she ran into trouble. At one meeting, during announcements, a male student stood to invite the fellowship to an upcoming Operation Rescue antiabortion rally. Then Lisa rose and encouraged her peers to volunteer with her at the homeless shelter.

When the meeting adjourned, the student promoting Operation Rescue confronted Lisa, reminding her that homelessness was "the world's issue" while abortion was "*God's issue*."[1] She was dumbstruck and struggled to reconcile the fact that Campus Crusade, which had

reconnected her to her roots and awoken in her a thirst for social justice, was simultaneously steeped in a white Republican evangelical culture with apparent apathy toward the poor.

Lisa didn't let these setbacks deter her. She continued engaging the
homeless community *and* her evangelical community. She volunteered
regularly at the shelter. She led the worship team. She and a male friend
from Campus Crusade co-led a regular prayer group.

Lisa was finding her voice, not only as a black believer, but as
a black *woman*. But her presence as a female leader of the worship
team and prayer group eventually came under sharp scrutiny. Many in
Campus Crusade were complementarian, believing that God forbade
women from leading men. When a new male staff worker was hired
to work with the fellowship, Lisa noticed that a longtime female staff
worker was suddenly stripped of many responsibilities. Then one day,
when Lisa showed up to lead worship rehearsal, the newcomer pulled
her aside and, harnessing the complementarian code, told her, "Because
a man is here to lead worship, you have to step down and learn how to
follow," Lisa recalled. It was a conservative Christian concept that Lisa
had not seen so blatantly practiced until now.

Meanwhile, a few close male friends invited her to their church,
which belonged to a Brethren branch that requires women to cover
their heads and prohibits them from speaking aloud in church. Lisa was
skeptical, but attended anyway. She looked on as the small congregation
invited members to share about how God was speaking to them. But
half of the congregation could not speak. Lisa, who had plenty to share,
respected the rules of the church and remained silent but left livid.

Toward the end of her senior year, those same friends objected to
Lisa's role as coleader of a daily prayer group that she and a male friend
had started. These friends, along with Campus Crusade staff and students, held a forum to discuss the appropriateness of Lisa's leadership
as a woman. Nearly a dozen students showed up in the student center
meeting room to air their grievances. They worried about breaching
orthodoxy. They worried that a woman could lead them astray. Lisa

could feel her emotions rising: anger, betrayal, pain. She wanted to object, to quote scripture, and to lay out her own arguments for why she was qualified to lead.

But she had her own doubts. "Looking back at it, I think I internalized a lot of the misogyny," she said. So she did the only thing she could in that moment. She ran out of the building crying. Outside, under the lights and trees that lined the campus walkway, she fled from the meeting, and something within her cried out, *Forget you!* She walked back to her dorm, fuming. *Forget these people! I'm done!* Lisa thought angrily.

These had been Lisa's closest friends throughout college. "They were my posse," she told me, recalling all the ways they had spent countless hours together over meals, on spring break road trips, at conferences, in late-night heart-to-hearts, in prayer circles, at fellowship meetings. . . . Before this meeting, she had envisioned these friendships deepening well into adulthood. But they had broken her trust and, in her heart, she cut them out of her life.

Surprisingly, she attended the final fellowship meetings. "I stayed, but I checked out of the relationships," she explained. "I didn't have enough strength in me to leave altogether. I didn't have enough clarity." Once graduation came and Lisa walked off Rutgers's campus, she realized that the community she had worked so hard to build was no longer; she had to forge a future and a new community of her own creation. She made her way to New York City.

AWAKENING

Lisa's college experiences changed the course of her adult life. The writings of John Perkins, the impact of her summer urban project, and her conflict with conservative evangelicalism had huge ramifications. Politically, her brief confrontation with the Operation Rescue student marked the beginning of her break from the Republican Party. The forum on her leadership led her to further question the conservative teachings she had readily adopted in her youth.

She began studying the Bible with fresh eyes. "It was really about the gospel and rediscovering Jesus and God's heart," she recalled. This new gospel took her to places she hadn't expected: to New York City, where she met an evangelical Democrat for the first time in her life—she could hardly believe those two worlds could coexist; then to Los Angeles, where she attended an evangelical church with Republicans, Democrats, and independents. Again, she saw the political demarcations of her past dissolve. She reevaluated everything. Politically, she found her way back to the Democratic Party—but more importantly to Lisa, she experienced a spiritual transformation through discovering the social justice roots of the gospel.

After graduating with an MFA in playwriting from the University of Southern California, Lisa took a volunteer staff job at InterVarsity Christian Fellowship, the same campus ministry I was a part of in college, where she would work directly with college students. For Lisa, InterVarsity represented a progressive departure from her past. She witnessed a woman (of color, no less) preach to hundreds within the evangelical organization. Still unable to shake the anti-women-in-leadership message from her college Campus Crusade days, "My first response was, 'This is heresy.'"

InterVarsity is a national, interdenominational, evangelical campus ministry with a robust publishing arm and a colossal missions conference, which is held every three years and draws upward of twenty thousand attendees. Among evangelicals, InterVarsity is considered moderate because it promotes women in leadership and, especially since the 1980s, has made concerted efforts to make multiethnicity a core InterVarsity value.

In the late 1970s and early 1980s, as the country and campuses saw increasing diversity, InterVarsity launched ministry arms dedicated to reaching Asian American, black, and Latino students. In the 1990s, John Perkins's urban community mission model garnered attention, and "racial reconciliation" became the buzz phrase in evangelical circles. InterVarsity leadership launched a task force that worked on a new theological framework for multiethnicity and began hosting regular conferences for minorities.[2] The organization has since attracted more leaders of color, who currently account for about 30 percent of its 1,200-member staff. (Today InterVarsity has close to a thousand chapters and about forty thousand active students every year, of which 38 percent identify as ethnic minorities.)[3]

Of course, the impact of this message across the ministry was uneven. It drove some chapters to engage with communities of color, but other chapters merely boasted ornamental multiethnicity. Lisa joined InterVarsity's UCLA chapter in 1998, the same year I joined as a student at the University of Illinois. Among my InterVarsity peers, many agree that our group largely ignored racial issues, which led to an undercurrent of racial strain. Lisa had a very different experience, driven in part by her very different context (diverse, liberal Southern California, versus my world of farm-town Illinois, which drew many students from small, mostly white, conservative towns, suburbs, and rural areas).

During Lisa's first four years at InterVarsity, she served as a volunteer staff worker, then as a paid staff worker, counseling and leading students at the UCLA InterVarsity chapter.[4] The students actively engaged with campus justice initiatives. When racial tensions tore across campus after news broke that a black woman had been kicked down a stairwell, called a "nigger," and told "We don't want you here," Lisa's InterVarsity community worked through its own mixed reactions, joined the march through campus led by the black student union and camped outside the UCLA president's office to speak to him about dealing with campus racism and protecting vulnerable students.

The need for more leaders like Lisa became increasingly important as diversifying chapters—like mine—sought guidance through this tricky terrain. Lisa helped develop "Race Matters," an educational and conversational tool to equip the broader InterVarsity community with methods of engaging racial issues in its chapters and schools. Her impact led to a promotion to divisional director of racial reconciliation for the greater Los Angeles area. Her job entailed running ethnic reconciliation training conferences, consulting on race issues with InterVarsity chapters across her region, and reporting on trends she saw in her fieldwork. She also trained staff and spoke to students across the country.

In 2003, Lisa took a trip with twenty-five other InterVarsity staff that would change the trajectory of her life. Together, these staff members and their families went on InterVarsity's inaugural "Pilgrimage for

Reconciliation," a bus ride across the South which retraced the Cherokee Trail of Tears and the African American experience from slavery through the civil rights movement. They crossed ten states in four weeks and spoke to people who had experienced, or descended from people who experienced, "some of the most evil moments in American history at the hands of people who called themselves followers of God and Jesus," Lisa told me, her voice rising with emotion. As Lisa and her colleagues gazed out their bus windows, the changing scenery passed them by and they grieved the country's terrible racial landscape.

"I came to the end of that and just realized, *My Gospel is too small. My God is too small to deal with this. My gospel . . . had nothing to say at the end of the Trail of Tears . . . or to African Americans on American soil from slavery to civil rights. My gospel, the gospel I understood as the Four Spiritual Laws had Nothing. To. Say.*"

A MOVEMENT BUILDS

In the years that followed, Lisa began to notice a similar awakening taking place among her peers in the broader evangelical world. This was a post-9/11 America with an evangelical president at the helm. But over the course of George W. Bush's tenure, Lisa heard more young evangelicals echo the dissatisfaction expressed by so many Americans. While many backed the wars in Afghanistan and Iraq, by Bush's second term droves of believers—even those from the most entrenched war-endorsing faith communities—withdrew their support of the wars. Revelations of faulty intelligence, wiretapping, and torture drove a deeper wedge between the administration and its followers of faith, who began grappling with the moral ramifications of these actions. Republican policies had been losing their sway among evangelicals, and the marriage forged by the Religious Right and the GOP was on the rocks. In an ironic twist, the evangelical president had prompted something of an evangelical fallout among a small but growing segment of believers.

"The Religious Right is beginning to collapse," said religious historian Randall Balmer in an interview with me at the time, adding that younger, less conservative evangelicals were speeding up the demise of the old guard. And they were not acting alone—believers of all ages were helping push the new movement forward.

At the grassroots level, pastors decried the subservient role the church had played to the GOP. Theologians called for a return to the faith's social justice roots. Young believers distanced themselves from conservative faith and sought other options, including participation in online Christian forums, intentional communities, and alternative churches, ranging from casual house congregations to groups embracing ancient practices, like prayer labyrinths (walking paths designed to facilitate prayer). Faith communities, which once held Bush in messianic regard, openly criticized his policies and called for a broader evangelical agenda. A telling sign that a mass evangelical market was ready for this new message came when Jim Wallis's 2006 book *God's Politics: Why the Right Gets It Wrong and the Left Doesn't Get It* climbed in sales and sat solidly on the *New York Times* best-seller list for fifteen weeks in a row.

"It felt like a door opened in the universe," Lisa recalled. "It wasn't until the 2006 midterm elections that progressive evangelicals came out of the closet in a public way. For the first time since I've been a Christian you could say you were a Democrat and really have an honest conversation and speak the unthinkable."

Lisa is quick to clarify that not all progressive evangelicals identify as Democrats. In fact, many leaders like Lisa prefer to call themselves "prophetic evangelicals" as opposed to "progressive evangelicals" to emphasize that theirs is a gospel-rooted movement, not a political one. They insist that today's evangelicals share less of a political framework and more of a spiritual—and in many ways cultural and generational—heritage. Though raised during the reign of the Religious Right, the younger, more technologically connected generation grew up exposed to varied ethnic and racial cultures and alternative ways of thinking. Add to that the rise in evangelical service trips like the one Lisa embarked on in college, and out comes a generation with firsthand exposure to systemic inequality, an immersive experience crucial to building empathy. Urban mission trips have helped more sheltered believers understand the discrimination many communities, especially communities of color, face. For suburban kids who have not dealt with a crippled public school system, dangerous streets, routine police harassment, drug laws that penalize poor black and brown men more than others, and a whole host of other issues that make the playing field uneven, these urban service trips are transformative. Among her fellow evangelicals, Lisa has seen this firsthand. "The thing that's so powerful about going on an urban project is you actually know those people," Lisa said. Those personal relationships make the lightbulb go off for evangelicals.

During the Bush administration, Lisa took part in a generational awakening of believers whose faith journeys, missionary experiences, and other cultural engagement had prompted them to leave the Religious Right and embrace a broader agenda. Their faith shaken, they began reaching out to each other, organizing, and finding ways to redefine what it means to be evangelical.

AN ACTIVIST IS BORN

For Lisa, this new awakening led to a major career shift. Informed by her work at InterVarsity and utilizing the connections she was making with the broader evangelical world, Lisa set out to mobilize evangelicals to address the real life, daily systemic injustices faced by vulnerable communities today, such as police brutality and environmental contamination, and the difficulties people encounter in trying to navigate the immigration process.

In quick succession, she left her job at InterVarsity and obtained her master of arts degree in human rights from Columbia University in 2006, then launched her own organization called New York Faith & Justice, which mobilized faith communities to work directly as the bridge between vulnerable New Yorkers and government entities.

The night Lisa launched NYFJ, in the autumn of 2007, she circulated among the crowd of five hundred supporters gathered at a community college in the Bronx. Tall and attractive, Lisa stood out in the crowd, with her burst of curly hair, bright smile, and poise. Even in its nascent stage, Lisa's organization was attracting the attention of progressive evangelical luminaries, key figures who attended the seminal Thanksgiving Workshops in the 1970s. Jim Wallis, founder of Sojourners and celebrated progressive evangelical forefather, had traveled from Washington, DC, to deliver the keynote address at the NYFJ launch. Lisa received a book deal with the New Press; her book crafted a vision for how the next generation might carry the progressive evangelical torch. The research put her in touch with John Perkins, Tony Campolo, Ron Sider, and many other movement founders. People were watching her because she represented something big—a new generation informed by their progressive evangelical forefathers, carving out a movement of their own. The advantage these young and middle-aged believers had was an actual following.

When the din of Christian rock sounded, Lisa took her place off-stage as the attendees filled the auditorium to celebrate the NYFJ launch. They undulated to the worship melodies. They belted "Hallelujah!" After a few prayers and introductions, Lisa walked to the podium and addressed a mixed-race crowd of college kids in graphic tees, smartly dressed young professionals, and older evangelicals wearing professorial attire. She spoke their language, drawing from Christian aphorisms and harnessing the rhetorical flourish of a feisty Pentecostal preacher, all to drive home her ultimate point—there is a new model of evangelical faith, an alternative to the one so aggressively defined by the Religious Right. For this audience, she hit all the right notes. To a chorus of "amens," she called them to join her organization's growing list of initiatives. Lisa's message was well timed, striking one year before President Bush's departure from the White House and as presidential primaries heated up. Issues of faith, activism, and politics were flashing wildly across the evangelical radar screen as the Right plotted for another victory, and a growing contingent stirred up talks about an exodus from the Republican Party.

"I think the massive failure of the Bush years has really caused a lot of people to reconsider things," explained NYFJ volunteer Matt Dunbar, a white, twenty-six-year-old community activist. Other activists spoke excitedly about pushing for stricter environmental policies and mobilizing young believers to work in the inner city.

At one table, thirty-two-year-old Tony Gabaton stood armed with a clipboard hoping to recruit the faithful to his labor rights group, Jobs with Justice. He explained that his group works to mobilize congregations to fight for workers' rights, corporate accountability, and a living wage. He was hopeful that the shifting tone in evangelicalism would motivate more churches to prioritize these issues. "The church is beginning to regret the choices they've made in terms of politics," he said.

After the launch, NYFJ operated like a bridge between young people of faith, community members, and city leaders. Lisa organized the group's regular meetings in the South Bronx, where community members and the local officers met to openly discuss concerns about police misconduct and racial profiling. She joined other faith leaders in meetings with the offices of the mayor and state senators, where they advocated policies that would eliminate food deserts (areas with scarce access to healthy food) in impoverished neighborhoods. She mobilized congregations to join in marches calling for comprehensive immigration reform. She spoke to the media, she got arrested at protests, and she fired up large crowds with impassioned sermons.

In addition to her local activism, Lisa worked to support this movement on a national level. She had networked, read, and traveled enough to know that a new generation hungered for a new evangelical movement. She made phone calls. She sent e-mails. She introduced activists to theologians to pastors to young believers. Soon a group of them began to organize around a common vision: to host national gatherings that would lay the groundwork for a new progressive movement. The conference, which took place annually from 2008 to 2010, was called Envision.

SOONG-CHAN

Over the course of planning Envision, Lisa and her colleagues gathered some of the most influential evangelical and mainline Christian leaders on conference calls, in seminary boardrooms, and in her cozy apartment living room. They met with immigration activists, feminist theologians, scholars of evangelical racial history, influential DC lobbyists, living-wage advocates, church historians, and justice workers of many stripes.

One of the speakers Lisa invited to Envision was Soong-Chan Rah, an evangelical scholar of modern-day church growth and multiethnic churches. As a professor at North Park Seminary in Chicago, consultant to evangelical institutions, and author of a series of books exploring these issues, Soong-Chan is on the cutting edge of explaining this new era of evangelicalism—and not only because he's an astute observer, but because his story is emblematic of many fellow believers.

Soong-Chan has a round, friendly face outlined by an anchor-shaped beard and close-cropped black hair. If you look closely, you'll see the blurry scribble of a scar over his left eyebrow. It has faded in the decades since adolescence, when he tried to stop a fight between Korean and black kids in inner-city Baltimore, where they had begun hurling rocks at one another. Back then, life was tumultuous. As immigrants from Korea with little money, Soong-Chan's family lived in a rough neighbor-hood where racial tensions ran high and resources were scarce. After his father walked away from the family, Soong-Chan's mother had to work two jobs to keep the family afloat. He eventually climbed out of pov-erty, and accumulated the trappings of American success: Ivy League degrees, home ownership, a wife and children, and a professorship in a major American city where he has the freedom to write books and work his ideas into the larger evangelical conversation.

But his scar is a reminder of where he is from, that he once lived in the other America. Back when he attended seminary at the conser-vative evangelical Gordon-Conwell Theological Seminary in the early 1990s, he quickly realized how gravely white evangelicals misunder-stood his America.

During one discussion about poverty, Soong-Chan recalled, white classmates spoke disparagingly about "freeloaders," "welfare queens," and single mothers on food stamps exploiting the government. Soong-Chan looked around the classroom, speechless. As the only nonwhite student, he felt outnumbered. There was so much he wanted to say. He wanted to talk about his mother's backbreaking twenty-hour workdays—ten hours behind the Plexiglas barrier at the inner-city sand-wich shop followed by ten hours working as a nurses' aide at the local nursing home. He thought about the hunger that gnawed at his small stomach as he stared into the barren refrigerator. He remembered how food stamps and the free lunch program for low-income kids helped him survive. So as he listened to his seminary classmates—future pastors—spew, as he called it, "vitriolic venom" and judgment toward "freeloaders," he felt incensed.[5] Little did he know that this experience would shape his career path and put him at the forefront of upending these very views in evangelical culture.

THE HOMOGENOUS UNIT PRINCIPLE

Soong-Chan's classmates reflected the views of typical white evangelicals at the time. Those raised in homogenous, well-off faith communities face little exposure to other ways of life, which limits their worldview, according to sociologists Michael Emerson and Christian Smith in their book *Divided by Faith*. "We were struck by how racially homogenous the social worlds of most evangelicals are, particularly those of white respondents," the authors write. "With a few notable exceptions, none lived in worlds that were not at least 90 percent white in their daily experience."[6] The sheltered, white evangelical environment does not foster empathy for "the other," as media, isolation, and limited points of view tend to reinforce stereotypes.

Homogeneity has long been the status quo of the Christian church in America, so much so that evangelical seminaries have actively encouraged future ministers to perpetuate segregation. This was codified in the predominant "homogenous unit principle," which encourages churches to maximize growth by forming homogenous church communities. Missionary specialist Donald McGavran introduced this principle in his 1955 book *The Bridges of God*. The book lays the foundational concepts for what would become known as the "church growth movement," a pivotal evangelical expansion strategy.

Racial and economic segregation made this movement flourish. Borrowing from the sociological principle of homophily, which says that people tend to stick to their own kind, McGavran encouraged the church to maximize growth by harnessing these tendencies and forming uniform communities. "It does no good to say that tribal peoples ought not to have race prejudice. They do have it and are proud of it. It can be understood and should be made an aid to Christianization."[7]

The evangelical movement thrived by self-segregating, contributing to a Christian America increasingly divided by race, according to Soong-Chan's research. A hunger for growth justified the homogenous unit principle, he explained. "It's easier to do evangelism with people who are like you. So if you look at Rick Warren's book, *The Purpose Driven Church,* he actually identifies—*these are the people we want.*" (Warren's Saddleback Church in Southern California attracts about twenty-thousand people.) Soong-Chan pointed to a photo in Warren's book captioned "'Saddleback Sam'—Our Target" that portrays an educated, upper-class white man dressed in business casual attire, holding a cell phone to his ear. "The photo is about as blatant as it can be," said Soong-Chan. "That's the homogenous unit principle at work."

As a seminary student in the 1990s, Soong-Chan listened to his classmates excitedly talk about this principle, which dominated class discussions. Soong-Chan understood the need for some monoethnic churches, such as churches that catered to people who didn't speak English or to communities facing unique needs as immigrants. After all, as a young boy, Soong-Chan found faith at a Korean immigrant church.[8] But he also saw how the homogenous unit principle was used for nefarious purposes—to justify white separatism and the benefits white communities reaped from turning a blind eye to inequality.

During his studies at seminary, Soong-Chan developed a very different vision. Not only did evangelicals dominate the population, their network reached wide and their resources were abundant—they didn't have to segregate to grow. Multiethnic churches could serve various immigrant communities. They could also commit to racial and economic justice. And as a witness to the world, they could reflect Christian unity across cultural and economic divides. Multiethnic churches could do it all.

But as Soong-Chan remembers it, "I was probably the only person out of anybody in the seminary saying we need to do multiethnic churches." Though he felt alone, he pursued this vision in the years that followed seminary, often feeling like he was preaching into a void. After all, the American church had a checkered history: it had consistently failed at forming multiethnic congregations.

MULTIETHNICITY: A HISTORY OF FAILED ATTEMPTS

Over our country's few centuries, attempts to form multiethnic churches have been stymied. In the eighteenth century, when Christian clergy zealously sought new black converts, segregated seating quickly became the norm. White church members were torn between Christian fellowship and the system of slavery.[9] Church historian Lester B. Scherer's reflections on race relations from 1619 to 1919 summed up the tension white believers faced: "In Christian imagination the blacks were a people apart, to be assessed by different criteria from whites. That perception tainted all approaches to black people, even those designed to . . . liberate them."[10] In response, a subculture of black Christian faith emerged.

In the early 1880s, a white minister named Daniel S. Warner partnered with Julia A. J. Foote, an African Methodist Episcopal Church preacher, in spreading a message of Christian unity. The two led revivals, which broke down many social barriers by attracting men and women, along with whites and blacks.

Warner was a prominent leader in the Church of God movement, a nondenominational movement whose many leaders established biracial congregations across the country. But at the turn of the century, Church of God congregations began to split by race. At the 1912 Church of God annual convention, white leaders encouraged black leaders to spearhead their own separate event because white attendees did not want to attend a convention with so many African Americans present.[11]

Of course, evangelicals do not own the market on racial conflict. Integration was and remains a problem for American society as a whole.

In the Christian realm, every group, from Catholics to Pentecostals, experienced similar imploding events.

By the 1920s, roughly forty thousand pastors had become members of the Ku Klux Klan, bringing white supremacy to pulpits across America. By then, segregation in the country and the church had been firmly established.[12]

Around the middle of the century, a handful of churches managed to maintain multiethnic congregations, but these were liberal outliers, mostly Unitarian churches, according to a 1959 study conducted by the Southern Regional Council.[13]

African American activists tried to challenge the status quo. In the 1960s teams of mixed-race or black activists attempted to attend segregated white congregations, but were routinely turned away, arrested, or placed in separate seating. Many evangelicals in the South supported segregation, echoing justifications such as the one declared by Galloway Memorial Methodist Church, which ejected black students from worship: "It is not un-Christian that we prefer to remain an all-white congregation. The practice of the separation of the races in Galloway Memorial Methodist Church is a time-honored tradition."[14]

As we've seen, white evangelicals not only participated in our country's larger racist patterns, but they also relied on them in order to attract more people to their churches in the second half of the twentieth century.

After Donald McGavran introduced the homogenous unit principle in his 1955 book, the church growth movement became the paramount evangelical strategy for dominating the American religious landscape. In the 1970s, Peter Wagner gave new life to McGavran's gospel with the release of his book *Our Kind of People*. The back cover sums up why this message held such great appeal to white evangelicals, explaining that the book "attacks the Christian guilt complex arising from the civil rights movement." Wagner argues that Jesus himself employed the homogenous unit principle when he selected his inner circle, adding that breaking from this principle threatens "a higher rate of conversion growth." From there, the homogenous unit principle fueled the church growth movement, which caught fire and gave way to the megachurch landscape, single-ethnic congregations and churches catering to specific economic classes—and it established the massive evangelical base we know today.

ANOTHER ATTEMPT AT RACIAL RECONCILIATION

In the 1990s, the racial reconciliation movement forged by black evangelicals such as John Perkins gained mainstream appeal when large evangelical organizations like InterVarsity Christian Fellowship, Chicago's Urban Reconciliation Enterprise, and many others began promoting racial reconciliation as a core evangelical initiative. The enormously influential male-only evangelical group Promise Keepers seized on this priority when it formed in 1991, and by 1997, 30 percent of its 437-member staff were people of color. Promise Keepers, which attracted over one million men to its twenty-two stadium events in 1996, helped make "racial reconciliation" a household term in evangelical circles.[15]

Bill McCartney, the white leader of the group, preached about loving across racial lines, and his 1996 event was dubbed by some Christians as "historic" for its show of unity across racial and denominational lines. *Christianity Today* reported that "a real breakthrough had indeed occurred: Pentecostals and Baptists prayed together; Anglos and men of color embraced. In perhaps the most moving event of the gathering, PK leaders invited men of color down to the [Georgia] Dome floor, while white ministers stood and cheered them."[16]

But these were flimsy gestures that failed to rigorously grapple with historic and institutional inequality. As Carl Ellis, leader of the Christian ministry Project Joseph, put it: "Tears and hugs and saying I'm sorry is a good first step, but for me, the question is not one of changing the hearts of individuals as [much as] it is dealing with the systems and the structures that are devastating African-American people."[17]

McCartney himself admitted that the popularity of reconciliation didn't last long. In his book *Sold Out* he explains that after the racial reconciliation message at Promise Keepers peaked in 1996, about 40 percent of participants reacted negatively to the reconciliation theme, and that likely played into the diminishing attendance numbers in 1997. "It is simply a hard teaching for many," McCartney writes.[18]

SPLINTERING

Today, new multiethnic initiatives, along with other attempts to bolster church membership, have formed against the backdrop of rapidly shifting generational and racial demographics within the evangelical world. On one hand the mass exodus of white millennials has leaders wringing their hands about declining membership. Currently, only 10 percent of young Americans are white evangelicals, whereas 30 percent of Americans sixty-five and older are evangelicals, according to data from the Public Religion Research Institute.[19] But looking at white evangelicals alone does not tell the whole story: today, more than half of younger Christians are people of color. In other words, young Christians have flipped from being mostly white to mostly nonwhite. In another twist, the "nones"—people with no religion—now represent the largest religious group among young Americans.[20]

Simply put, "What you have in American religion today are the nonwhite Christians and the Nones," according to Mark Silk, a Trinity College professor of religion in public life, in an interview with Faith-Street.com.[21] As a result of these two major demographic shifts, two movements within evangelicalism have evolved: one tailored to young, hip believers interested in making Christianity culturally relevant to white evangelicals walking out the door, and a second driven by people of color making multiethnic churches more possible and urging the church to embrace their unique values and causes.

The contrast and conflict between the two movements was starkly evident at a conference I attended in 2011. The Jubilee Conference was geared toward college and post-college evangelicals. It was a sea of flannel and tousled hair, interrupted by the occasional crisp oxford shirt. Two keynote speakers, Gabe Lyons and Soong-Chan Rah, took the stage on separate days. Gabe pitched his vision for a new evangelicalism, one that reached beyond politics and permeated all corners of culture. To demonstrate his point, he invited his friend, Michael Braeger, a smoldering Giorgio Armani male model chiseled from head to toe, to join him on stage to talk about staying true to God in the weedy world of high fashion.

Michael recounted in disappointingly vague terms a time he felt compromised at a photo shoot and had to walk away; then he quickly moved on to a story about living out his faith through volunteer work. Some audience members listened intently. Others sat transfixed by the Jumbotron display of Michael and a female model dashing across a glitzy cityscape. Still others looked confused about the point of it all. There were mixed feelings about Gabe's talk. For many, his male-model schtick rang hollow. Minority leaders I spoke to felt disconnected from Gabe's message. One shook her head and wondered aloud, "What was the point of that?"

When Soong-Chan took the stage, he had nothing sexy to offer. Instead, he blamed American evangelicals for perpetuating conservative white values—"cultural Christianity"—instead of a true gospel message of peace: "biblical Christianity." He urged his audience to examine the core principles of their faith and to change the legacy of the church.

"For example, the Bible does not directly say that you have the right to bear arms, yet I have found at least one hundred passages that talk about caring and showing justice for the alien and immigrant among us," Rah said. He wondered why the "typical evangelical church" seemed to have more members of the NRA than people advocating for immigration reform. "Is that cultural Christianity or biblical Christianity?" The audience answered Soong-Chan's question with a mixture of applause and audible contempt.

Rah and Lyons represent two sides of a new evangelical movement battling to win the next generation at a very impressionable time. Soong-Chan explained the disparity this way: "There is a racial and socioeconomic divide between ministries." Lyons and Rah respectively embody a conservative faction with a slick, pseudoprogressive message and a scrappy progressive movement working to bring believers into the difficult, complicated work of racial justice. Soong-Chan believes the rising population of evangelicals of color holds the key to motivating the church to effect real systemic social change.

TOKEN MINORITIES

In working on racial reconciliation, Soong-Chan is entering the long legacy of leaders trying to integrate evangelical churches. In the decades since seminary, he has established new churches (including his own multiethnic urban church), led his community in racial reconciliation and social justice initiatives, worked for InterVarsity Christian Fellowship, become a seminary professor, served on the board of major evangelical outfits, and traveled the country speaking about racial issues in the evangelical church.

More recently, the topic of multiethnic Christian communities has gained traction among mainstream evangelicals, but Soong-Chan has worried that the folks jumping on the bandwagon are more interested in embracing the multiethnic label than the content.

When Christian colleges invite him to speak, he often feels like a token minority voice promoted to assuage white guilt. Soong-Chan has witnessed only marginal institutional change in response to his message. Sometimes a few individuals—typically students of color—will thank him and keep in touch. On the other end of the spectrum are those who bristle at his message, often with angry editorials. At a speech delivered to students at Wheaton College in Illinois a decade ago, Soong-Chan asserted that Christianity masked Western imperialism and criticized the colonialist tendencies of missionaries. Afterward, a student created a website dedicated to the talk, printing Soong-Chan's name below a big picture of Karl Marx. "When you clicked on the picture, they had taken words I had said out of context—'colonialism,' 'imperialism'— and they had looped it with the Soviet Union national anthem playing in the background," Soong-Chan recalled. It was a troubling response, but Soong-Chan, toughened by decades of facing this kind of hostility, laughed as he recalled this story. He was more deeply disturbed by the "95 percent of the middle that couldn't care less."

Even as multiethnic churches become the next evangelical hot topic, Soong-Chan worries that many initiatives are superficial, with an eye toward church expansion and not much else. That creates "a level of mistrust," Soong-Chan said. "You didn't want us in your churches. You didn't want to hear what we had to say. And now all of a sudden you say, 'Oh, come to our churches.' And you want us to adapt to your style of worship and style of teaching just so you can call yourself a multiethnic church so your churches can grow? It's like, where did this come from? Where's the depth to it? Where's the sincerity to it? Is it just another fad that you're latching on to?"

The heart of Soong-Chan's critique comes down to how many white evangelicals adopt issues that impact minorities (multiethnicity and racial justice, for example) but fail to invite minorities to lead these initiatives. Take for example the recent popularity of justice-themed conferences, Soong-Chan said. Today, these conferences extol white celebrity leaders—like megachurch superstar Rick Warren and David Platt, the wunderkind preacher who barred women from church deaconship—as headliners, but rarely include speakers of color like John Perkins, "who has embodied justice for his entire life," or pastors of African American churches who confront racial injustice day in and day out, said Soong-Chan. These leaders have been addressing issues of prison reform, church segregation, and inequality for decades, paying a steep cost through beatings, imprisonment, or economic hardship, but they're almost never keynote speakers. As a result, white evangelical leaders give speeches, make names for themselves, and call evangelicals to "a pretty simple and easily attainable form of justice." Christian conference speakers don't call attendees to civil disobedience to protest systemic racial injustices like police brutality, where there may be a real cost. Instead, they urge followers to write checks for orphans. "Of course it's a good thing to feed an orphan," Soong-Chan said. "But you don't have to change your life." A rough 2013 survey of popular evangelical conferences found that only 13 percent of 775 speakers were people of color.[22] And these conferences tend to rely on the same minority speakers who will reliably back the theological and ideological views of the organizers, said Soong-Chan, pointing to celebrated preachers like Billy Kim, who spoke adoringly about American triumphalism through its wars and made a jab at President Obama ("Even if President Obama comes from Chicago, may God *still* bless Chicago!") at a 2015 conference at the conservative Moody Bible Institute.[23]

The omission of real diversity—diversity of perspectives, of theology, of culture—bothers Soong-Chan. On one hand, demographic changes suggest that minorities will soon make up the majority of the church, and Soong-Chan absolutely believes that the American church must embrace diversity in order to survive. Still, he can't help but feel cynical at times about the way this is being done.

Soong-Chan has sometimes wondered, "Are we just being co-opted by the majority culture to simply advance the majority culture's agenda without actually reflecting who we are in your communities?"

DEBORAH

This is a question I've heard evangelicals of color ask repeatedly. It's the same question I asked as I made my exit from evangelicalism. I've known all along that racism happens on many levels. I've experienced a range in my life, from microaggressions to violence. And while most of the racism I faced in the evangelical world played out in subtle ways, the buildup over the years eventually drove me away. A pivotal moment came my senior year of college, when many in my group attended a year-end retreat in northern Michigan.

One night, our group was winding down after an evening service. Several dozen of us milled around the open room socializing. There was a small platform at the front of the room, where decorative cloths hung beside a blank screen that had earlier displayed worship song lyrics. I had joined an impromptu drum circle in one corner. The rows of chairs that once filled the room had been put away, so most students sat in clusters on the floor. The sound of laughter and conversation filled the room.

Suddenly, the screen flickered with light. I looked up and saw a familiar image. *Where had I seen this before?* And then it clicked: this was the music video from India. Just a few months earlier, I had explained to my old roommate Rebecca that the way the students wanted to dance to the video—fake turbans, silly dancing—seemed hurtful, like they were ridiculing another culture. My feedback was ignored. I found out later that the performance came and went. I expressed my disappointment, and then moved on. I didn't think it would come up again.

Rebecca and Toby had both missed the earlier performance and had been egging on the dancers to perform an encore, the two later explained to me. That night at the retreat, the students decided to share their dance with the entire chapter.

As the music filled the room, my eyes darted between the rapt crowd and the four students who were excitedly tearing down the cloth decorations and wrapping them around their heads like turbans. The students began dancing, their arms flailing wildly, their voices intoning apishly to the melody. They could hardly keep their composure because they were laughing so hard. It was mocking, insulting, and utterly cringeworthy. I ran to the back of the room, my mind racing, tears filling my eyes, unsure of what to do. I watched some friends roar with laughter. Then I saw John, a staff worker of Indian descent, watching the terrible display, his arms crossed. I stood beside him and apologized. I told him I had tried to stop this months ago. He responded sharply, his voice trembling with anger and pain; I had never seen him look so enraged. We turned our gaze back to the dancers. I couldn't take it anymore, so I ran to the bathroom and cried helplessly in a stall. Just a few moments later, I heard the music come to an abrupt stop. I returned to the room to find two young female staff workers, one white and one Asian American, standing before the room, explaining why what had just happened was offensive. I was surprised and impressed that anyone had done anything at all.

After they spoke, they opened the floor for a discussion. A number of people, including John and me, shared our feelings of frustration with the group. Many white students were defensive, explaining that they meant no harm. Eventually, we went our separate ways. Rebecca had been holding my jacket, and when she handed it to me, I could barely look at her.

The next day, our staff members scrapped the original itinerary and devoted the remainder of the time to processing the conflict. First, they split white students from students of color. People in both groups objected to this decision, but others found it helpful. Among the students of color, some saw no issue with the dance and felt that those hurt by it were overreacting. Others explained that it was problematic to mock another culture. Slowly, people began sharing the ways they had been ridiculed for their race or ethnicity. It was a tense, but moving time. I realized that many others shared my pain and had experienced similar tales of bullying. When we reconvened with our white peers, we told a few of these stories. It felt uncomfortable and it brought a lot of tears, but it seemed necessary in explaining why such insensitive behavior cut so deep.

I studied at the University of Illinois for an extra semester after my senior year and dedicated those final months to generating more rigorous racial dialogue. Many students of color pulled me aside to thank me for what I was doing, and it was exciting to feel a new sense of community forming. A consensus was building: many of us suddenly did not feel so alone anymore. But many white peers—even people I considered friends—began to distance themselves from me. Some called my efforts a distraction. I noticed others who exchanged eye rolls with their friends when I made announcements about racial reconciliation events, such as lectures, Bible studies, and discussions, that I and another leader were hosting. One acquaintance asked me to lunch to inform me that she and others were bothered by the white guilt this curriculum made them feel. I explained that reconciliation took time and would not be easy. It was a strange, uncomfortable conversation.

One could argue that the evangelical race problem is simply a reflection of our culture's larger race problem—Hollywood, boardrooms, and seminaries share this in common. I agree with this, but when I was in college, I naively believed that Christians could rise above the culture. After all, our prayers connected us to a God of justice and mercy who taught us how to break free from cultural norms, go against the flow, and do what is right despite popular opinion. Not only did I believe faith could give us the strength to do this, I believed it could give us the insight to see what was wrong in the first place. Shouldn't Christians easily understand systemic injustice, discrimination against people of color and women, and the ways queer people suffer? But Christians were just like the rest of the country, and in many cases, far worse.

I walked away from InterVarsity understanding that you can't integrate by just putting different people in the same room. Recruiting for diversity differed greatly from forging healthy, inclusive mixed communities. The latter takes effort and gets messy. You have to acknowledge that people come into the room with their own experiences and history. If the majority culture is not ready to acknowledge those experiences, it's not going to work. It's going to be superficial.

At the end of college, I was glad to be done with InterVarsity. I spent the next few years trying to revive my relationship with the church, slipping through all kinds of chapels and oversized worship halls, letting the serenades of ancient hymns, African spirituals, and dated Christian rock wash over me. I grasped at fleeting moments of hope, but that familiar spirit of injustice always seemed to find me: at one church, in the scornful looks thrown my way when I declined to sign a "defense of marriage" petition; in sermons that blamed feminism for the glut of deadbeat dads. Even at a hip, youthful congregation, where the communion line resembled a Diesel fashion show (picture a trail of gorgeous hipsters dunking artisanal bread in wine), the church denied ordination and marriage to LGBTQ people and, in one sermon, the pastor drew from the 2007 Virginia Tech massacre sweeping conclusions about the perils of "strict" Asian culture. I met the pastor for coffee after that sermon. In the gentlest, yet most forthright way I could muster, I told him that I found his decision to use the Virginia Tech massacre as a window into Asian culture deeply disturbing. He said that an Asian friend of his agreed with his interpretation, so that was that. Shortly after, I left the church altogether.

SIGNS OF HOPE

Over the years Soong-Chan has encountered his share of frustration with the establishment's treatment of ethnic minorities, from those who promote overtly racist content to those who make shallow attempts at addressing race issues in the church. In 2003 he battled LifeWay Christian Resources, an agency of the Southern Baptist Convention, for its children's Bible study curriculum Rickshaw Rally, which promoted racial stereotypes of Asians. In addition to lyrics such as "Wax on, wax off, get your rickshaw ready," the program used stereotypical imagery such as chopsticks, take-out boxes, and karate uniforms. Pictures from participants include white adults in yellowface dressed in conical hats and kimonos. It's baffling why they chose to stereotype Asian culture for a children's Bible study; the material was not some misguided attempt to appeal to an Asian Christian audience. The Asian references, it seems, were simply part of the program's "motif."

Soong-Chan set up a website explaining why the material was offensive and gathered over one thousand signatures from supporters opposing the curriculum. In response, the Southern Baptist Convention defended itself, justifying the material with familiar claims of theological orthodoxy and evangelism. "We believe our materials are biblically sound," LifeWay's communication director Rob Phillips said.[24] Soong-Chan would have to wait a decade for a sincere apology from LifeWay.

That apology came in 2013, in the wake of rising tensions between Asian Americans and white evangelical leaders. In September, Rick Warren, the celebrated megachurch pastor who delivered President Obama's 2009 inaugural benediction, posted to his Facebook account an image of a smiling, industrious-looking Chinese Red Guard with the caption, "The typical attitude of Saddleback Staff as they start work each day." This came just days before Warren launched his megachurch's expansion into Hong Kong.

Thousands of his followers liked the image, but many others criticized the post for its lack of cultural sensitivity. During China's Cultural Revolution of 1966–1976, Chairman Mao's Communist youth, known as Red Guards, violently oppressed, tortured, and killed millions of Chinese.

Warren defended his Red Guard post: "People often miss irony on the Internet. It's a joke people! If you take this seriously, you really shouldn't be following me!" But this only brought fiercer criticism from Asian American leaders like seminary professor Sam Tsang and Kathy Khang, a multiethnic ministries director with InterVarsity, and many others. On her blog, which went viral, Kathy wrote, "Please reconsider your comments that essentially told many of your brothers and sisters in Christ to get over it, to get a sense of humor, to lighten up, etc."[25] Others echoed her critique, and Warren eventually took down his original post and issued this statement as an apology: "If you were hurt, upset, offended, or distressed by my insensitivity I am truly sorry. May God richly bless you."[26]

A few weeks later in October, Christine Lee, an evangelical Episcopal priest from New York City, attended Exponential West, an evangelical leadership conference that featured a short video skit about the Christian mentor-apprentice relationship.[27] In an attempt to parody *The Karate Kid*, a white person used a mocking Asian accent and made karate-chop gestures against a backdrop of stereotypical "Oriental" music. Though a self-described conflict-avoider, Christine found a conference leader and voiced her disapproval. The leader dismissed her concerns and explained that the video was intended to be funny—it was a parody, that's all.

Christine left that conversation angry and posted her frustration on Facebook and Twitter, where a flurry of supporters flocked to her side. It caught the attention of other Asian American evangelical leaders, like Kathy and Helen Lee, an author and an editor at InterVarsity Press. The two began reaching out to others at the conference, connecting with Asian American evangelical leaders and drafting an open letter to express their dismay over evangelical culture's broad disregard of Asian American concerns. Two days after Christine's social media posting, a group of Asian American leaders met with the Exponential organizers to discuss why the skit triggered so much pain.

"I gained new and helpful insights into some of my own blind spots," said Exponential president Dave Ferguson in a blog post recounting the incident.[28] The next day, Exponential issued an apology.[29]

Shortly after Rick Warren's Facebook post and the Exponential discussion, Asian American evangelical leaders published "An Open Letter from the Asian American Community to the Evangelical Church" calling out these and past offenses by the evangelical church and garnering close to a thousand signatures. The letter was covered by *Christianity Today* and major media outlets such as National Public Radio. It called for the inclusion of Asian American voices in *Christianity Today*, examined the institutional barriers keeping out Asian American voices in the larger evangelical conversation, and demanded higher standards for respectfully reflecting Asian American culture. The letter also called out past high-profile incidents such as the 2003 LifeWay Rickshaw Rally curriculum. The following month, LifeWay finally issued the apology Soong-Chan had asked for a decade earlier.

This rapid progression of events underscores not only the growing number of Asian American evangelicals, but also to their increased activism around racial justice issues. Highly networked with each other, with major institutions, and with the media, these Asian Americans are not only speaking out against offenses to their culture, but also standing in open, vocal solidarity with other ethnic minorities and their justice issues.

A PLACE OF OUR OWN

Envision 2008, the conference of national progressive evangelical and mainline Protestant leaders that Lisa helped plan, was to be the antidote to evangelical ignorance, a galvanizing force that would propel an inclusive evangelical movement forward. The planning meetings were filled with energy. Lisa and a handful of committee members would gather in the living room of her uptown Manhattan apartment, contact lists open, pens poised over notebooks, speaking excitedly as they charted out the weekend that would change everything.

They crafted a vision for the "postwhite, radical, evangelical but generously ecumenical vision of the kingdom God" for the twenty-first century, as one member put it. They expressed gratitude that crowd-grabbing white speakers like Jim Wallis and Brian McLaren had agreed to speak, but also called them "just fronts for the next generation." Lisa's coplanner, the Reverend Peter Heltzel, a professor at New York Theological Seminary, elaborated: "The women, the people of color, the voices that have been marginalized, we're going to put [them] forward to say where do *they* think we need to go?" Peter, a white forty-something with wild brown curls and unconfined energy, looked like a caffeinated disciple of Jesus. His voice boomed and his body gyrated as he spoke about how the Religious Right's "days are numbered" and about how the younger generation is "reinventing North American Christianity."

"I think the political landscape has been shifting for the past two years and it's still unstable," said Rita Nakashima Brock, a licensed minister at the Christian Church (Disciples of Christ) and longtime feminist activist, at a meeting in November 2007. Brock believed that this moment represented a ripe opportunity for a major change in the religious-political realm, and that their group could play a major role. "I see this as not a one-shot deal, but as the beginning of a long-term initiative. I see this as a decade-long thing, at least. I see this as building that kind of movement. I want us to think big."

The first Envision weekend drew a modest crowd of a couple hundred curious Christians. Speakers heralded the demise of the Religious Right, younger evangelicals spoke about the inevitability of progress in their churches and many speculated about what the future held. And while it didn't feel history-making in the moment, the connections forged, especially among the leaders, gave birth to a community of female evangelical leaders and evangelical leaders of color that would slowly transform some of the most influential evangelical organizations and conferences in the years to come.

In year two, Envision ran a scholars' conference at which the progressive mainline Protestant leaders, who were pushing liberal views on sexuality, and progressive evangelical leaders, who were comparably more conservative, realized just how great the gap was between their theologies. The evangelical leaders knew they would need to move at their own pace if they wanted to reach their constituency—

conservative evangelicals. So Lisa and a handful of other evangelicals, including Soong-Chan Rah, formed a new group, Evangelicals for Justice. (The Envision conferences ceased after three years, but E4J carries on to this day.) This collection of like-minded progressive evangelical leaders met monthly on conference calls and annually in person. Together, they discussed the race and gender challenges in the evangelical world, and devised strategies for breaking the long trend of superficial racial reconciliation. Lisa did not know just how far their influence would reach or how deeply they'd be transformed by their own initiatives. But she looked forward to each monthly phone call, thankful for a place of belonging. She had finally found her tribe.

FIVE

Submit No More

DARKNESS AND SPOTLIGHTS

It was June. Every seat was filled at the palatial Wright Fine Arts Center auditorium at Samford University. The Miss Alabama Pageant was in full swing and excitement rattled the building as the crowd awaited the swimsuit competition. Backstage, Jennifer Crumpton sat at her stage mirror making a masochistic wonder bra. She pressed her breasts together, applied silicone inserts ("chicken cutlets"), and held everything together with duct tape stretched across her tender skin.

By her late teens, Jennifer found herself thoroughly steeped in the conservative, complementarian values of Southern Baptist Alabama. Gone was her early childhood confidence. Gone was the feeling of being limitless. In their place was a rigid sense that as a woman, she was valued for her obedience, public grace, and beauty.

Jennifer embodied these qualities so well that during her freshman year at Samford University, a Baptist-affiliated school a Bible toss from Jennifer's home, her sorority sisters encouraged her to enter the Miss Samford beauty pageant. They saw her as "the full package"—a skilled ballerina and a good Christian girl who was undeniably gorgeous. Blond hair cascaded down her back, and she had the kitten eyes and angled cheekbones of a cover girl. After she placed second in her first pageant, the pageant coordinators came calling, pushing her toward bigger, more prestigious competitions. Jennifer rode the wave, taking all their advice to heart: never leave the house without makeup, avoid scandal, live a godly life, excel at everything, work intensely, and think about the pageant "every minute of every day." Within a few years, Jennifer found herself at the top of the state pageant circuit, a favorite in the 1997 Miss Alabama Pageant.

Around the backstage dressing room, other Miss Alabama contestants were applying the same MacGyver resourcefulness to their breasts. They tore ribbons of duct tape, dusted blush into their cleavage, and sprayed a chemical adhesive to their bottoms to keep their suits from riding up. Later, they would have to peel the tape and hardened fabric from their bodies, the sound of ripping skin mingling with muffled cries. With the Miss Alabama title in the balance, it was a small price to pay.

Jennifer wasn't concerned about pain. She looked at her reflection and shot a worried look at her chest. *What if the chicken cutlets slide down my bathing suit?* She said a quick prayer.

Praying was appropriate in this setting. The Alabama pageant world, as Jennifer put it, "was all about Jesus." Churches hosted competitions, turning altars into catwalks where girls learned to weave faith sound bites into interview answers and stride around in high heels. Pageants served a higher purpose: they extolled the community's most "upstanding, outstanding" Christian women.

Backstage at the Miss Alabama Pageant, it looked like a tent revival, only with heavy eye makeup and big hair. Girls paced and prayed for victory, some mouthing their petitions, others aggressively whispering their savior's name. "Je-sus. Jeee-sus!" The ultra devout girls even saluted each other by holding up their fingers in a "V," calling to each other, "Virgins 'til marriage!"[1]

Just before the swimsuit competition began, Jennifer took one last look at herself: her bright pink one-piece hugged all the right curves. Her hair and makeup were in place. She looked stunning—but under the duct tape, silicone, and chemical spray, she felt like a "disaster waiting to happen." It wasn't just the duct tape and the lights that were uncomfortable; between pageant and church culture, she was tired of the demands that she be perfect. She had grown so used to living according to the expectations of others, she hardly knew what she herself wanted in life. She was ready to find out. Whatever the outcome of Miss Alabama, she had already decided that this would be her last competition.

When I met Jennifer more than a decade later, in 2011, she still had the perfectly coiffed hair of a beauty queen, but none of the rehearsed rhetoric. She told me about her pageant background in the embarrassed tone reserved for confessionals.

"I look back on that and I'm horrified," she said. "I can't believe that I did this. I can't believe my family was proud of me."

Pageants heightened the narrow definition of women in which her community, family, and church strongly believed. Internalizing these values made for some dark years in Jennifer's life. At one point in her young adult years, a boyfriend raped Jennifer, sending her into a tailspin of post-traumatic stress. Part of her felt at fault. On one hand, the responsibility to remain "pure" rested with her, the woman, or so she was taught. On the other hand, she had learned to never challenge a man's authority; this time was like any other. Still another part of her began to view these ideas as dead wrong. Deep inside, a quiet, angry voice cried out: *He did this to me.*

Beleaguered by the trauma of being raped and by pageant pressure "to be perfect," everything felt bleak to Jennifer, as if there was no way out and she had no control over her own life.

In the last few minutes of the Miss Alabama competition, two contestants remained: Jennifer and another woman. An exciting moment, but Jennifer felt only dread. "If you win the pageant you literally become theirs all year. You had a chaperone at all times. You lived with somebody. If you had a boyfriend, you had to break up. You couldn't leave the house without makeup."

Beyond Jennifer's world, the feminist movement had been shaking the country. A decade before Jennifer was born, Betty Friedan's *The Feminine Mystique* awoke a generation of unhappy housewives to "the problem that has no name," the notion that female fulfillment came from homemaking. In 1966 the National Organization for Women was founded. In 1971 *Ms.* magazine began publishing, and in 1972 the Equal Rights Amendment to the Constitution had passed both houses of Congress and was awaiting ratification by the states. In 1973, the same year Jennifer was born, the Supreme Court established the right to abortion in *Roe v. Wade*.

Though the feminist revolution had yet to reach Jennifer, in her own way, she was experiencing an internal awakening. She realized she did not know who she was—she hadn't known for years. To some she was the beauty queen. To others, she was the idealized Christian woman. But she knew if she told anyone about being raped, she would suddenly be the slut.

Jennifer wanted to run far away from the pageant system. Though everyone she knew thought this was "the pinnacle of womanhood," by her last year, "I was like, 'What the fuck?' I had finally begun—barely begun—to have a mind of my own: *These people can't be right.* I started listening to myself a little more: *This is wrong.*"

Moments away from being crowned Miss Alabama or deemed the runner-up, Jennifer looked out at the audience. Her family was watching, but all she saw were the blindingly bright stage lights. The other contestant grabbed Jennifer's hand and looked heavenward, her face trembling with expectation. Jennifer nearly groaned, but she forced a smile as the anticipation swelled. There was a long pause in the announcer's voice. And then she heard her name. She was the first runner-up. A wave of relief washed over her as she hugged the winner and stepped to the side. Just like that, her pageant days were over.

PURITY

So much of what Jennifer had longed to escape was evangelical purity culture, which links a woman's self-worth to her sexual history and presentation. At InterVarsity I learned an identical message: a woman's virginity was her greatest virtue, a gift for her future husband. We read books like Elisabeth Elliot's seminal *Passion and Purity*, in which she writes, "I did not want to be among the marked-down goods on the bargain table, cheap because they'd been pawed over. Crowds collect there. It is only the few who will pay full price."

Purity culture stems from a long history of Christian theologies that cast women as sexually controversial. One early church father called women "the devil's gateway," and monastic fathers associated men with spirit and women with sinful flesh.[2] The contemporary purity movement sprouted in the 1990s. It can be read as a reaction not only to the aftermath of the sexual revolution, but to the AIDS epidemic, and the media focus on teen pregnancies in the 1980s.

In 1993, the Southern Baptist Convention launched the True Love Waits campaign, which quickly became a global sensation. Denominations adopted its sex education curriculum (abstinence only), hundreds of thousands of teens signed virginity pledge cards, and in 1994, the campaign displayed 210,000 cards on the National Mall during a rally that attracted twenty-five thousand youth.[3] With each passing year, the rallies drew more cards and teens.

Fathers bought their daughters (but not their sons) "purity rings," which the young women wore on their left ring finger as a symbol of their virginity, only to be removed when replaced by a wedding ring. It symbolized the patriarchal idea that a woman transfers her guardianship from one man to the other. The fact that men didn't have purity rings underscored the gravity of a woman losing her virginity before marriage (she's damaged goods) compared to the redeemable act of a man doing the exact same thing (he merely stumbled). It's a system where women's bodies are controlled and their voices are silenced, and men hold the authority.

Purity culture places the responsibility of sexual morality on women. It creates a dangerous framework in which, even if a man behaves badly, a narrative would be constructed to lay blame on the woman. In cases of consensual premarital sex before marriage, repenting men can undergo a redemption process (confession, prayer, renewal) while repenting women tend to face rebuke for shirking their duty and shame for irreversibly "defiling" their bodies.

Tina Sellers, director of the Medical Family Therapy Program and instructor at the evangelical Seattle Pacific University, has researched the psychological impact of purity culture. Her research began when she saw its negative impact on her students. As part of her course, Sellers has asked students to write a sexual biography. In the past decade, she has noticed "horrendous amounts" of sexual shame expressed in these assignments. "The self-loathing that people were feeling and describing about themselves really paralleled the kind of self-loathing that you often see with somebody who's experienced childhood sexual assault," she said, according to TheOtherJournal.com, a publication in partnership with the Seattle School of Theology and Psychology.[4]

The consequences of purity culture escalate when applied to actual cases of sexual assault; again, adherents typically justify the actions of men and blame women. Nowhere is this more plainly evident than in headlines about how certain Christian colleges have responded to sexual violence. At fundamentalist Bob Jones University, an alleged rape victim filed a report only to be met by a dean who inquired, "Is there anything you did that made him do that?" reported Al Jazeera America in 2013.[5] Soon afterward she was expelled.

In a 2014 *New Republic* article, Kiera Feldman writes about a sexual assault case at Patrick Henry College.[6] Famously nicknamed "God's Harvard," it is a feeder school for conservative political jobs in Washington. When a female student reported that a fellow student had sexually assaulted her, the dean laid blame on both of them, reportedly saying to the female student, "You are in part responsible for what happened, because you put yourself in a compromising situation. Actions have consequences."

Patrick Henry College leaves its female students especially unprotected because, as Feldman reports, it is "one of only four private colleges in the United States that eschews federal funds in order to avoid complying with government regulations."[7] This means the school is exempt from policies aimed at protecting victims, such as the Clery Act, under which schools must release campus crime reports; Title IX, which mandates an independent investigation by the school and accommodations for the victim; and the Campus Sexual Violence Elimination Act, which requires prompt proceedings, transparency and accountability from the school. These regulations don't guarantee proper handling of sexual-assault cases, but their absence at Patrick Henry show how little legal recourse the school's students actually have.

At its core, purity culture advances the conservative evangelical goal of curbing female independence. By controlling a woman's choice in reproduction, sexual expression, attire, and overall behavior, the patriarchal establishment robs a woman of the authority over her own body. In fact, independent women are set apart as sinful and rebellious. And if female autonomy in itself is sinful, acts that violate it, like rape, are less likely to be viewed as clearly wrong or criminal. The confluence of purity culture, deficient sex education, and pervasive patriarchy leaves young evangelical women dangerously vulnerable.

"I JUST WANTED TO DIE"

In the months after Jennifer's boyfriend raped her, Jennifer's world turned upside down. The symptoms of post-traumatic stress set in—the flashbacks, the depression, the self-hate, the hopelessness. She numbly went through the routines of her life; she even continued dating her boyfriend for a little while. "I just had no context for how to handle what had happened," she recalled. Her brain worked overtime, constantly in crisis mode: *I can't get out of this. I don't know how to change my life. I hate myself. Nobody can know about this. I must act perfect.* The self-destructive thoughts seemed to never cease. "I definitely had moments where I just wanted to die." Even when she finally found the strength to leave her boyfriend, her family grew angry with her for ending what seemed to be a good thing. "I was turned into this huge villain." But she couldn't tell anyone why she did it because she knew she'd also be blamed for the date rape.

For years, she felt haunted by the idea that she had prompted the trauma. "Throughout my twenties I never addressed it because I was so unequipped to assess what had happened," she says. She grew depressed, anxious, and crippled by "staggering self-doubt" and the inability to make decisions about anything. "Everything just got really hard."

CONSERVATISM WINS OUT

Evangelical feminism failed to reach the young Jennifer because the conservative evangelical message drowned it out. As evangelical feminists gained backers of the Equal Rights Amendment (ERA), they, along with secular feminists pushing for state ratification of the amendment, did not predict the overwhelming influence of the anti-ERA movement, STOP ERA, led by Phyllis Schlafly.

The ERA passed both houses of Congress in 1972 and then awaited ratification by state legislatures. Early in the decade, the majority of evangelicals backed the ERA's basic feminist thrust of securing equality for women in all realms of society, according to Seth Dowland, religious historian and author of *Family Values and the Rise of the Christian Right*.[8] But soon after, Phyllis Schlafly and other conservative Christians reframed the ERA, and feminism as a whole, as fundamentally antifamily. Nationally, this strategy won over men and women across the country and across denominational boundaries, creating a tidal wave of anti-ERA activism aimed at halting ratification by state legislatures; passage of the ERA was ultimately defeated.

The success of Schlafly's STOP ERA efforts shifted political alignments. "The disproportionate representation of the Old South demonstrated the importance of conservative evangelical southerners to the STOP ERA coalition, yet this list of states also indicated the linkages among conservative activists in the Midwest and Sunbelt that defined the Republican Party in the second half of the twentieth century," writes Dowland. "The alliance of women opposed to ERA signaled the shifting landscape of religion and politics in America."

This shift laid the groundwork for the antiabortion movement. In the coming decades, this issue would help secure the evangelical vote for the Republican Party. The evolution of evangelical opposition to abortion is a story all its own. Evangelicals had not always taken an antichoice position. In the 1960s and 1970s, evangelicals were largely silent, if not supportive, of abortion rights. At a 1968 symposium on birth control, sponsored by the Christian Medical Society and *Christianity Today*, evangelical leaders declined to categorize abortion as sinful. They released a statement that acknowledged their diversity of opinions and declared that certain situations justified abortion. "When principles conflict, the preservation of fetal life . . . may have to be abandoned to maintain full and secure family life."[9]

In 1971, representatives at the Southern Baptist Convention concurred, passing a resolution that declared, "We call upon Southern Baptists to work for legislation that will allow the possibility of abortion under such conditions as rape, incest, clear evidence of severe fetal deformity, and carefully ascertained evidence of the likelihood of damage to the emotional, mental, and physical health of the mother."[10] Even after the *Roe* ruling, Southern Baptists reaffirmed this position repeatedly, in 1974 and 1976. In a *Baptist Press* piece, W. Barry Garrett wrote, "Religious liberty, human equality and justice are advanced by the Supreme Court abortion decision."[11] Leading intellectuals from the most esteemed evangelical institutions agreed. In a *Christianity Today* piece, Robert P. Meye of Fuller Theological Seminary, wrote that evangelicals "must reckon with the fact that there are those within the Christian community who can see no final offense in abortion when entered into responsibly by a woman in consultation with a physician."[12]

Architects of the evangelical Right themselves admit that their mid-1970s efforts to galvanize evangelical opposition to abortion flopped. Their constituency was divided over the issue, but most of all, they were apathetic. Ringleader Paul Weyrich noted that when he tried to get evangelicals mobilized around abortion, school prayer, and the Equal Rights Amendment, "I utterly failed." As late as 1980, the evangelical publication *Moody Monthly* lamented that, when it came to abortion, "evangelicalism as a whole has uttered no real outcry. We've organized no protest."[13]

This changed in the 1980s, when Jerry Falwell used his new, influential position as cofounder of the Moral Majority and capitalized on the widening Religious Right network to spread the antichoice gospel. Revered evangelical intellectual Francis Schaeffer provided the theological infrastructure for evangelical political action, citing abortion, secular humanism, and pluralism as enemies to unite against in his 1981 book *A Christian Manifesto*. These leaders paved the way for a massive antiabortion movement among evangelicals. In the 1980s, groups such as Operation Rescue mobilized evangelicals to demonstrate at abortion clinics, protest events like the 1988 Democratic National Convention, and distribute graphic images of aborted fetuses. By the late 1980s, the Religious Right had firmly cemented a new, absolutist evangelical position against abortion.

As the conservative message overtook the evangelical community in the 1980s, the evangelical feminist movement began to fracture along ideological lines. At first, divisions formed over contrasting methods of biblical interpretation. Conservative feminists argued that correct biblical interpretation (one that accounts for historical and cultural context) points to a consistent message of gender equality, while liberal feminists respected the Bible's authority while also acknowledging the human error in scripture. In other words, the conservatives blamed patriarchy on flawed biblical interpretation and the liberals blamed it on flawed biblical authors.[14]

In the broader evangelical world, the conservative feminists received some criticism, but the liberal feminists faced the harshest blowback for departing from biblical inerrancy. Critics questioned their hermeneutics, or method of interpretation, saying they appeared less guided by the Bible and more influenced by the surrounding culture.

Within the evangelical feminist movement, these theological differences fully came to the surface when the Evangelical Women's Caucus broached the subject of homosexuality. In 1978 Letha Scanzoni (who cowrote *All We're Meant to Be*) and Virginia Mollenkott published their groundbreaking book *Is the Homosexual My Neighbor?* in which they argue for acceptance of gays and lesbians within the church. They were pioneer Christian voices providing an evangelical audience with a thorough exegesis of biblical passages addressing homosexuality. But they also gave weight to stories, scientific data, and the authority of reason, which turned off many biblical feminists who thought their methodology strayed far from the practice of relying on biblical authority alone.

Disagreements over homosexuality had stayed largely beneath the surface. But once, at the 1975 EWC conference in Washington, DC, a woman raised her hand at a workshop titled "Woman to Woman Friendships" asking how she might respond to a coworker who came out as lesbian.

The workshop coleaders, Nancy Hardesty and Virginia Mollenkott, looked around the crowded room. Nancy saw a former student who had recently told her she was gay. Behind her sat Elisabeth Elliot, the conservative evangelical author of the widely acclaimed book *Passion and Purity*. Unbeknownst to those around her, Nancy, thirty-four at the time, had recently discovered that she too was a lesbian. But she wasn't ready to come out. She and Virginia skirted around the issue, neither endorsing nor condemning homosexuality. Still, the talk sparked debates and "quite a furor in the halls because we were not immediately and emphatically condemnatory," recalled Nancy.

Between 1984 and 1986 this issue divided the caucus. The lesbians of EWC had been meeting with each other, informally hosting "lesbian and friends" gatherings. A few group members wanted the EWC to recognize and support them, so they submitted a resolution for the group to vote on at a meeting in 1984. EWC members would sometimes submit resolutions for a member vote; the ones favoring the Equal Rights Amendment and women's ordination dependably passed. But the gays and lesbians proposal, along with a few others, were set aside, as some believed these issues went beyond the scope of the caucus's gender equality mission. For this meeting and future meetings, the EWC banned resolutions outside of supporting the Equal Rights Amendment.[15] But during the business meeting at the 1986 EWC conference in Fresno, a few members of the "lesbian and friends" gathering tried forcing their resolution through. Despite a chorus of opposition, these members swayed the EWC to pass three resolutions, which pledged to support racial justice, fight domestic violence, and, lastly, recognize the group's lesbian minority while taking "a firm stand in favor of civil rights protection for homosexual persons."

Those opposed to the final resolution worried that the vote suggested approval of homosexuality and would hurt the EWC's outreach to conservative evangelical churches. Others worried they might lose their jobs at Christian organizations. Those behind the resolution, like EWC's national coordinator, Britt Vanden Eykel, insisted that the resolution was "not any kind of endorsement of the gay lifestyle or comment on biblical interpretation."[16] Others expressed concern that the EWC was broadening its scope too much and weakening its core mission of bringing gender equality to evangelical churches.

Other members felt caught off guard by the introduction of resolutions, or had walked in after the votes had gone through. Several members left in tears. Soon, leaders, members, and then whole chapters submitted their resignations from the EWC out of opposition to the gay civil rights resolution. As one leader put it, she did so to maintain credibility among evangelicals. By February 1987 former EWC member Catherine Kroeger and roughly two hundred women formed a new group, and by August of that year they voted into existence Christians for Biblical Equality.[17]

THE SECRET TO SUCCESS IN THE EVANGELICAL WORLD

After the split, the fate of each group served as a powerful lesson for how to make a mark in evangelicalism. In short, the EWC faced consequences for its convictions, and CBE, by staying within the boundaries of conservative beliefs about sexuality, remained credible to the evangelical community.

In the years that followed, EWC's membership dwindled and the group almost disbanded in 1992. Eventually, the group regained its footing by scaling back its activities and overhauling its identity. The organization changed its name multiple times as it sought to include a broader range of theological views and drew increasingly from liberation theology, which is grounded in the belief that Christians should challenge unfair social systems. Today, EWC is known as EEWC-CFT, for Evangelical and Ecumenical Women's Caucus—Christian Feminism Today. Its justice initiatives for women and sexual minorities live on, but the organization lost clout in the evangelical world. Since the split following the 1986 conference, it's been pushed to the margins.[18]

The women at Christians for Biblical Equality fared much better. Chapters flourished across the country, with strong attendance at its biennial conferences. By 2000, it counted 2,300 members, a mailing list of sixteen thousand, new international chapters, two publications, and memberships from churches as well. Internal surveys revealed that membership skewed young and was committed to biblical inerrancy, with strong beliefs that the Bible backs egalitarian marriages and the ordination of women but not homosexuality or abortion. A statement affirming heterosexual marriage as God's design was folded into CBE's statement of faith to prevent another controversy.[19]

By adhering to conservative methods of biblical interpretation, Christians for Biblical Equality earned acceptance into the evangelical establishment. Prominent evangelical leaders, such as Bill Hybels of Willow Creek, Ron Sider of Evangelicals for Social Action, and many more helped CBE launch, and they signed CBE's declaration, which was published in *Christianity Today* in 1990. CBE leaders were invited to international evangelical events, and its egalitarian message made its way into some of the most influential churches, including Willow Creek, which by 2000 reached an estimated fifteen thousand people weekly.[20]

Today, CBE continues to hold influence. It has 1,500 members and has interacted with the nearly 35,000 individuals, organizations, schools, and churches in its database. CBE serves as the gender consultant for World Vision and plays leading roles in major networks such as Evangelicals for Justice, the Coalition for Christian Colleges and Universities, and the Evangelical Theological Society, which it has lobbied to embrace the leadership of women scholars.[21] Its members include major institutions such as InterVarsity Christian Fellowship, and its egalitarian statement of belief has been adopted by roughly three hundred evangelical and Christian groups.

"What we do is mostly theological," said Mimi Haddad, current president of CBE. "We provide theological materials that help churches, denominational leaders, Christians make holy and biblical decisions about gender and leadership and authority. We believe that the shared leadership and authority of men and women is just part of the biblical teachings from Genesis to Revelations. We believe male leadership is patriarchy and stands against the teaching of scripture and very easily leads to abuse."

CBE's success appears, in part, due to its narrow focus on promoting egalitarian marriages and women's ordination to the exclusion of more controversial causes, such as the advancement of reproductive rights or the inclusion of sexual minorities. Mimi told me that within CBE today there is a "diversity of opinion" when it comes to reproductive rights, but the group itself has not taken a position. "We just talk about how women have the right to make decisions," she said. On issues of LGBTQ equality, the group maintains in its "core values" that heterosexual marriage is part of God's design. When a CBE couple in their thirties (Emily Rice, a CBE board member, and her husband, Daniel Fan, also an E4J member) recently lobbied to have this language removed, they lost their battle and left the organization. CBE's commitment to limiting marriage to heterosexual couples reflects a harsh reality—that in order to maintain a voice within the evangelical world and make progress on a single issue, one must toe the conservative line on every other issue, lest she or he be cast out as a blasphemer. As Daniel explained, CBE retained its statement on heterosexual marriage because "it's a way that they prevent their identity from being mischaracterized by propatriarchy groups as too liberal."

That threat is real, and has been real for decades since propatriarchy efforts launched in the 1980s. In 1987, after the EWC-CBE split, an opposition group formed to thwart the spreading impact of evangelical feminism. The Council on Biblical Manhood and Womanhood launched with John Piper, a widely read author and pastor, and Wayne Grudem, a professor at Trinity Evangelical Divinity School, at the helm. CBMW's goal was clear: reassert biblical manhood (defined by authority over women) and womanhood (defined by submission to men), prevent women's ordination, halt gender-neutral Bible translations, and show how egalitarian beliefs the family and church. They catalogued their arguments in the Danvers Statement, which earned endorsements from Southwestern Baptist Seminary, the Presbyterian Church of America, and other church affiliates. Two years later they advanced this viewpoint by publishing a collection of supporting articles in the book *Recovering Biblical Manhood & Womanhood.*

In 1998 the Southern Baptist Convention made a single revision to its statement of faith, the "Baptist Faith and Message": in a new section about the family, an amendment establishes the marriage relationship as a model of God's relationship to his people, with the husband called to "provide for, to protect, and to lead his family," and the wife called "to submit herself graciously to the servant leadership of her husband, even as the church willingly submits to the headship of Christ."[22]

By 2000, the Southern Baptist Convention revised its statement of faith to announce that women should no longer work as pastors.[23]

From there, the attacks against evangelical feminism fanned across the country. Other major complementarian groups formed, amassed large followings, and made it their mission to discredit egalitarian principles. Their ideas have been applied in disturbing ways. Some actively lobby against efforts to advance women's rights (CitizenLink, Focus on the Family's lobbying affiliate, has fought to defund Planned Parenthood and mobilized against the Violence Against Women Act), while others promote oppressive messages about the relationship between men and women. Take, for example, Mark Driscoll, pastor of the now-shuttered Mars Hill megachurch empire, which boasted fifteen satellite locations.

Driscoll has credited *Recovering Biblical Manhood & Womanhood* for shaping his ministries. Known as a bombastic hipster preacher with a fixation on hypermasculinity and sex, he prohibited women's ordination, declaring women "unfit because they are more gullible and easier to deceive than men." He urged wives to dutifully give their husbands blow jobs. ("Ladies, your husbands appreciate oral sex. They do. So, serve them, love them well. It's biblical.") He lambasted effeminate men and, in addressing marital infidelity, he has said, "A wife who lets herself go and is not sexually available to her husband . . . is not responsible for her husband's sin, but she may not be helping him either."[24]

After Driscoll founded Mars Hill in the mid-1990s, his influence soared—that is, until he was accused of plagiarism in 2013 and was found to have used church funds to pay a firm to game his book sales figures. He lost his immunity to criticism from current and former church staff and members. He resigned in 2014, and the church dissolved shortly thereafter.

Though Driscoll's church died out, complementarian values live on, thriving in some of the most influential evangelical institutions, such as the Gospel Coalition and the Acts 29 Network, a national church-planting organization that Driscoll founded. Today, the complementarian-egalitarian debate rages on, with groups like CBMW and CBE competing for evangelical influence.

WHO AM I?

In certain evangelical enclaves, including Jennifer's Southern Baptist community, the complementarians have held their ground. That remained true through Jennifer's upbringing, and even in adulthood. As a twenty-something female in the mid-1990s, she did not have feminist blogs or social media to challenge her understanding of gender roles. So she struggled alone. Even after breaking up with the boyfriend who raped her, she fumbled through other relationships, unhealthy in their own ways. She did not assert her opinions. She felt constantly unsure of herself. She stayed in relationships far past their expiration dates.

In her mid-twenties, when she married a sweet, wholesome Christian man, her family celebrated this crowning achievement. Jennifer flashed her bright, happy smile through the marriage, all while a black cloud of dissatisfaction mushroomed within.

Jennifer and her husband loved each other, but their different expectations for marriage quickly drove them apart. Her husband expected the traditional markers of a Christian family: a presentable Christian wife and a warm home filled with their babies. Jennifer was not ready for children but tried in other ways to fit the wifely mold. Even though they both worked full time, Jennifer made sure to have cooked meals ready for her husband when he arrived home every night. But often he worked late or spent whole Saturdays playing golf with his friends, and during this alone time, Jennifer enjoyed her first taste of total independence. No longer under the scrutiny of the pageant system or her parents, Jennifer began exploring her interests.

She joined community theater and found herself surrounded by a new group of fun, raucous theater friends. Experimenting with other forms of self-expression, she double pierced her ears and later got a tribal design of an angel tattooed on her back. She proudly shared all this with her husband thinking, *He'll love this; I'm finally being me!* But her husband did not like the new Jennifer. One night, he tugged at her fresh double piercing, waking her from slumber. "Are you trying to look like a stripper?" he asked angrily. Later, when she revealed her new tattoo, he called it a tramp stamp and asked how she planned to explain it to their future children.

His reaction shocked Jennifer. She thought her husband was liberal, unconditionally supportive, and eager to help her grow into her own. Before they married he had said as much. But in retrospect, "that was bullshit," Jennifer said. "That was lovely in theory. But he married this pageant girl. When I got a tattoo or I started theater, he couldn't handle it and he would call me a whore."

For the first time in her adult life, Jennifer had close female friends with whom she confided her marriage woes. They urged her to take care of herself. When she wondered if her husband's insults were deserved, they shook their heads; he was treating her badly and unfairly, no question. When the differences between Jennifer and her husband became irreconcilable and Jennifer began looking at apartments, she felt guilty but her girlfriends backed her up.

Finally, she broached the subject of divorce with her husband and the two began the process of separating. When her realtor walked her into the apartment that would soon be her own, she could taste her freedom. The quaint, two-bedroom apartment was worn with character, and immediately Jennifer could envision the space decorated to her liking, a cocoon in which she could grow into herself. Feeling simultaneously excited and scared, she put down a deposit and signed the lease.

Jennifer broke the news to her parents by letter; they were so devastated they refused to help her move. Some in her family told her she was going to hell. From the outside, she had the perfect life—a beautiful home, a Christian husband—and had chosen to throw it all away. In the broader community, rumors began to fly. *There must have been another man. She just didn't appreciate her husband.* "Again, I was the villain," Jennifer recalled. According to Jennifer's friends from Alabama, divorce in Birmingham was "a modern-day scarlet letter." It's just "so scandalous," said her friend India Ramey. "I felt like anytime in my life I did anything good for myself, I got vilified," Jennifer said. "That was being a woman."

Thirty days after signing her lease, Jennifer left the house she had bought with her husband. As she moved her cardboard boxes into the tiny apartment she would rent on her own, a mix of feelings orbited her mind—feelings of loss for the life she had left behind, of fear for the unknown future, of relief for getting out of an unhealthy relationship, and of satisfaction for forging a fresh new journey for herself. But Jennifer wasn't alone. Half a dozen girlfriends helped her move in that day. They poured wine and mixed mimosas. They blasted Shakira's *Laundry Service* album on repeat, belting out girl-power anthems. "We all rallied around her," recalled another friend, Jacinda Carlisle. "It was like you could see the life coming back into her." In the swirl of celebrating and moving in, something powerful hit Jennifer in the gut. She realized, "I have no idea what's about to happen, but this is where I'm supposed to be." Newly single and unsure of what lay ahead, Jennifer wondered what she would make of her future. She did not yet have the answers, but she knew she was off to a good start. For the first time in her life, "I made a decision for myself. I made it happen and it felt really good."

SIX

Coming Out

THE QUEER UNDERGROUND

Tasha's plan to transfer out of Biola was already in motion when she met Will, who was a year ahead of her. It was early in the second semester of her sophomore year and, while she continued attending classes, Tasha had emotionally checked out. She became a ghost student, fading out of relationships and drifting through campus without a trace. All she could do was daydream about packing up and never looking back.

That's why it surprised her when she found herself at a Biola house party, deep in conversation with a guy she had only met in passing. Ever since a mutual friend had introduced Tasha as "my lesbian friend," Will had grown curious about her. As their classmates splashed in the pool, Will and Tasha came out to each other. A new friendship was born.

They began hanging out at Will's apartment, spending hours commiserating over tea and biscuits. They swapped stories about encounters with campus homophobia, and strategies for faking straightness. Delighting in their new best-friendship, they eagerly took inventory of all the ways their lives mirrored each other's—homeschool upbringing, conservative Republican parents, intense faith, antigay churches, self-loathing, the gay Biola experience.

They ranted a lot. Mostly about the school. They hated the chapel messages that told gay people to remain celibate and the way professors compared homosexuality to pedophilia. They hated that dating and love, the open aim of so many straight students, was grounds for their own expulsion and public shame.

"Fuck this place," they'd say angrily to each other. But then they'd lock eyes over their teacups and catch a wave of something new, something unfamiliar; it was the feeling of being completely known and still completely loved.

In the weeks that followed the pool party, morsels of joy began to slip into Will and Tasha's days. "I loved being in the hallways with him in Sutherland"—the honors building—"whispering about gay things together," Tasha recalled. "It's like you're holding your breath at school and you could finally let go for two minutes in the hall with Will. It felt like this tension was released and I could laugh. It's really weird when you've been lying so often to be honest with someone. I felt like I had a genuine friend."

Suddenly, the secrecy, which previously tormented them, became fun. They were hungrily curious about who else at school might be gay and how they might find out without exposing themselves or others. They began keeping a list of any student who said something even mildly queer-friendly in class. They huddled around a laptop in Will's apartment, scrubbing through Facebook profiles, looking for clues. With so little to go on, they admittedly relied on stereotypes: Short hair or "really butch" attire on a woman. Effeminate men. Women who raved about Tegan and Sara, the openly gay indie rock duo. Men who posted gushily about Sufjan Stevens, an attractive folk-indie musician with sensitive, spiritually infused lyrics. As their list grew, Will and Tasha began reaching out. They had a plan. They wanted to build a secret queer society.

When they noticed a student wearing a Reading Rainbow shirt in a Facebook picture ("This guy totally has to be gay because he has a shirt with a rainbow on it!"), they sent him a private message asking if he'd be interested in joining their underground group; and if not, he should just ignore the message. That student, Christian Ortega, was elated and joined their meetings.

Will networked with his theater friends ("Are they gay or just, like, a theater person?") and more members began attending. News spread by word of mouth. Hushed voices in dorm rooms. Oaths of secrecy. Friends brought friends; and those friends brought more friends. On a weekly basis, anywhere from five to fifteen people would arrive at Will's apartment, sit in a circle, and share their gratitude for having found "group," the shorthand they'd use to describe their pseudo-group-therapy fellowship. Of course, there were no licensed therapists at the sessions, just a collection of lonely students.

"There were a lot of tearful moments in those early days when people were just coming out of complete isolation and finding a group of relatable people," Will told me, recalling his heartbreak when, week after week, he realized that nearly everyone in the group had a history of suicidal thoughts or behaviors. One student confided in Will that before he discovered group, he tried to kill himself by drinking a bottle of bleach. "He felt guilty just for existing."

"What was really, really hard," Tasha later told me, "was being nineteen years old, having no resources, no older adults sitting in the circle, and having people share that they were suicidal. It's like, what do I do? These people were looking to *me*. All I could do was refer them to the Biola Counseling Center, but they were sometimes afraid to go there and they couldn't afford to go to an outside therapist. It was really hard and it stressed me out a lot."

Will knew Tasha had applied to transfer out of Biola, and he bristled whenever the subject came up. Tasha seemed so keen on leaving Biola behind. Would Will and group be forgotten?

That desire to abandon Biola *had* been a driving force in Tasha's life ever since her first day. But in those early meetings with Will and group, she could sense something changing inside of her.

"I loved those first meetings," recalled Tasha. "They even stand out as some of the best because all of us in the room had this expectation of something new starting. It was like, *Oh my gosh. We're not alone.*"

As membership grew and people increasingly looked to Will and Tasha for guidance, Tasha began to question her decision to abandon Biola. Suddenly she saw Biola in a new light: it was a project, a place she could fix. It was the kind of broken world that unleashed her missionary zeal. "I kind of felt like it would be unchristian of me if I just left these people and didn't try to change Biola."

Tasha also saw her commitment as an act of giving her faith "one last go." For years, her Christianity had felt precarious, as the constant assault of antigay remarks reinforced her outsider status. She felt angry. She stopped praying. But now, with the eyes of so many hurting peers on her and Will, she realized she owed it to them, and her faith, to give herself over. "My whole life I've seen my Christian faith as being willing to take huge risks for the sake of other people."

So Tasha emotionally checked back in to Biola. She went from autopilot to activist mode. She and Will gave the group a name: the Biola Queer Underground.

As the group cultivated its mission, it became clear that its primary goal was to create a safe, loving space for LGBTQ students and straight allies. And keeping their group safe included keeping the members anonymous and the group underground. They established a multistep process for vetting potential new members. Bottom line: be vague, don't give names or details, watch for their reaction, and get the group's approval before inviting others.

Anonymity was crucial to members because they feared the school's snitch culture. Through alumni contacts, they had heard rumors of past expulsions and disciplinary actions targeting LGBTQ students. Then, when one BQU member was reported to a campus official for "homosexual behavior," the others doubled down on their efforts to hide their sexuality.

The story of the reported student goes like this: Rory, the student's preferred name, is a female-to-male trans student who passed on campus as a petite female dressed in tough, tomboy attire—backwards baseball caps, camo-tees, a septum piercing. One night, after a difficult day, Rory burst into the dorm room of his secret girlfriend (we'll call her Dahlia) and spent the night crying in her arms.

When Dahlia's roommate returned in the morning and saw the two curled up in bed, she knocked on the resident director's door to report their "same-sex behavior." Rory was brought in for questioning. He felt nervous, but adopted a casual tone of voice and played it off as an uneventful girl slumber party. It worked, but it left him feeling exposed and scandalous.

"It's just tough to feel like you're sneaking around even if it's a legitimate relationship. You can't just be, like, cute together or go on dates."

Based on my interviews, I understood Rory's experience to be the exception. Most queer students told me they were way too careful to ever get caught. (When I asked the dean of students about Rory's questioning, he couldn't confirm or deny that this happened, but he said, "That doesn't sound like a process that we would do here.") Nonetheless, Rory's story was enough to drive the group further underground.

Because the BQU was a lifeline for so many members, by the end of the semester they agreed they needed to make a concerted effort to advertise the group to attract other closeted queers, while maintaining their secrecy. True to their millennial ways, they turned to anonymous blogging and created the *Biola Queer Underground* blog. Channeling old-school activists, they designed splashy handmade signs and leaflets to scatter around campus.

On the blog, club members described the LGBTQ experience at Biola. A lesbian student wrote about her alienation and anger. Another writer explained heterosexual privilege. Others wrote about their faith, romantic longings, and suicidal thoughts.

One entry publicly rejected the school's condemnation of same-sex relationships, and another appealed to their target audience—closeted LGBTQ Biola students.

"We desperately want you to know that your desire for intimacy and human connection is beautiful, and nothing about you is a mistake. To those of you in the closet, we may not know you yet, but we are fighting on your behalf and constantly praying for you."

On its face, the plan seemed simple: launch the website early Wednesday morning during finals and then, when the entire campus was at chapel, plaster the campus with the signs and leaflets.

But no one in the BQU was willing to do that. They were too afraid of getting caught. Members of the BQU never hung out on campus as a group; they barely acknowledged each other, outside of exchanging knowing smiles. They communicated through a secret Facebook group and met at Will's apartment, then later at a site far from school. The idea of arriving on campus with a fistful of queer fliers was out of the question.

Even Will and Tasha weren't willing to risk it. The week before the website had launched, a professor had paused her lecture on homosexuality, locked eyes with Tasha and announced her suspicion that *some* students at Biola were in "secret lesbian relationships." Another panic attack lurched inside Tasha as she fought back tears.

The whole semester had been like this. As the BQU expanded its reach, Tasha's anxiety attacks had grown frighteningly debilitating. Her mental health was frayed, and by the end of the semester, she realized she had to transfer to another school. But she wasn't leaving Biola behind—she vowed to stay on as Will's coleader and run the BQU from the outside.

Before she left, she had this one last play—letting the world know about the queer students at Biola. She convinced two people to distribute BQU fliers and hang posters all around campus: Emiko Woods, her best friend, who attended Azusa Pacific University (a neighboring Christian school), and Christian Ortega, of Reading Rainbow legend and the only willing BQU member.

On that fateful Wednesday morning, the two met Will and Tasha in a nearby park to discuss strategy. After Tasha published the website it was go time. She drove Emiko to Biola. Christian returned on his own, nervously watching the time pass. When he was sure chapel was well underway, he hopped out of his car, flipped up his hoodie, and darted into the hushed campus.

A NEW MOVEMENT

The Biola Queer Underground is one of several dozen LGBTQ groups that have formed among Christian college students and alumni in recent years. For decades, secret groups have coalesced and disbanded in the shadows, but technology and greater acceptance among younger evangelicals has fueled their recent nationwide emergence.

One of many groups that has propelled the rising queer Christian movement is Soulforce, an LGBTQ advocacy group that engages religious communities. In 2005 Soulforce launched an initiative called the Equality Ride, in which activists traveled the country by bus to present to Christian colleges arguments against campus antiqueer policies, host workshops, and meet with administrators. Haven Herrin, the executive director of Soulforce, told me that since the program's inception Equality Ride volunteers have visited 101 schools, engaged in "thousands of conversations," and played a role in seventeen school policy changes. For example, Birmingham-based Samford University deleted "homosexual acts" as a punishable offense a year after Soulforce visited, according to Herrin.[1] And though many factors besides the Equality Ride were in play, "I don't think it's entirely a coincidence that student groups, alumni groups, and policy changes have started coming out of the woodwork [over the course of the same period] we've done the Equality Ride. We provide a spark on campus that really helps students organize because they are able to see who their allies and kin are."

For Sabrina Valente, the inaugural Equality Ride "was such a huge moment in my life." At the time, Sabrina was a senior at Eastern University, a school affiliated with the American Baptist Churches with a slight progressive bent. Its tagline is "Faith, Reason, Justice." When the Equality Ride fanned across the country, Eastern University allowed them on campus despite the fact that many Christian schools barred Soulforce volunteers or had them arrested. While the school prohibited sexual intimacy outside of marriage between a man and a woman and had its own share of homophobia, it was more open to dialogue than other Christian schools were.

The talks hosted by Soulforce helped Sabrina sort out questions about her sexuality. She met Jacob, a Soulforce volunteer, who listened to her and treated her with a kind of life-changing love. "I remember looking at Jacob and just saying to him, 'This must be what Christ's love feels like. If there's a God and God loves us the way we're told he does . . . that's what you're giving off right now.'" Jacob looked at Sabrina and began to cry. "He took my hand, and through his tears he said, 'Sabrina, no one else ever said that to me before. Everyone has always told me that I'm an abomination.'"

When Sabrina finally came out as bisexual to her friends, they left her. "I had friends with standing lunch dates who just didn't show up or said they were busy. They just walked out of my life."

All across campus, the Equality Ride was sparking controversy. Friendships were tested. Professors clashed. According to Eastern psychology professor Yolanda Turner (whom we heard from in chapter 3), "We had a lot of people who were totally against it, but the general consensus was, 'Of course we'll let them come here.'"

Turner, sprightly and middle-aged, with a salt-and-pepper pixie cut, has seen Eastern travel a bumpy, yet willful path toward progress on queer issues. In the mid-1990s, LGBTQ students confided in Turner, but didn't dare come out of the closet. But a decade later, a new crop of students formed Refuge, an LGBTQ support group for sexual and gender minorities, which Turner has been attending as an unofficial faculty advisor. The group kept a low profile, but the Equality Ride blew the LGBTQ question much wider and "changed a lot of folks here on campus," Turner said.

Even though the school still upholds anti-LGBTQ policies, Turner has seen a tide change, especially among the student body. At a 2012 panel discussion, in which Turner defended same-sex marriage and a professor of political science opposed it, Turner had expected to be interrogated for her views. Instead, "nobody challenged me. Everybody was saying to him [the other professor], 'Help me understand how you think this way.' I was like, *OK, this is wild.*"

To Soulforce's Haven Herrin, the Equality Ride acts as a "kind of Rube Goldberg of social change." Soulforce kicks off the conversation, LGBTQ students and their allies emerge from hiding, they organize, and a culture begins to shift. It's a pattern that's playing out across American evangelicalism.

In Christian college circles, queer alumni have burst on the scene in recent years, offering support to current students and graduates. Graduates of Wheaton College, which has topped the Princeton Review list of "the most LGBTQ-unfriendly schools," formed the group OneWheaton. Alumni from dozens of other Christian colleges have followed suit, forming OneGeorgeFox, BJUnity (for Bob Jones University folks), and OneEastern.

According to Ryan Paezold, founder of OneEastern, alumni can play a critical role in influencing campus policies. "Where the students can't challenge administration directly, alumni can," Paezold said. "So when we get the call [for donations, we can say], 'No, we're not donating money until you change your stance on sexuality.'"

For now, the balance does not hang in favor of LGBTQ-affirming alumni. "The power differential is so mighty when the school is connected to a denomination . . . (and) to a treasure chest," explained Herrin. In 2013, with the help of Soulforce, about forty-five LGBTQ-ally groups responded by uniting under one umbrella called Safety Net, a coalition working to support students and change campus policies at Christian colleges. A few of these groups have seen recent victories: Wheaton College and Fuller Theological Seminary have both sanctioned LGBTQ clubs on campus (though the schools officially hold to the traditional view of sexuality), and after nondenominational Belmont University sanctioned a campus LGBTQ discussion group (which isn't a part of Safety Net), it added "sexual orientation" as a protected class to the school's nondiscrimination policy.[2]

But these triumphs are the exception, not the rule. LGBTQ students typically report that administrators ignore or deny their requests for official club status. Some even crack down on visibly queer groups and individuals. In 2012, Patrick Henry College threatened to sue the alumni writers behind the blog *Queer at Patrick Henry College* for copyright infringement. Administrators at North Central University, Grace University, and California Baptist University have expelled LGBTQ students in recent years. In the latest affront, schools are targeting queer or affirming faculty. The incendiary nature of the subject makes it difficult for sexual minorities to come out and connect, which is part of what makes the blossoming queer Christian movement so staggeringly brave.

GOING VIRAL

At first blush, Biola's campus could pass as any small college in Southern California. Between the leafy walkways and nondescript buildings, nothing screams "Christian university." Espresso machines whir beside flannelled baristas. Students in oversized sunglasses and flip-flops glide around in packs. Even dressier students don't look conservative; they look stylish and twee, like little Zooey Deschanels hugging laptops instead of ukuleles.

But at the center of campus, a striking two-story mural of Jesus brings the school's religious mission into sharp focus. In it, a radiant, crimson-robed Christ clutches a Bible and looms over every passerby. The campus is also distinctly conservative Christian in how it requires every public posting—like fliers for clubs, concerts, and other events—to conform to the school's religious values. Every leaflet undergoes an official approval process; if it's out of line, it's banned from campus. Unlike secular schools, with their cluttered, unregulated bulletin boards announcing rock shows and political protests, at Biola signs for campus-sponsored events (like the seminar Call to Manhood: Masculinity and Perseverance) are laminated and affixed to wooden posts that neatly line the walkways. For the BQU, there was no upside to seeking approval, so they never tried. They knew their signs would be denied and that they'd be outing themselves.

On the day of the website launch, when the chapel service cast a hush over campus, Emiko and Christian scurried around distributing their illicit little ads. Christian scattered BQU business cards in empty classrooms and bathrooms. Emiko left small leaflets on tables and affixed a glittery poster right outside the chapel doors. "Read your fellow queer students' stories," the signs urged, alongside pictures of celebrity couples like Ellen DeGeneres and Portia de Rossi.

When chapel let out, the news of the BQU went viral. Soon after, campus security rushed to the scene to tear down the signs and fliers. But it didn't stop the controversy from taking on a life of its own, surging through the efficient veins of gossip, social media, and even national media coverage. On campus, the student newspaper, the *Chimes*, put out a story the same day and drew a barrage of comments. Even in the hours after the blog went public, the community response sent the BQU website statistics skyrocketing, which Tasha watched from off campus, wide-eyed and hyperventilating.

JASON

Jason Brown learned about the BQU the way most people did, through the breathless dispatches that followed the launch. The group intrigued him, and it just so happened that the very next day, he had an appointment with the administration to discuss LGBTQ issues.

Jason was a slightly older transfer student with a lithe figure, wispy hair, and black-framed transition glasses. He deliberately identifies as queer because he prefers the flexibility of the inclusive term and says he is interested in men and women. Unlike Will and Tasha, Jason entered Biola at age twenty-two, having experienced a much wider breadth of Christian and LGBTQ cultures, from Lutheran and evangelical services to the San Francisco queer scene and the ex-gay conferences held by Exodus International, which he attended at his parents' behest.

Jason found Exodus's ex-gay message problematic, but it didn't deter him from embracing the Christian faith and attending Biola, where he hoped to explore his questions about faith and sexuality in an evangelical setting. From the get-go, Jason carefully shared his queer identity with a few close friends and even to a larger group of guys from his dorm.

"They were pretty wide-eyed and didn't know what to say, but I remember the RA . . . told me that he saw me as a brother and friend and that they very much respected me."

To his dismay, outside his small circle, Jason found it difficult to explore these questions. Most Biola students seemed poorly versed in their understanding of queer issues "beyond the fact that homosexuality is a sin and . . . that homosexuality and evangelical Christianity are . . . [mutually] exclusive." In his sociology class, students presenting research on "homosexual subcultures" displayed images of shirtless gay men clad in leather and body paint. Jason noticed all of his classmates nodding as if to say, *Well, yes, this is what it means to be gay.* Jason left class upset and vowed to take up his concerns with the administration.

By pure coincidence, the day after the BQU website went live, Jason met with the dean of students, a thin, crisply dressed, middle-aged man named Danny Paschall. Danny had just come from a meeting in which the school's administrators finalized the school's statement on human sexuality. Jason wondered, *Will he think I'm part of the BQU? Will I get in trouble?* But Jason plowed ahead and was surprised by Danny's genuine interest.

There was something reassuring about Danny, Jason recalled. He seemed to empathize with his pain, even if he remained firm on Biola's position on sexuality. The two spoke about meeting regularly in the coming year to build a plan for change and deeper campus dialogue. Jason left the meeting satisfied by the progress they had made and could feel his interest in the BQU waning. He was glad the group existed, but was wary of underground movements. He worried that if he joined, he'd be climbing back into the closet. He wanted to tackle these issues head on, out in the open, and believed he'd be more effective partnering with the administration.

That same day, the administration released two documents: the first was a letter vowing to host campus-wide educational forums on human sexuality; the second was the school's statement on human sexuality, which holds firm to the view that "God designed sexual union for the purpose of uniting one man and one woman . . . in the context of marriage." In the statement, and again in Biola president Barry Corey's chapel talk the next week, it was made abundantly clear that the school views "any act of sexual intimacy between two persons of the same sex, as illegitimate moral options for the confessing Christian."[3]

In the remaining weeks of the school year, a wave of debate crashed over the campus. But the BQU members lay low, nervous that they'd be found out. Could the school trace their IP address? Could the website get hacked? Could security footage reveal Tasha driving Emiko around campus or Christian distributing fliers in the empty classrooms? They assured each other that everything would be fine. They had so been careful.

Then, a few days after the launch, Christian was awoken in the middle of the night by his ringing cellphone and a deep male voice on the other end.

"Is this Christian?"

"Yeah," Christian mumbled sleepily.

"I'm going to kick your ass."

Christian assumed it was a prank call. As he recalled, he was about to hang up, but the caller said something that made him sit up straight.

"Faggot."

Could this be about the BQU? Christian wondered.

"You go to Biola, right?" the voice asked, before listing off everything he knew about Christian—where he worked off campus, where he worked on campus, where he was from, where he lived.

"I'm going to kill you."

Christian's stomach flipped and the call ended. He staggered toward his computer and frantically typed a message to some BQU friends still on Facebook. Within moments two of them were at his door.

The two students, who asked to remain anonymous because they're not out publicly, told me that Christian looked nervous and shaky. "At that point we were also scared to call campus safety," one student recalled in an interview. "How are we going to explain *why* we had a death threat? Because we can't associate him with the underground. We were super paranoid."

Christian made the call and told a campus safety officer a vague version of what had happened, excluding the gay slur.[4] Nothing came of the investigation, Christian said, but campus security did offer to drive him between classes and his dorm. Christian chose to spend the remaining weeks of the year hiding out at Will's apartment. From there, the two observed the online debates raging in the school newspaper's comment section, in the BQU in-box, and in updates from their BQU friends. And among the rubble of hate speech and hand wringing over their sexual immorality, they found something tremendously hopeful in all the reactions: there were Christians on their side.

DEBORAH

If the 1990s represented an era when vilifying the LGBTQ community galvanized evangelicals, this past decade stands for a period when that very tactic has divided the church and alienated a generation.

Today, sexual minorities come out earlier in life, which means more young evangelicals have encountered LGBTQ people as friends, room-mates, and youth group buddies and not as the threatening outsiders conjured by older evangelicals. When Tasha came out to her two best friends from her homeschool community, they listened and became al-lies. Emily Ulmer, a mid-twenties straight woman I met at a conference, echoed the sentiment of so many Christian allies: the issue hasn't fazed her for years. Her close friends are gay; two would be married that coming summer. "That's part of life for me," she said. For so many, their shift was more than just a casual adjustment to social patterns, it was a deliberate, meaningful decision they made as an extension of their moral beliefs.

It's a journey I identify with, but, as difficult as it is to admit, one that took a few faltering years. In college, I woke up to the fact that my spir-itual quest had taken me to the heart of the culture wars. I was attend-ing the University of Illinois, Urbana-Champaign, living in the legendary outcast dormitory, Allen Hall, which attracted shaggy-haired musicians, paint-smeared artists, and self-proclaimed weirdos. The dorm's nick-name "Alien Hall" was a badge of honor; we were a commune of mis-fits, a cradle of diversity on a campus dominated by the Greek system. I made gay and lesbian friends; I also made Christian friends. But at the turn of the millennium, these worlds felt very far apart.

One gay resident advisor told me that he immediately distrusted all Christians he met. One Christian friend compared my affirmation of same-sex relationships to slipping a flask to an alcoholic: I was feeding someone's disease. Of course, these are extreme examples. Most of my gay and lesbian friends said little about Christians and vice versa. But when they did, the subtext, especially from the Christians, was always clear: the two sides were at war; I needed to choose a side.

I wondered if I could bridge the two groups, but then something happened. I became subsumed in my evangelical community. For the uninitiated, here's something you probably don't know about the subculture: politics aside, the people can intoxicate you with love. I had friends who prayed for me daily, leaders who mentored me, a community that asked the big questions about life, death, and meaning. When I wanted to learn to play the djembe, my friends took up a secret collection and, on my birthday, dozens of them surprised me with the gift. At a nearby Pentecostal church I attended, the worship leader, destroyed by the cancer that had crawled across his body, had lain in bed at home with a phone against his ear while my pastor, who had called him from the pulpit, pointed a cordless phone toward the congregation; we all wept and sang him love songs as he lay dying. During all of the ups and downs of college life, my closest Christian friends and I loved each other and prayed for each other. *You will never be alone when you have brothers and sisters,* we said.

But like any family, we had disagreements that we didn't always handle well. As I wrote in previous chapters, I grew increasingly disturbed by the group's troubling racial and gender dynamics. As a leader, I made these issues central to the weekly messages, drawing criticism from people I cared about. Some students of color thanked me for my work, but among many others, I lost support and felt bonds begin to fray.

We shouldn't focus on race—it's distracting us from our central purpose of converting people to Christ.

Of course there is a hierarchy: God's at the top, then man, then woman, then child. This is biblical.

I hope you don't become another angry feminist.

To my critics, I had become a caricature of minority victimhood, and a "backslider."

It's tempting to self-mythologize my college years (Embattled activist! Feminist outcast!) but I'll be the first to admit that I messed up a lot, especially when it came to LGBTQ issues. Instead of bridging two communities or standing strong in my nascent pro-LGBTQ convictions, I began to wonder if the Christians were right. The unbending message that "homosexuality is a sin" overwhelmed me. In my doubt, I felt too uncertain about my beliefs to do anything or to say anything.

Sometimes, I try to excuse myself. *I was so young. The issue didn't come up often.* And while those things are true, the bigger truth, the truth that I carry with me to this day is this: as a straight person, my privilege made this issue easy to ignore, and in my silence, I was complicit in the culture's condemnation. What I did—or rather, what I *didn't* do—was wrong and weak. I wish I had been stronger in my convictions and less cowardly. Especially when Roger called me.

Roger (not his real name) was a younger student in my fellowship who asked me to meet at Espresso Royale, a cafe halfway between our dorms. Sitting in the darkened loft of the cafe, he handed me a printout of something he wanted to share with the fellowship. Would I carve out a few minutes for him to speak at the next group meeting?

As I read, I realized he wanted to tell a room of more than a hundred Christians that he was gay. His bravery made my heart quicken and I put him on the schedule. But in my hasty reading of his story, I missed something crucial at the end of his speech that I didn't grasp until I heard him share his story aloud to the group: he was asking us to pray that he be healed. This troubled me; it seemed wrong and dangerous. When Roger handed the microphone back to me, I didn't know how to articulate my concerns. I was so plagued by uncertainty, so worried about saying something heretical, that I said little. I didn't make waves. I didn't find Roger later and say, "You're OK. You're perfect." I did nothing.

Roger and I were friendly in college, but not close. Only years later, when we reconnected, did he tell me about the depression and suicidal thoughts that unspooled in his mind after coming out. He started "freak-ing out," he explained, from all the pressure he felt to change—from the ex-gay books he read and the Christian psychologist who encouraged him to fantasize about women. Roger received sympathy from folks in our fellowship and leaned on a few Bible study friends for real support, but he also felt "a little bit abandoned" after he came out. Most people treated him politely, he recalled, but in their silence, they seemed quietly complicit with disapproving Christian attitudes toward gay people. He was talking about the group, but he might as well have been talking about me.

It was only after college, when I began giving credence to my beliefs about LGBTQ equality, that I came to regret my actions with the kind of ache and shame that comes with waking up to one's own bad behav-ior. I made amends with Roger and another gay friend. I learned about the broader, uglier impact of antigay theology and vowed to live a more loving life. I sought an affirming church, but ran into dead ends. At one vibrant, multiethnic church, the pastor testified about his metamor-phosis from gay basher ("I hated my gay cousin so much I wanted to punch him!") to a pastor who wants to help convert gay men into "real men." At another, congregants pressured attendees to sign a marriage amendment petition on the way out of service. I had begun to wonder if I would ever find a church home.

And then my close Christian friend came out to me. Charlie and I had known each other through our college fellowship, and we later lived in neighboring apartments the summer we both got internships in Milwaukee. As neighbors, we grew close quickly, and in our roaming postcollege years, we met up regularly in different cities. We were the kind of friends who spent most of our time together goofing around, but one night, walking through the East Village in New York, we found ourselves stopped on a street corner ranting about the absurd conserva-tism of evangelical culture. It was raining and the streets were a shiny black. We huddled under a shared umbrella and, for the first time, I saw Charlie's anger and he saw mine. Charlie wasn't out to me yet, but I could sense the sharpness of his pain, even if I couldn't trace its origin. Later, he would come to terms with his sexuality, find a gay-friendly church, and come out to his family, who would embrace him. And then he would come out to me.

"I'm gay," he told me over dinner one night. There was a calmness in his face that hadn't been there before. The edge in his voice was gone. He was smiling. I felt myself smiling back. But later I felt a sadness stab me as I thought about all the years Charlie was alone with his secret. I had been right there, sitting next to him in prayer circles, laughing at his jokes as I rode shotgun, bursting through his apartment door like a wacky sitcom neighbor. Yet I offered no indication that I would have accepted him if he came out as gay. How good a friend was I if that much wasn't clear?

Later, I would ask Charlie how he survived our fellowship's anti-gay culture, and he would tell me about the countless times he held his tongue when others called homosexuality sin, about how he stayed closeted and dated a girl because he didn't want his friends to put him in the "unsaved" column of their prayer lists, about how peer pressure kept him in the Christian fold, about how he broke down when Roger came out of the closet, and about how he internalized the advice others were giving Roger: *It's OK, just be celibate; we love you, we accept you, but you must defeat this.* And when he looked at me, standing in front of our fellowship every week, all he saw was, as he put it, "Debbie Lee, super Christian." Charlie listened for an alternative message, but there was none. "I thought we were like-minded," he said. But how could he be sure?

Charlie doesn't hold my silence against me. He doesn't tell me that, if I had spoken my convictions as a leader, I could have made life easier and less horrible for other closeted Christians. He gave our friendship time, and saw the best in me. "As I got to know you I was like, here's a person who I've had this impression about, but I feel like I share a lot more with her than I've ever thought." I'm lucky to have such a patient friend.

Today, Charlie is happy. He has support from his family and a tight-knit community. He is married to the love of his life. And when they exchanged vows and swayed to *Glee*'s slow version of "I Wanna Hold Your Hand," I stood among his group of friends, smiling and wiping my tears.

I devoted so much of my postcollege life to trying to make amends for my past and escape fundamentalism. But the more churches I attended, the more I began to doubt that I'd ever shake all that off. When I steered a ten-foot moving truck from Chicago to Manhattan, I had the naive idea that New York City would be different. I spent my first year there retracing the steps of my pre-evangelical, spiritually searching youth, entering the sacred temples of different faiths, reading spiritual literature, and meditating. When I fell in step with an Episcopal church, I felt like I had finally jimmied my faith from its twisty dogmatic roots. In the evangelical world, Episcopalians were the defiant liberals, with their gay bishop and female priests. And this church defied the stereotype of an aging, shrinking, irrelevant mainline Protestant outfit. Its community was a hotbed of youthful social justice activism. Its pews were lined with educated New Yorkers who had eschewed lucrative careers for full-time jobs at homeless shelters, justice coalitions, and high-profile nonprofits.

But with time and conversation, the mirage evaporated. Soon I realized that this church was Episcopal in attire but more evangelical in ethos. My disbelief in the Bible's inerrancy made conversations come to a record-screeching halt. I was scolded for suggesting that Paul's teachings perpetuated misogyny. But the real kicker came when I discovered that for some years the parish had not paid its dues to the state diocese in protest of the denomination's ordination of a gay bishop. This shattered my world. Fundamentalism seemed to lurk at every corner and it was clawing my faith to shreds. With a lot of private mourning, I decided to leave the church for the preservation of my own faith, a faith that today feels more authentic and thriving despite being vagrant and nameless.

I am a statistic. Countless recent studies show rising religious disaffiliation among the young. It's a narrative arc I've encountered repeatedly in my reporting. And evangelical leaders woke up to this when the data came from one of their own. In 2007, the Barna Group, an established

Christian research organization, published an extensive study that showed a sharp decline in the image of American Christianity and a hemorrhaging of young people, many of whom attributed their exodus, in part, to Christianity being too "antihomosexual." In raw numbers, 60 percent of young people are leaving the church permanently or for long periods after age fifteen. Barna also found that between high school and age thirty, about eight million once-active Christians have abandoned the church or Christianity.[5] This movement away from institutionalized Christianity is explored by the authors and evangelical leaders David Kinnaman and Gabe Lyons in *unChristian: What a New Generation Thinks about Christianity . . . And Why It Matters*, which expands on the Barna studies.

The years since the Barna findings have been marked by a concerted effort by evangelical leaders to rebrand conservative Christianity as less exclusive, more compassionate, and, somehow, *the* panacea for the wounded LGBTQ community. Leaders took the Barna results on the road to publicly lament the error of their ways. *We screwed up, and Jesus can fix us all.* They pointed to the exodus of their youth as a reason for the church to chart a new course. Their message, which often slammed the Religious Right, went wide and was heralded by some as a progressive shift, or at least a "new face" for evangelicalism.

But their heartfelt calls always had a caveat. They preached a backhanded compassion, calling for love while calling same-sex love sin. Despite the soul searching, the evangelical reaction from the top continued to exclude even the *possibility* that the church's "traditional marriage" theology could be wrong. Stepping outside "tradition" would be heretical and so beyond the realm of any "true" Christian's imagination. Instead, the self-appointed gatekeepers of evangelicalism crafted a rebranded message, basing it on an outdated psychological interpretation of the LGBTQ experience.

WHEN BAD PSYCHOLOGY WON'T DIE

When writer Jonathan Merritt, the son of a former Southern Baptist Convention president, characterized past evangelical screeds against homosexuality as "vitriolic polemics" but stopped short of demanding full church inclusion of the openly LGBTQ, he channeled the voice of many evangelicals who want to distance themselves from the Religious Right but still harbor doubts about the morality of "homosexual behavior."[6] Then, in 2012, a gay blogger who was frustrated with Merritt's large platform and steadfast "homosexuality-is-sin" message wrote about his brief fling with Merritt, which involved flirtatious text messages and, as Merritt later put it, "physical contact that fell short of sex but went beyond the bounds of friendship."

Merritt addresses that experience in his 2014 book *Jesus Is Better Than You Imagined*, by writing about the childhood sexual abuse he endured at a young age, his suicidal tendencies, and his sexual confusion. "Did the childhood abuse shape my adolescent and young adult experiences, or were those parts of me already there? I'm certain I don't know the answer to this question, and I'm not sure anyone does except God." The *Christianity Today* excerpt of this story went viral in Christian communities.[7]

Merritt offers his story as a personal account of his abusive past and the messy working-out of his questions, not as "a bludgeon in anyone's debate," as he put it.[8] Despite my disagreements with many of his conclusions about LGBTQ equality, I value his story and don't have a problem with it on its own.

But I do take issue with how evangelicals universalize stories like Merritt's and ignore the vast diversity of queer experiences, like the stories of folks like Will and Tasha, who had nontraumatic childhoods. Merritt's is the kind of blanket narrative historically used to back up misguided theories about homosexuality, namely that same-sex attraction is sinful and caused by troubling childhood events and can be reversed with Jesus's love. By excluding the stories of healthy gay Christian couples, affirming churches, and countless other LGBTQ lives, leaders perpetuate a flawed, dangerous view that hurts church members, especially LGBTQ congregants.

This theory has been strengthened by its relentless, uniform messaging and is widely held among lay people, theology professors, Christian therapists, pastors, and today's most visible evangelical leaders, both progressive and conservative. When I interviewed Gabe Lyons, a nationally recognized evangelical voice and the coauthor of the Barna Group's *unChristian,* he spoke at length about compassion "shaping the tenor of the conversation," and seemed genuinely heartbroken by his LGBTQ friends' stories of struggle. Still, he remained skeptical toward the idea that homosexuality was something people were born with.

Drawing from conversations with his gay friends, Gabe pointed to a litany of potential triggers for homosexuality: molestation, unhealthy same-sex relationships in childhood, or situations where a child "can become over-sexualized."

"It taints them to see the world through a lens that may not have been how things were designed to be, but it is what their journey has been," he told me in an interview.

The origins of this viewpoint date back to discredited psychological research from more than fifty years ago that Christians have popularized over the decades.

In the 1960s, when psychiatrists widely believed that homosexuality was a disorder, psychoanalyst Dr. Irving Bieber surveyed the lives of more than a hundred homosexual men and concluded that homosexuality sprouted in men whose families were "characterized by disturbed and psychopathic interactions."[9] Their fathers were typically detached and hostile while their mothers gravitated toward a more smothering, sometimes "seductive" style of parenting. Bieber's findings were widely acclaimed and he held them up as authoritative proof that homosexuality was a pathology.

Over time, this theory lost traction with the psychological community. Researcher Evelyn Hooker made an important observation: prior to her work, scientific research on homosexuality exclusively examined the lives of mentally ill and incarcerated men, creating a false correlation. Hooker forged a study that drew from a broader population of homosexuals and heterosexuals of comparable age, IQ, and education levels, and ran her subjects through a string of personality tests. Then she asked experts in those tests to analyze the results and spot the gay men. They couldn't. In fact, the expert clinicians found that an equal two-thirds of the subjects in the gay group and the straight group were well-adjusted human beings.

Hooker's findings eventually played a role in the American Psychiatric Association's 1973 decision to strike homosexuality from its *Diagnostic and Statistical Manual of Psychiatric Disorders*. Today the vast majority of mental health experts agree that efforts to change sexual orientation, popularly known as "reparative therapy" in religious communities, are not shown to work and may cause psychological harm.[10]

But in Christian circles, Bieber's claims live on. As Gay Christian Network founder Justin Lee writes in his book *Torn: Rescuing the Gospel from the Gays-vs.-Christians Debate*, Christian theologian and psychologist Elizabeth Moberly built on Bieber's theory by adding the concept of "reparative drive." She argued that a child with a detached same-sex parent would subconsciously seek to repair that rift, and that effort—the "reparative drive"—was the source of same-sex attraction.[11]

Lee points out the holes in this theory.

> Distant fathers and overprotective mothers are extremely common in American society, so this allows a larger percentage of gay people to say, "Hey, that sounds like me!" But these same dynamics are very widespread among straight Americans as well, and they are not at all present for many gay Americans. If distant fathers and overbearing mothers made people gay, there should be far more gay people in American society than there are.

Lee, who writes at length about his loving, attentive parents, concludes, "Meanwhile, I should have been the straightest guy in the world."

CULTURE WAR 2.0

Today, evangelicals are more divided than ever on the issue of sexuality. Out of this new era, three distinct groups are emerging: a strengthening progressive faction, conservatives resisting the change, and those caught in the middle parsing through mixed feelings, according to Jeremy Thomas, a sociology professor at Idaho State University who has studied the evolution of evangelical beliefs about homosexuality since the 1960s. Among those moving away from the conservative hard line, skepticism over the reparative drive theory is growing. More evangelical youths are standing by their gay friends. Ex-gay empires are shuttering and renouncing ex-gay therapy. The nation's laws are turning to protect sexual minorities. And a trickle of evangelical leaders is publicly supporting gay marriage.

Fearing this shift toward acceptance, conservative evangelical stalwarts are launching a sort of Culture War 2.0. They've conceded defeat on the gay marriage battle, but they've launched a new directive aimed at protecting individuals, businesses, and religious organizations seeking to deny services, housing, or employment to sexual minorities—once again, all in the name of religious freedom. With no national laws prohibiting these forms of discrimination (and in the absence of sexual orientation and gender identity protections in civil rights laws in more than half of the states) local communities have taken up this issue, with a number introducing ordinances aimed at protecting those who discriminate against queer people on the basis of deeply held religious beliefs. Evangelical leaders made this Culture War 2.0 strategy explicit when, after President Obama signed an executive order banning federal contractors from LGBTQ discrimination, some of the most politically influential evangelical leaders publicly demanded a religious exemption.[12] And in this new era of national legalized gay marriage, these efforts are only intensifying.

What's striking about Culture War 2.0 is that this message is coming from evangelicals across the ideological spectrum, including progressives. It's not a shock that Focus on the Family's lobbying affiliate CitizenLink defends the rights of businesses to refuse service to gay weddings. But it is surprising to read similar sentiments in PRISM, a publication of the left-leaning Evangelicals for Social Action. In the November 2013 issue, progressive evangelical forefather Ron Sider points the church toward a new frontier: protecting the tax-exempt status and "rights" of religious organizations who refuse to hire "practicing gays."

On the argument of how to handle sexual minorities, the distance between many evangelical leaders on the Left and Right has collapsed. And their posture in this new debate is one of defensiveness; any critique of their views is cast as intolerance toward Christians. When the Reverend Louis Giglio faced backlash for previous denouncements of the gay rights movement and withdrew from delivering President Obama's 2013 inaugural benediction, Gabe Lyons wrote, "Mr. Giglio is the victim of a kind of hate crime." After other evangelicals criticized his choice of words, Lyons amended his "hate crime" language and wrote that Giglio lost his First Amendment right and was a "target of intolerance—the kind of prejudice that many in the LGBTQ community have suffered themselves."[13]

Evangelicals on the defensive seem to have forgotten their history. They've lobbied to criminalize gay sex; they support the right of businesses to deny services to same-sex couples; they fight for exemptions from employment nondiscrimination policies; they uphold church policies that exclude LGBTQ members from communion, marriage, and the pulpit—all while perpetuating the grand myth of Christian persecution.

They argue that opposition to same-sex marriage is a deeply held religious belief, and withdrawing support, whether it's by declining to photograph a gay wedding or refusing to hire a married lesbian woman, is a rightful expression of their faith. But the logic doesn't extend beyond the LGBTQ issue: evangelicals aren't out pushing for the right to discriminate against divorced couples, unrepentant gossips, or gluttons, all people in blatant violation of Christian tenets.

In addition to being defensive, the gatekeepers of evangelicalism are quick to punish those who venture outside their boundaries. Like the jolt of an electric fence, the evangelical machine is swift and exacting, as evidenced by top evangelical lobbyist Richard Cizik's 2008 dismissal from the National Association of Evangelicals after he voiced support for civil unions. Cizik violated what I like to call the "orthodoxy ultimatum," a litmus test that determines who is allowed into top evangelical roles.

"To be a senior level . . . highly respected evangelical leader, still seems to require affirming the traditional position" on homosexuality, explained leading Christian ethicist David Gushee in an interview with *Religion Dispatches*. "It's a matter of orthodoxy. You're . . . still in the community, if you can do it. If you're not so sure about it anymore, then you're pushed to the margins of your own community."[14] Gushee himself, a longtime proponent of the homosexual-conduct-is-sin camp, came out in 2014 as a "pro-LGBTQ" straight ally vowing to offer full acceptance of sexual minorities, to fight religion-based harm, and to help churches become more safe and welcoming to everyone. Theologians and denominational leaders predictably condemned him.

The pressure doesn't come just from the higher-ups. In 2014, when the behemoth Christian charity World Vision announced it would hire employees in same-sex marriages, antigay donors pulled "several thousand" sponsorships of Third World children to protest the decision, according to World Vision president Richard Stearn. Despite the praise from queer and ally Christians, Stearn issued an apology days later and reinstated the old policy barring gays and lesbians from employment.[15]

All of this might not sound like progress, but beneath the noise, there's a swelling signal of hope. The defensiveness, the backlash, the tightening grip on conservative theology—it's all a reaction to the groundswell of LGBTQ progress taking place in society and within the evangelical community.

Today, the majority of young evangelicals support some form of legal recognition for gay couples, according to the Public Religion Research Institute.[16] And when it comes to same-sex marriage, young white evangelicals are more than twice as likely to lend support than the oldest generation of white evangelicals, according to a 2014 study by PRRI.[17] Unlike a few decades ago, when few evangelicals vocalized support for the queer community, today's efforts to stamp out LGBTQ rights have been met with resistance among younger believers.

This shift has led to a very public tug-of-war for power and credibility among evangelicals. In early 2014, after lawmakers in Kansas, Arizona, and a handful of other states pushed bills that would have allowed businesses and individuals to deny services to same-sex couples on the basis of religious beliefs, Jonathan Merritt and Fox News political analyst Kirsten Powers, also an evangelical, penned articles opposing these moves. And after the Supreme Court legalized gay marriage in 2015, nearly one hundred evangelical leaders signed a statement that not only supported the decision but also called for stronger legal protections for LGBTQ people in housing, employment, and education. Their celebration struck back against the damning rhetoric from the evangelical right. In 2014, after World Vision recanted its decision to hire married gays and lesbians, a wave of criticism from evangelical LGBTQs and allies came crashing down. Rachel Held Evans, a popular feminist evangelical blogger, wrote in a blog post shared more than three thousand times, "I don't think I've ever been more angry at the Church, particularly the evangelical culture in which I was raised and with which I for so long identified."[18]

A decade ago, there were no such divisions. Conservative leaders had no need to cloak their efforts to eradicate LGBTQ rights with saccharine talk of compassion. That's because progressive believers kept quiet, fearful of getting sidelined as godless heretics. But today, those voices are out and gaining traction among mainstream evangelicals.

AFTERMATH

To understand the spectrum of evangelical thought surrounding LGBTQ issues, look no further than the BQU in-box. In the months that followed the group's blog launch, Will and Tasha fielded a steady stream of e-mails. Many e-mailers offered the typical compassion-condemnation bait-and-switch, like the pastor who wrote "I LOVE YOU" before warning them of their destiny, "the lake of eternal fire." Some criticized their splashy advertising stunt, believing it had stifled campus discussion. And many asked them to leave Biola and form segregated "gay schools," to prevent the alleged oppression of straight people.

The BQU also heard from admirers. "I used to be strongly against homosexuality," wrote one straight supporter, "but through looking at the issue more, I have come to see that I was wrong. Please always remember that someone's got your back and that each of you is deeply loved."

One graduate wrote to them "with tears in my eyes" and recounted the years it took "to learn to live without the self hate that they [Biola] taught me."

In the comments section of the BQU article printed in the Biola student newspaper, the *Chimes*, readers clashed over their opinions of the group.

"Can someone please explain to me how a person can be a devout follower of Christ and at the same time be professing he/she is LGBTQ . . . Sin is sin, right?" wrote a reader by the handle "Stephanie."

The consensus Side B response (you can be gay, but you must remain celibate) was captured by commenter "John Kruckenberg": "@Stephanie . . . Struggling with LGBTQ temptations and feelings is not a sin . . . if a person who is struggling with LGBTQ temptations gives in to their sin or does not acknowledge the sinfulness of a LGBTQ lifestyle, then they are living in sin."

"Cary—Class of 1981" suggested liberal conspiracy was at the heart of this group. "I guarantee, this is an infiltration at best. . . . I am sure some were able to slip through the cracks of admissions, with the soul [*sic*] purpose to start this attack from within."

While some supported this conspiracy theory, others dismissed these claims as hyperbolic nonsense. And others supported the BQU members, calling them "honest, god loving people, hurt by the church."

Will and Tasha could not resist reading all of the reactions, which sent them on a swooping roller coaster of emotions. But what settled them, and assured them that they had done the right thing, were the private notes from closeted LGBTQ students who saw the group as their lifeline. In one e-mail, a student wrote, "I am just so sick of feeling alone." Another told them about the "insane amount of guilt" she felt all the time. To some hurting queer students, this mysterious, anonymous club was their last hope. "I have NEVER been ashamed of who I am UNTIL I transferred to Biola. I desperately want to meet someone I can relate to. Im [*sic*] literally at my ends here. Please help."

That summer, Will tried talking to his mother about his sexuality. As Mrs. Haggerty recalled in an interview, she told Will, "I'm not going to talk about this with you until you tell your father." It had been a year since Will had come out to her. The news had shocked her, but she kept it to herself. "I did not tell anybody that I knew because I did not want to accept that lie," she told me.

Later, Will approached his father in the garage and told him about his sexual orientation and his role in launching the BQU. After Will came out, Mr. Haggerty pulled his wife into the conversation.

From there, things unfolded strangely. First, Mr. Haggerty thanked Will for sharing. Then he announced that he was divorcing Mrs. Haggerty. Will's mother began to cry. As Will remembered it, his father explained that he was trying to make a point: this is how it felt to hear news that was outside of God's design. Mr. Haggerty clarified his intentions to me, explaining that his purpose was "shock value." Will's coming-out was not news he wanted to hear. Delivering the divorce news was "like saying: 'Here's what it feels like when you drop something like this on us.' Maybe my approach wasn't the best." (Will's parents were not, in fact, getting a divorce.)

From there, things got ugly. They yelled. They cried. Will said his parents probably *should* get divorced. His father compared homosexuality to pedophilia. His reasoning: "Homosexuality is being more embraced and the media is showing it. Well, what's next? What's wrong with having sex with boys and girls under eighteen? To me it's Pandora's box." Will's parents love him deeply and unconditionally, they stressed in our interview, but as Mr. Haggerty put it, "At this point, I can embrace him and I can embrace his friends, [but] I don't think I can get to the point where I can accept something that leads to a destructive lifestyle."

At the end of their emotional conversation, Will's parents left him with an ultimatum. As Will recalled, they said he must leave the BQU or else he'd lose his home, many of his possessions, and their financial support. Will's parents deny that they kicked him out of the house, but they confirmed the rest.

As they saw it, they were paying over $30,000 a year in Biola tuition and Will, by running the BQU, was violating the school's code of conduct, risking expulsion and huge financial consequences. "We gave him a choice: you either go to another university, or you drop the underground and we finance your last year in school," said Mr. Haggerty. "Or you're on your own."

They gave Will the summer to think it over, and in the end, he decided to stick with the BQU. "I had prayed about it," he told me. "I couldn't abandon these people. I wanted to be there no matter the cost." Will scrambled to secure a loan from the bank, a job serving coffee on campus, and a room at school. His parents cut off their tuition payments and took away his car, laptop, and cell phone. Mr. Haggerty explained that they took back these possessions because they knew Will would use his computer and car to advance the BQU, which they couldn't support. (After Will graduated, they returned the car to him.)

"I felt like we were getting a divorce," Will recalled with a sad laugh, "but they got mostly everything."

But what Will had lost was outweighed by what he had gained: a new family that adored him and relied on him. Will and Tasha had replied to the desperate e-mails in the BQU in-box and welcomed new members. As soon as school started, their group met weekly, bonding for hours over heavy confessions and silly icebreaker games. Some members began to date and fall in love. Others found true friendship and a space to finally breathe. For many who had lost their faith, the group had helped them rediscover it.

As the year progressed, that giddy feeling that Will and Tasha shared at the start of their friendship had infected the entire group. They piled in front of the television and cried together as they watched movies like *Brokeback Mountain* and *Milk*. They gave each other drag queen names: "You take your street name you grew up in and your first pet's name—so mine is Yukon Star," Will explained. Every Sunday, they attended a queer-friendly church together. Their carpool ritual involved discreetly meeting on campus, hopping into two cars, and tearing down

Interstate 5, racing, cutting each other off, and shouting through the open windows. In those moments, when Will looked at his friends, their laughing faces splashed with morning sun, he knew his sacrifice was worth it. He had found his family.

That fall, the group grew even tighter after Biola staff members spoke on a panel about the school's view on sexuality. The panel, titled "Sexuality Matters: A Discussion on Homosexuality, Biola, and Jesus," drew roughly five hundred students and included Dr. Chris Grace, the school's student development administrator; Dr. Erik Thoennes, a professor of theology; and Dr. Tamara Anderson, a professor of psychology.[19] The student newspaper billed the panelists as "diverse," but the BQU balked; there was not a single pro-LGBTQ voice. (The school had hosted interfaith panels in the past that let atheists present arguments contrary to the school's values. The BQU wondered, Why couldn't they make room for a queer Christian voice?)

As a result, homosexuality remained invariably cast as sin, dysfunction, perversion, and "a sign of the fall and the curse," according to Thoennes. When an audience member asked why the panel lacked LGBTQ representation, Thoennes paused and replied with a hint of annoyance, "Because we think it's a sin." In an audio recording of the talk, the audience titters.

"We wouldn't want a proracist person sitting on this panel if the question were about racism," Thoennes continued. "I wouldn't want someone advocating, proclaiming, or talking about the goodness of racism. Or lying. This [homosexuality] is a fascinating sin in our culture. There's no other sin I know of that has parades celebrating it. And days at Disneyland. Can you imagine having 'dishonesty day' at Disneyland?"

The room roared with laughter. Thoennes, on a roll, continued. "I am not concerned about giving more voice to something that seems like a tidal wave in opposition to the way God has designed things."

Later, when I spoke to the administration about the panel's messaging, I expected it to distance the school from Thoennes's incendiary comments, which had been circulating in a Gay and Lesbian Advocates and Defenders petition that demanded Thoennes's apology. But the administration didn't recoil. It explained that the purpose of the panel was to explicitly lay out Biola's theological perspectives to the student body.

COMING OUT

The panel disappointed Jason Brown, the older queer student who met with the dean of students, Danny Paschall, one day after the BQU launched its website. That school year Danny invited Jason and two other queer students to meet with him regularly to discuss LGBTQ issues on campus. Jason attended, hoping that by appealing directly to the administration he could convince the school's leaders to adopt a more welcoming attitude toward students like himself. But as the months went by, Jason began to doubt the effectiveness of Danny's meetings.

Others in the group felt differently. Atticus Shires, a nineteen-year-old sophomore who identified as "struggling with same-sex attraction," described Jason as "wildly above us academically and intellectually." While their meetings left Jason unsatisfied, Atticus, who had thus far done little research on queer issues, felt empowered and educated by the group's discussions. Eventually, he began to form his own opinions. "Side A wasn't there for me theologically," he said, and Side B theology denied essential elements of his humanity. As a result, Atticus declared himself Side Neutral, a new category that embodies the fact that, "I'm not really concerned with pushing myself to find a side to fall in right now. I'm comfortable without knowing."

Eventually, Atticus decided to form a safe space for other queer students at Biola. Because he found the BQU's posture toward the administration too aggressive he and another student began drafting plans to form a group on campus called NakID, which would be publicly Side B ("A lot of the reasons NakID is Side B is political," he admitted. "We quickly learned that the only way Biola would allow [a group] was if it was professing Side B") but operationally Side Neutral (everyone across the spectrum would be invited). Danny's office supported Atticus's efforts and in the fall of 2013, NakID officially launched as a

Side B alternative to the BQU. Danny, Atticus told me, is "definitely the driving force for a lot of good happening at Biola."

But while Atticus formed his beliefs in the Danny meetings, Jason grew increasingly agitated by the group's limited scope. In the fall of 2012, still reeling from Professor Thoennes's comments, which Biola officials did not apologize for, he began to wonder if Danny and the administration had any real interest in welcoming queer students and whether he could safely express to the others that his Side A convictions had been growing stronger.

The broader campus climate seemed more defined by Professor Thoennes's attitude than by Dean Paschall's willingness to listen. Among classmates, Jason heard questions about the presence of queer students. "Why are these people here?" they'd wonder in annoyed tones. And the words of Professor Thoennes began to infect his sense of self. If Jason came out, would everyone see him as a pervert? A sign of the fall and the curse? Was he as bad as a racist? A liar? Did he deserve the audiences' laughter? If anything, campus felt *more* hostile, Jason recalled. In October, fed up with the administration, Jason e-mailed the BQU.

By then, Tasha had left Biola and had been charged with screening the BQU in-box for potential members and conducting in-person interviews off campus before allowing new members to join. Tasha and the others suspected some e-mailers had asked to join the club simply to expose its members; but "moles," as she called them, were easy to weed out. Their language was contrived. When Tasha read Jason's e-mail, she could tell he was sincere. She met with him and before long he was a regular attendee.

Like the many other new BQU members, the world of queer Christians was unlike anything Jason had ever seen on campus. In sharp contrast to Biola's culture, the BQU had a strong female leader, members spoke openly about working out their faith and sexuality or gender identity, and they introduced themselves by indicating their preferred pronouns. The BQU had almost a year on record, forty members, and vibrant weekly meetings. Its efforts had been covered by MSNBC, *The*

Huffington Post, and the local CBS station. Will and Tasha had rehearsed talking points for reporters and documentary filmmakers and made connections with outside LGBTQ activists like Soulforce. Later Tasha would win ten thousand dollars in grant money to support public events cohosted by the BQU. Before, Jason had felt like a lone sailor, crushed by the waves of a powerful anti-LGBTQ culture. But now he felt part of a vast armada that was advancing steadily, wind in sails. By the end of second semester, he signed on to colead the BQU with Tasha.

Will wanted to keep the momentum going through the end of the year, especially as graduation neared and questions about his legacy began to prod him. He knew that, like so many LGBTQ Christian-college students before him, graduation marked the end of his closeted life. He could grab his diploma, come out to the world, and live his life free from the dictates of Biola's student contract.

And then it hit him: Why wait until *after* graduation? Why give the doubters any more reason to believe that the BQU was a conspiracy orchestrated by godless outsiders? Why not humanize the queer community on campus by publishing their names and faces? Why not force the administration to deal with them, not in theory, but in real life?

That's when Will made a daunting proposition to his BQU colleagues: *Let's have BQU's graduating seniors and students transferring out of Biola publicly come out of the closet during finals week, while we are all still officially students.* Tasha was stunned by Will's suggestion. He had always been the risk-averse one; she had always been the envelope-pusher. But here he was, leading the group into uncharted territory.

Eventually, Will and Tasha convinced fifteen members to publish their names and photographs online in what they called the *BQU Yearbook*. The final product was an eight-page, web-based booklet that opened with a letter from Will and Tasha explaining the group's desire to "take its first step out of the closet." Their message: "To the queers at Biola and those worldwide, know God loves you." In the photograph printed at the end of the letter, Will and Tasha stare stoically into the camera lens, their arms slung around each other, their necks sharing a single rainbow scarf. The centerfold features the beaming faces of fifteen LGBTQ and ally members, each set against the backdrop of a rainbow flag. Their faces look youthful and full of promise. The yearbook closes with letters from Tasha and Jason, who planned to colead the group in the coming year, promising to work hard to make campus safer for the queer community.

I had been following the BQU story in the news ever since the group's blog launch the previous year. In an interview with Tasha, I learned about their plans to surprise the campus with their online yearbook, so I booked a flight to California.

The night before they published their online yearbook Will, Tasha, and Jason sat in Jason's bare-bones campus apartment, discussing their plans for the week. It was a Tuesday night. Wednesday morning they would meet at Panera and use the free Wi-Fi to publish their online yearbook. From there, they'd run around campus and distribute fliers that linked to the yearbook and hope that their publication would go viral again. On Thursday the school's student newspaper, the *Chimes*, would run an article about the BQU's big reveal. Will and Tasha had given advance notice to Elizabeth Sallie, the *Chimes'* editor in chief, who had been covering the BQU as part of a broader series, "Homosexuality on Campus."

Elizabeth was a fast-talking senior with cat-eye glasses and a full laugh. She had grown close to Will and Tasha over the course of their interviews and the BQU leaders were under the impression that she would tell both of their stories in her coverage. But then Elizabeth sent an e-mail suggesting that based on her conversations with the administration, she was having second thoughts about profiling Will. This news came as a major blow to Will, who wanted to show the school that the BQU was indeed a club led by Biola's very own queer community. Focusing the article on Tasha, who was no longer a student at Biola, seemed to reinforce the conspiracy theory that the BQU was a club run by outsiders.

Sitting in Jason's apartment, Will scrolled through Elizabeth's e-mail, rereading excerpts aloud to Tasha and Jason. The three sighed and speculated that the administration had intimidated Elizabeth into silence. They made plans to meet with her the following night, after they had published the yearbook.

On a classic blue-skied California morning, Tasha and I settled into a corner table in the outdoor patio at Panera. It was 7:30 a.m., too early for most of humanity (like Will and Jason, who were running late) but Tasha had her game face on. She pulled out her laptop and began to put the finishing touches on the BQU's online yearbook.

Will and Jason arrived with bed head and sleepy eyes, plopping down on the metal chairs. Jason announced that moments earlier he set his Facebook status to "interested in men and women." He smiled sheepishly and looked around the table, but his friends didn't say anything; they were preoccupied and tense. Tasha's eyes were trained on her computer screen, her fingers tapping the keyboard. Will hugged his messenger bag, folding his lanky body at awkward angles. He looked rigid and fragile, ready to shatter.

I asked him how he was feeling, and he told me that he hadn't eaten a meal in days. His stomach burned. "I've been shivering since I woke up this morning; I'm not cold." Tasha and Jason exchanged concerned looks.

"Can you drink some water?" Tasha asked hopefully.

"I drank out of the tap in the bathroom sink," Will said, trying to laugh. "Does that count?" Jason touched Will's arm and shook his head.

And then it was time. Tasha took a deep breath, swiveled her laptop around, and revealed the finished online yearbook. There was the tough-as-nails photo of Will and Tasha. There were the smiling photographs of their fellow BQU friends. There were the senior quotes, like "No day like today" and "Birds born in a cage think flying is an illness." Jason let out a quiet squeal. Will clenched his jaw.

"So are you guys ready?" Tasha asked. The three looked at each other feeling giddy, breathless, astounded by their own audacity.

"My heart's going like a rabbit," Will said.

"Are we sure we want to do this?" they asked each other, half joking.

And then Tasha pushed the launch button. They leaned in, eyeing the slow-loading blue bar. It was up.

"Oh my gosh. That's beautiful," Jason whispered.

After their moment of admiration passed, Tasha gave instructions for where to distribute the fliers, which were palm-sized printouts emblazoned with the words "LGBTQ AND ALLY MEMBERS COME OUT," along with a link and QR code to their yearbook.

Before parting, the three hugged and made plans to meet at the fountain at the center of campus when they had finished.

"Fountain at nine!" Will shouted to Tasha as he bounded toward Jason's pickup truck.

"Fountain at nine," she called back. "Good luck! I'll be praying the whole time!"

"Thank you!" Will said. "I'll be pissing my pants everywhere!"

PART 3

Radicals

SEVEN

Made in the Image of God

LISA

Lisa's racial justice career is a storied one. It took root when she locked eyes with Johnny just outside the Love Kitchen in New York City; it sprouted to life during her InterVarsity years as she confronted racial conflict on campuses and in American Christian history; and since dedicating herself to full-time advocacy, it has branched wide to encompass a range of racial justice matters, from minority representation to immigration to police brutality. In her current role as the chief church engagement officer at Sojourners, Jim Wallis's influential social action group, Lisa has worked to advance these concerns. She has convinced major conference organizers to include these issues, along with leaders of color, on their main stages, she has gone twenty-two days without eating to press Congress to pass immigration reform, and, after marching alongside black youth in the streets of Ferguson, she has built a network of local faith leaders and equipped them to support the city's disenfranchised residents. These key moments in Lisa's career offer a significant look into the complicated, sometimes dreadful yet sometimes hopeful evangelical racial terrain.

AN INCLUSIVE ORTHODOXY

When we last left Lisa's story, she had helped form Evangelicals for Justice, a collection of leaders combating evangelical racism, as well as sexism. I watched E4J grow over the years. Lisa and other members often sought out like-minded believers at mainstream evangelical conferences, the kind that drew thousands to auditoriums that quaked with Christian rock and extolled celebrity evangelicals—typically white and male. E4J members would meet over drinks or dinners to privately sound off about the lack of minority representation. I've sat in on their conversations and found that, in the shadow of massive evangelical conferences, minorities have been commiserating, networking, and organizing for a more racially just evangelical world.

While their critique of evangelical conferences also applies to the broader evangelical world, E4J members pointed their attention to conferences because these events play a critical role in building cohesion across evangelical culture and dispensing ideas to the masses. Even as themes of "Christian social justice" have moved from the fringes to the center of this culture, they've noticed how people of color are rarely leaders; instead they are often used as props (for example, a photograph of a hungry African boy in a dusty landscape) to garner support for organizations run by white evangelicals. At these conferences, themes of "justice" often focus on problems that, though important, take place in other countries, rather than issues happening in our churches, our neighborhoods, or along our borders. E4J members represent the growing number of evangelicals who recognize these blind spots and critique the way white leaders shy away from local issues that the church had an actual hand in—pervasive, systemic ones, like the church's homogenous unit principle strategy, which encouraged racial and economic segregation, thereby perpetuating inequality—for the sake of church growth. By voicing their concerns, E4J members seek to tackle pressing local problems, such as flaws in immigration and the criminal justice system. By doing so, they hope to write a new evangelical history.

My formal introduction to E4J came in the summer of 2013 when Soong-Chan invited me to a private gathering in Chicago. The group consisted of core members, including Lisa, Soong-Chan, and others, along with a loose collection of like-minded progressive evangelicals. E4J has no website or official organizational presence in the evangelical community, but many of its members are directors or leaders at major evangelical institutions (InterVarsity, World Vision, Sojourners, and Christians for Biblical Equality), along with seminary professors, a Nobel Peace Prize nominee, pastors, authors, and seminary students.

They had been meeting by conference call every month, and in person once a year, but realized that, in order to effectively expand their strategy, they needed to more deeply know each other's personal experiences with racism and sexism in the evangelical world. So at this Chicago meeting, they gathered in a circle, passed around a flashlight—the "talking stick"—and spent several hours sharing their stories.[1]

Soong-Chan began, recounting the time when, after he criticized a conference organizer's all-white speaker panel, the organizer asked Soong-Chan to refer a few speakers of color, but made it clear that he didn't want theologians with their own ideas. He just wanted token minorities to parrot the conference organizers' theology.

Daniel Fan, an evangelical justice activist from Portland, Oregon, described the time he attended the 2011 inaugural Justice Conference, with its roster of mostly white men and nonprofits geared toward foreign concerns. He was disappointed that they didn't confront issues of "racism, colonialism, imperialism, indigenous land rights, and gender hierarchy" that he had come for. But the moment that appalled him came during a Q&A session that followed a lecture on the historic African slave trade. An African reconciliation minister asked the speaker if, in light of the damage caused by the slave trade, reparations were due. As Daniel summarized in a blog post, the speaker replied, "I find it morally questionable to hold people today accountable for what happened hundreds of years ago; we need instead to work toward a more just world today."[2]

As Daniel recounted this story to the E4J group, his face twisted with pain and he concluded with this kicker, "And a thousand white people stood up and clapped. And this was [supposed to be] the 'largest conversation on justice.'" (When I spoke to Ken Wytsma, the founder of the Justice Conference, he said that the audience applauded the speaker's entire presentation, not the comments on reparations, and that the speaker "critiqued all sides" and argued that "it was Christians themselves who were advancing the system of slavery." He also noted that the diversity issue of the first conference "wasn't driven by ideology, but [by] trying to cobble together a gathering" on a "shoestring budget.")

Lisa recalled the time her college fellowship peers held a forum to publicly object to her leadership because of her gender. Their reproach haunted her and for years she had internalized inferiority. "I still struggle with that to this day," she said.

One middle-aged woman, an accomplished writer, told the group about being invited to speak at a local presbytery, only to have a group of male pastors turn their chairs around—so their backs faced her—to protest the sacrilege of a woman teaching men.

Divinity student Brandon Wrencher, twenty-eight, remembered the time a pastor of a white Southern Baptist megachurch recruited him—one of the few black congregants—to "be that guy" to teach the church about diversity. Still a college student at the time, Brandon accepted the pastor's challenge, became his intern, and made multiethnicity the focus of his religious studies program. He devoured books by black religious scholars and contemporary thinkers. But very quickly the pastor "made it clear that I was transgressing, that I needed to put these thinkers down and read folks coming out of the Southeastern Theological Baptist Seminary and anything coming from a European Christian heritage."

Brandon gave the pastor's readings a shot, but they disparaged the black Christian tradition that Brandon was raised in and made him struggle with feelings of hatred for his heritage. But those feelings didn't stick. When his pastor urged him to attend Southeastern Theological Baptist Seminary—even offering to help secure him a full scholarship to steer Brandon away from "transgressive theological traditions," Brandon was not swayed. He eventually turned down the offer in favor of a progressive seminary program. As a result, his pastor stopped talking to him. "I got thrown aside," Brandon recalled.

The discussion moved to Jimmy Spencer Jr., a young white male pastor at the E4J meeting. He added that even those, like himself, who "look the part" get discarded if they fail to "adopt the message of the empire." After an aging, shrinking white congregation in the Chicago suburbs hired Jimmy to revitalize the Saturday evening youth program, he built a thriving four-hundred-member congregation. But over time, Jimmy said, the church elders took issue with the people he was attracting—young people of color, immigrants (many undocumented), and low-income families. They criticized Jimmy for coleading with a woman and for not asserting his authority over her. After a few years, Jimmy's conflict with leadership came to a head and he decided to leave, which meant shutting down his service. Jimmy's eyes were red and rimmed with tears as he told his story.

"What I've discovered is we have all been handed something that we call Christianity, or evangelicalism, that is very much a brand. The rules that people in charge set, we call that biblicalism," Jimmy said. To him, those who push the boundaries on race and gender would be ostracized. "If you fail to advance the agenda of people who want you on stage, then you have no use to them."

The common thread in all of these stories was the way those in charge used theology to exert power. The dominant theology, crafted by white men, said women were inferior and excluded from Christian theology the values of people of color, all while denying the existence of white privilege and racial inequality. Those in control wielded theology as a weapon to protect institutions and systems that keep certain groups in power. White evangelical men accomplished this, Soong-Chan explains in *The Next Evangelicalism*, by anointing Christian beliefs based on Western individualism as universal, orthodox theology while shelving beliefs that call for corporate responsibility under special labels (for nonstandard groups), such as liberation theology, black theology, feminist theology, and so on.[3] It was clear from the group's stories that this problem infected evangelical culture at many levels—from tiny churches to megachurches to conferences that reached thousands.

After sharing and shedding a few tears, E4J members discussed strategies for overcoming this deeply ingrained theological myopia. As someone who made his own shift away from "white orthodoxy," Jimmy explained that the key component involved disentangling white evangelicals from the idea that they embody and own all of evangelicalism. His own turning point came through working with people from different backgrounds, which helped him realize that he was "invited to be a *part* of the table like everybody else, without the false presumption that I somehow owned the table." The group agreed, adding to their goals an effort to move away from the hierarchical "platform" approach of conferences (one person talking at the masses) and replacing it with a "table" approach, which invited a diversity of voices to share and listen.

Others voiced concerns that the conference system itself is fundamentally flawed. It is hierarchical and capitalistic by nature, said Soong-Chan. Organizers are beholden to their funders, which include powerful Christian publishers and evangelical institutions with conservative agendas. Conference profit margins also came into play, Daniel explained later. More attendees lead to more ticket and merchandise sales. And how do you attract attendees? Feature white celebrity evangelicals. Daniel compared it to the entertainment industry's attraction to white actors. As he put it, "People don't want to see people of color on stage." Some in the group wondered if they'd be more effective by trying to change the conference system from within or by leaving it altogether.

Later, Andrea Smith challenged the group to assume some of the theological blame. "I think we are sometimes idolatrous," said the acclaimed indigenous feminist, author, activist, and professor at the University of California, Riverside. "I think idolatry is when we only presume failure. We don't believe that God can actually work through us to create a whole different church or whole different world." Yes, white theology can seem overpowering and inevitable at times, but she encouraged the group to "presume success" and let that transform the way they worked to assert change in evangelicalism. She also urged a complete paradigm shift in their organizing approach. Their work, she said, "isn't trying to replace the Christian Right agenda with a different agenda. It's trying to open conversation up," even to people beyond the evangelical world. "Let's not presume that evangelicals even know the right thing to do on things. Let's stop organizing around a party line. We might end up with a great idea with these conversations."

From there, the group hammered out four key goals. First, they wanted to bring more progressive women and people of color to conference stages and other leadership positions. They recognized that various people who shape theology—from theologians and pastors to heads of advocacy groups to authors—have the power to reshape evangelicalism by reaching thousands at a single conference.

Secondly, they sought to make *domestic* justice issues central to evangelical concerns across diverse communities. Even among minority groups, people tend to back issues that serve their own communities. For example, immigrants may focus more on immigration policy issues, and less on decriminalizing drugs or combating police brutality. But with a forceful justice agenda, the evangelical church could breed intersectional justice efforts and build support across communities.

Much of that can be accomplished through their third goal, forging multiethnic partnerships. By building bridges between white evangelicals and various groups among evangelicals of color, the church has a better chance at overcoming its deep racial divide.

Lastly, E4J leaders sought to provide a way for evangelicals of color to break free from the faith's white power structures. As Andrea put it, "Would there be a point where we realized, 'Hey we're actually the majority of the church? We get to kind of run things?'"

Over the years, E4J has helped reshape some important conversations. After a few members separately noticed problems with the Justice Conference (Daniel Fan took issue with the reparations comment; later, Mimi Haddad and Lisa Sharon Harper took issue with the dearth of female and minority speakers) the group began devising a strategic response on their monthly calls. From there, E4J members—including Daniel Fan; his wife, then CBE board member Emily Rice; CBE president Mimi Haddad; Lakota reconciliation minister and justice advocate Richard Twiss; and theology professors Randy Woodley and Paul Metzger—met with leaders of the Justice Conference, including its founder Ken Wytsma, to discuss their concerns about the conference's race and gender disparity. "It was a very profitable and bridge building time of sharing hearts," recalled Ken.

On a separate occasion, Lisa shared a three-hour lunch with another Justice Conference organizer in which, after they swapped stories, Lisa made her case for the importance of diverse speaker lineups. Lisa got personal, explaining that her family members were "seekers," as in, "they want to know the gospel; they want Jesus." But she couldn't invite them to a conference where her black family members and the issues they cared about were not reflected on the stage. She longed for the day when she could invite them to a Justice Conference, but that day had not yet come. By the end of the conversation, she had him convinced. The organizer reached out to Ken Wytsma, who called Lisa directly to discuss ways to address her concerns.

Ken joined the E4J meetings for a year, and as he put it, "The Justice Conference listened and engaged—was a positive example of interaction in a landscape of conferences which had no desire to interact at that time." By the next Justice Conference, Lisa and many of her E4J colleagues led workshops and spoke on panels from the main stage. And perhaps more significantly, Lisa and her E4J colleagues developed relationships with the conference directors. By sharing their stories, these evangelicals of color built trust, and for the next few conferences, the directors sought their counsel before making some big decisions.

This is the kind of change many progressive believers of color are trying to duplicate across the evangelical world, both at conferences and in every other corner they can reach. But in order to accomplish this and mobilize evangelicals around racial justice issues on a broad scale, they need to overcome the biggest hurdle: getting white evangelicals to recognize that institutional racial injustice truly exists.

In *Divided by Faith*, sociologists Michael Emerson and Christian Smith show just how steep a hill progressive believers of color have to climb. In their survey of more than twenty-five hundred Americans by phone and nearly two hundred evangelicals in person, they found that most white evangelicals are stubbornly unable to grasp how life circum-stances are a result of *both* individual choices and social structures. To most white evangelicals, one's fortune, or lack thereof, is entirely the sum of one's personal decisions. In other words, when explaining black poverty, most white evangelicals surveyed did not account for the leg-acy of historic oppression (slavery, Jim Crow), the influence of modern-day systemic discrimination against people of color in housing and employment, mass incarceration, and the long litany of other inequi-ties. Instead, Emerson and Smith found that nearly two-thirds of white conservative Protestants said "that blacks are poor because they lack sufficient motivation," and they found that, compared to other whites, white conservative Protestants "blame blacks more" for the black-white socioeconomic divide. On the flip side, black conservative Protestants, compared to other blacks (and whites), viewed the world through the opposite side of the lens; they were more likely to cite discrimination as an explanation of racial inequality.[4]

"It appears that *conservative religion intensifies the different values and experiences of each racial group, sharpening and increasing the divide between black and white Americans*," write Emerson and Smith. "How people explain racial inequality shapes how they vote, what pol-icies they support and the solutions they advocate."[5] We see this plainly in the way the vast majority of white evangelicals vote Republican and the vast majority of black evangelicals and Christians vote Democrat.

Furthermore, Emerson and Smith found that the white evangeli-cal worldview is inherently tied to a view of laissez-faire capitalism: economic advancement is perceived as equally available to all and be-stowed upon those who worked the hardest. "This helps us understand why our respondents, apart from being irritated at the racial inequality question, were not at all bothered by the racial inequality itself," they write. From their years of research, Emerson and Smith draw a rather withering conclusion:

> Given that white evangelicals—and Americans in general it appears—
> are both comfortable with the black-white gap and inclined to do noth-
> ing about it, we do not think it too risky to conclude that evangelicals

will make little contribution toward reducing the black-white gap. But we wish to extend our argument further to say that evangelicals, despite not wanting to, actually reproduce and contribute to racial inequality.[6]

Despite conservative evangelicals' shared religious beliefs, bridging the gap between white and black will require a dramatic theological paradigm shift, a task that white evangelicals have resisted for generations, especially when those changes lack economic benefits or direct rewards. Taking in the long view of history, this can seem like an irreconcilable difference. As long as white evangelicals, especially those in power, continue to see racism as something that happened in the past or as easily identifiable insults, rather than as an institutional issue, they will block any real progress on fixing unjust systems.

But the tasks of educating evangelicals and building bridges across the racial divide are precisely what Lisa and her colleagues have set out to do. By using their influential positions and their strength in growing numbers, E4J continues to press forward in this often daunting work. For Lisa, this is her life calling. It's what drives her racial justice career and has taken her across the country to tackle a variety of concerns. Despite the obvious obstacles, she has most recently taken up the controversial issues of immigration and police brutality.

IMMIGRATION

On December 2, 2013, Lisa gazed up at the US Capitol, her eyes tracing the dome crowning both wings of Congress. It was a surprisingly mild December day. Lisa felt frail as she made her way into the building. In an effort to demand changes to immigration policy, she hadn't eaten for twenty-one days—subsisting on only water, broth, and juice—and in recognition of her fast she and a small group of fellow activists participating in the 2013 Fast for Families demonstration had been invited as special guests to the House of Representatives gallery. Lisa felt overwhelmed by the honor and prayed that her example would move the hearts of the nation's leaders she'd face in just a few moments.

———

Despite the fact that Congress had effectively tabled immigration reform discussions for the year, weeks earlier these Fast for Families activists had pitched a tent in the shadow of the Capitol and had begun an indefinite fast to push for a vote on the issue.

Lisa felt humbled to partner with the leader of the fast, a successful labor organizer with the Service Employees International Union named Eliseo Medina, whom Lisa saw as a role model for his decades-long advocacy for labor unions and for his work with Cesar Chavez. Lisa and Eliseo began the fast with two other "core fasters": Dae Joong Yoon of the National Korean American Service & Education Consortium was a lanky immigrant advocate and father of two who spoke with urgency about the families affected by the broken immigration system; Cristian Avila of Mi Familia Vota was a baby-faced twenty-three-year-old whose eyes brimmed with tears whenever he explained why he was fasting. At age nine Cristian arrived in the United States with his family from Mexico. Later he qualified for Obama's 2012 Deferred Action for Childhood Arrivals program. While he and his siblings no longer fear deportation, their parents are still at risk.

Every day the fasters made their way through the winter chill, sat in their large white tent, and hosted a steady stream of visitors. Undocumented immigrants stopped by to talk about their loved ones' deportations. The Reverend Samuel Rodriguez, president of the National Hispanic Christian Leadership Conference, flew in from California and brought thirty evangelical pastors along. In a surprise visit, President Barack Obama and his wife, Michelle, came and hugged each stunned, teary-eyed faster. When Lisa set her eyes on the couple, she lifted her hands off her chair's armrests and froze. Then she began to cry. When the president took Lisa's hands, she told him that she long admired his work and thanked him for his support. He had just come from a meeting with Jim Wallis, Lisa's boss, and said he was glad to have "a Sojourner" in the room. When Michelle approached Lisa, the two embraced in a long, tight hug. "It was an 'I feel you' hug," Lisa recalled. Earlier, Michelle had tweeted about the fasters, which helped draw attention to their work. Through her tears, Lisa squeaked, "Thank you for your tweet."

More support continued to flood the tent over the course of their fast. Joe Biden also visited, and members of Congress took turns fasting in solidarity. Altogether, the Fast for Families demonstration drew support from more than two hundred fasters who visited the tent and four thousand fasters across the country and world.

When Lisa and the other core fasters arrived at the House of Representatives gallery on that balmy December day, they were nearing the end of their fast. Medical advisors had urged them to break their fast within the day. Lisa was waking up woozy every morning and found herself frequently on the edge of dizzy spells. Dae Joong had been hospitalized briefly. Onlookers watched Eliseo, then sixty-seven, faint once, go gray in the hair, and shed twenty-four pounds.

When the core fasters stood in the House of Representatives gallery to receive recognition for their work, the Democrats exploded with applause. Lisa looked out at the chamber and saw suited politicians on their feet, their hands thrown in the air, "clapping thunderously" for what felt like minutes. The other side, where the Republicans sat, looked like a still painting. It reminded Lisa of a similar scene in the movie *Lincoln*, when the Thirteenth Amendment is passed and slavery is abolished; the gravity of the parallels made her break down in tears.

TURNING TIDE

Lisa had not come to understand the issues surrounding immigration until after college, in the early 1990s, when she moved to Los Angeles. In 1994, Lisa learned about California Proposition 187, a ballot measure seeking to severely limit social services to undocumented immigrants. Proposition 187 went so far as to require law enforcement, health care professionals, and teachers to report the immigration status of individuals, including children. Lisa had been attending an evangelical church, LA First Church of the Nazarene, which was uniquely diverse politically, and its members threw their weight behind fighting the proposition. Lisa recalled one church leader, a doctor, delivering an impassioned sermon about the inhumanity of Proposition 187. Lisa herself had been working as the director of education at the church's nonprofit youth center, which served many undocumented children. That November, when Lisa heard that Proposition 187 had passed, she cried as she imagined the kids from her group getting picked up and deported. "It was personal," she recalled. "It wasn't just an issue. It was Maria and Eliana and José and John. It was the kids that I was mentoring every day and the ones that I had grown to really love. The thought of never seeing them again because of a vote, it just grieved my heart." (A federal court later found Proposition 187 unconstitutional.)[7]

More than a decade later, when Lisa made her big career move from InterVarsity staff to director of New York Faith & Justice, she put immigration reform at the top of the organization's agenda. In 2010, when Arizona passed its controversial SB1070, considered one of the strictest anti-immigration laws, Lisa joined the protests in New York City, singing "We Shall Overcome" alongside other religious leaders, speaking to the media, and getting arrested for civil disobedience. Lisa was carted away in a police wagon and held in a jail cell that May. She met other protesters there, heard their stories about people they knew undergoing the deportation process, and prayed alongside them. Lisa understood more deeply how this was not just an issue for immigrants—it was an issue for the church—and how the matter dovetailed with her broader pursuit of racial justice. Sitting in that jail cell "was my no-turning-back point," Lisa said. "This is my issue now."

Throughout the last century, evangelicals did little to build their reputation as advocates for the undocumented. The National Association of Evangelicals objected to the Immigration and Naturalization Act of 1965, a law that opened the process to non–Western European immigrants. Since then evangelical leaders have hammered home a hard-line stance—secure the borders, deport the lawbreakers—or they remained on the sidelines. They said little when President Ronald Reagan granted legal status to three million immigrants or when President George W. Bush failed to push through immigration reform during his second term. But all of that has changed over the past decade as rapidly shifting demographics have altered the face of evangelicalism, launching what Lisa calls "the browning of the evangelical church."

In a 2013 *Sojourners* article, the Reverend Wesley Granberg-Michaelson pondered the increasingly multiethnic landscape and its implications for Christianity: Asian Americans are the fastest growing racial group, and more than 40 percent are Christian; African immigrant congregations are flourishing in major cities; the country's Hispanic Protestants (85 percent of whom are Pentecostal and evangelical) number 9.5 million. "There are three times as many Latino Protestants in the U.S. as Episcopalians," he writes. "While millennials are walking out the front door of U.S. congregations, immigrant Christian communities are appearing right around the corner, and sometimes knocking on the back door." Immigrants, he concludes, "may hold the key to vitality for American Christianity."[8]

This revelation has swept the evangelical world, drawing immigration reform supporters from across the ideological spectrum, even from the most conservative enclaves. Not only do progressive groups like Sojourners back immigration reform including a path to citizenship, but so do conservative groups like Focus on the Family, the once anti-immigration National Association of Evangelicals, and the Southern Baptist Convention, a denomination that was founded on proslavery convictions.

"I believe . . . that the future of the Southern Baptist Convention has to be a multiracial, multiethnic future, or quite frankly, it has no future," said Paige Patterson, former president of the Southern Baptist Convention. The convention has seen its percentage of ethnic minorities jump to 20 percent, from about 4 percent in the 1990s.[9]

While evangelical elites have changed their tune, they're running up against opposition and indecision among their white followers. A 2013 survey shows that white evangelicals, compared to whites overall, have more fears about threats to the "American way of life," are more in favor of deportation, and dislike the idea of becoming a minority demographic.[10] But a month later a more nuanced survey by the same group revealed that support for a path to citizenship jumped from 45 percent to 60 percent among white evangelicals when the caveat "provided they meet certain requirements" was added.[11]

In an effort to gain more support, leaders have turned their focus to educating the masses. In 2012, a massive coalition launched the Evangelical Immigration Table. In 2013, just after political analysts linked Mitt Romney's presidential defeat to whiffing on the Hispanic vote, the EIT piggybacked on this sentiment and urged Republican lawmakers to support immigration reform (evangelicals want this, they argued). They also theologically tied immigration reform to biblical values through radio ads and direct outreach to pastors and churches, and through a viral forty-day challenge to congregations, an effort that involved studying the Bible verses addressing immigration.

EIT includes the heavyweight lobbying group the National Association of Evangelicals, representing forty-five thousand congregations from forty denominations. From the group's humanitarian arm, World Relief, two immigration advocates—Jenny Yang, an immigration lobbyist, and Matthew Soerens, an immigration counselor—have paved the way for this conversation with a three-pronged strategy for winning evangelicals: education, relationships, and scripture.

Even among the conservative white congregations that oppose more open policies, Matthew and Jenny do well by appealing to their listeners on the grounds of biblical compassion and evangelical self-interest by conveying these messages: immigrants share their values, immigrants are a boon to church growth efforts, immigrants can advance Christianity by being converted. Ultimately, "We find the response is really positive even in those churches because we go back to scripture," said Matthew. All white, conservative congregations seem to soften once they hear the evangelical pair speak. "They go from being slightly antagonistic to slightly supportive. Only a few become activists."

But among rapidly diversifying evangelical congregations, Jenny and Matthew are finding an emerging contingent of advocates. The two field calls from pastors grappling with the rising number of undocumented immigrants filling their pews. The pastors are baffled by the problem of how they might help these congregants, many of whom face difficulties navigating policies or have families divided by deportations. Oftentimes the pastors, and even their conservative white parishioners, emerge from these experiences supporting immigration reform. Meanwhile, immigration activists within the church have spent years building a wide base of white evangelical supporters, namely through programs that invite white evangelicals to work with undocumented children. "It's often that personal relationship combined with the words of scripture that turn people into really strong advocates for systemic change," said Matthew. "It's hard to argue with relationships."

The impact of this flurry of activity is still unknown. A number of polls with mixed results came out in 2013, some showing a decline in negative attitudes toward immigrants among white evangelicals,[12] others showing that white evangelicals still harbored the most resistance to immigration reform.[13] The following year a survey showed that, in 2013, the majority of white evangelicals supported a path to citizenship.[14] But that figure slipped in 2014, a shift that some experts attributed to pragmatism: perhaps respondents favored legalization (but not full citizenship) as a first step, "so it doesn't kill immigration reform," said evangelical pastor and immigration advocate Gabriel Salguero to the *Atlantic*.[15]

In a separate study, Michele Margolis, a political science professor at the University of Pennsylvania, found that, at a baseline, white evangelicals are more persuaded by antireform messages, regardless of the inclusion of religious language. However, the EIT's message pushed against this trend. According to Margolis's study, white evangelicals became more supportive of immigration reform when they were exposed to the voices of respected evangelical leaders *and* to a biblical justification for a proreform position. The religious language and institutional backing "can help liberalize attitudes on immigration" among white evangelicals.

But, Margolis says, "the EIT is facing an uphill battle," especially since the results of the study split along racial lines, with white evangelicals more persuaded by antireform discourse and nonwhite evangelicals more inclined toward a proreform message. "In both cases, they moved in the way that suited their needs," regardless of religious rhetoric. In short, the EIT message had an impact, but did not revolutionize the racial-political landscape.[16]

This theme of politics dividing across racial lines brings us back to the arguments made by Emerson and Smith in *Divided by Faith*: when it comes to grasping the kind of inequality that's built into society, knowing people of color makes all the difference. White evangelicals from white communities struggle to understand systemic inequality, but those from diverse communities more easily grasp it. In other words, relationships and community have political ramifications.

As demographic changes pull more diverse communities together, Emerson and Smith's findings are playing out. From megachurches to storefront churches, pastors are watching their pews diversify. Many are launching separate ethnic-specific congregations within the church, and many others are combining with neighboring ethnic congregations that are thriving. One church emblematic of Emerson and Smith's findings is a large evangelical church in San Diego called Solana Beach Presbyterian Church.

JUAN-DANIEL

SBPC is a 1,300-member evangelical church that is predominantly wealthy and white. It also has a small Hispanic community that over time has grown, found its voice, and influenced the broader congregation to back immigration reform.

A major turning point came in 2007, when the church hired pastor Juan-Daniel Espitia to lead the separate Hispanic congregation. It was a small congregation whose forty members met in a modest classroom with little more than a piano and some chairs. Although the church had nonprofit youth tutoring and an immigration services program, Juan-Daniel did not see the broader congregation or leadership engaged with the policy flaws that made life so hard for his parishioners.

Furthermore, beyond the church walls, Juan-Daniel saw a growing immigrant community that occupied impoverished enclaves on the fringes of their mostly upper-class town. Surely, the church could be doing more, he thought. That's when he made a plan.

Juan-Daniel's family story is rooted in the intersection of American evangelicalism and American immigration policy. His father, Silviano Espitia, participated in the country's *bracero* program, a guest-worker agreement that brought Mexican laborers across the border to temporarily fulfill US labor demands. During his time in the States he was converted by young American evangelical missionaries. Silviano took his new faith home to Mexico City, and soon his entire family was attending the local Presbyterian church, a departure from the norm in their heavily Catholic society.

Faith became a driving force in young Juan-Daniel's life. It took him all over Europe and Latin America as a traveling missionary, then to the United States, where he finished college and obtained his master of divinity from Princeton Theological Seminary, his license in clinical social work from Rutgers University, and his US citizenship.

Today Juan-Daniel is in his fifties and, in addition to pursuing his pastoral and mental health work, he has dedicated his life to immigration activism. He has served on the board of an immigrant advocacy group, worked alongside families struggling through undocumented life, and pressed the Presbyterian Church (in which he is ordained) to more actively care for the welfare of the immigrant community. But for decades he has grappled with the crushing culture of indifference among much of the Presbyterian community, even where there are Hispanic congregations.

Despite his frustration, when Juan-Daniel joined SBPC, he continued to work hard to build bridges between the immigrant community and his church. He and the church's outreach pastor, Tom Theriault, began regularly distributing lunches to day workers living in the nearby canyons. The two collected, translated, and published stories in Christian publications to educate fellow believers.

They invited congregants to their annual *posada fronteriza*, or border posada. A posada is a traditional Christmas celebration in Mexico in which neighbors travel in a procession from house to house, reenacting Joseph and pregnant Mary's search for an inn. For the *posada fronteriza*, Juan-Daniel and other organizers hosted this celebration at the US-Mexico border, helping broken families reunite across the divide. They'd sing hymns, share testimonies, and sometimes pass communion over the fence. There would often be tears as separated family members found each other and touched fingers through the chain links. Nonimmigrant evangelicals from the United States often attended with Juan-Daniel, their perspectives transformed by the heartbreak and humanity of it all. For example, one white SBPC congregant named Leslie was so moved that she began helping with the church's monthly volunteer visits to a geriatric center in Tijuana, offering her time, car, work, and money.

The project that put Juan-Daniel's church on the map was an immigration focus group that he and Tom launched in 2011. When they began, the group was just a collection of a dozen immigrants and nonimmigrants sharing stories over homemade enchiladas and chicken mole. They had no idea that their work would transform the church and gain the attention of the president of the United States.

In the beginning, Juan-Daniel and Tom handpicked focus group members, with the intention of drawing people from a variety of backgrounds. Some members were undocumented; some recently received their paperwork. Others were citizens with varying degrees of knowledge of the immigration system. One woman had written a book about immigration policy, based on her graduate studies. Other people were complete newbies. There were conservatives and liberals, advocates and the undecided. They listened to each other's origin stories and slowly grew to understand the world from other perspectives.

In my interviews with the group's participants, one particular member's story of transformation repeatedly came up. Don Stapp is a conservative white evangelical in his early seventies with a military and business background who prefers a limited government. Others in the group characterized him as a businessman who expressed resistance to immigration reform early on, concerned that providing a path to citizenship simply rewarded lawbreakers. When I spoke to Don, he disagreed with that depiction but said, "I very much believe in the rule of law." He explained that, despite his early skepticism, he turned a corner when Gordon Hansen, an economics professor from the University of California, San Diego, explained in cold, hard numbers how undocumented immigrants give as much as they take from the economy. The professor went on to show how policy inaction is costing the country a lot of money and how the rapidly assimilating Hispanic community actually helps the workforce and the economy. "It wasn't an emotional presentation," Don recalled. "It was analytical." This appealed to Don, who excitedly asked Hansen for a copy of the presentation to share with his friends.

Don was moved also by the story of Pedro, a young undocumented congregant and member of the focus group. After hearing this young man detail the challenges of living life in the shadows, Don said to himself, "I still felt, *You need to follow the law,* but then you look at this and you say, *How can a reasonable person follow the law in the situation he's going through?*" Don realized that the issue was not the people crossing the border; the issue was the country's broken immigration system.

From there he joined with the others in bringing the focus group's findings to the attention of the lead pastor, Mike McClenahan, who brought the broader congregation to the discussion. They invited Dr. Richard Mouw, a respected professor and former president of Fuller Theological Seminary, to speak to the main congregation about immigration. Gordon Hansen also returned to deliver his presentation to an audience of about a hundred. Later, Matthew Soerens came to address the church and some San Diego community leaders. Soerens debunked common myths about immigration and teased out Bible passages that call Christians to "welcome the stranger." In addition to all of this, undocumented parishioners began sharing their stories with the congregation, putting a human face on the national issue.

From there, the church's involvement in advocacy snowballed. It added more members to its focus group. The church expanded its outreach to the surrounding immigrant community. Church members asked to get involved. They met with local immigration advocates and engaged their political representatives, and they joined the Evangelical Immigration Table's advocacy efforts. In November 2013, while Lisa Sharon Harper was fasting in a tent on the National Mall, she received a visit from Pastor Mike McClenahan. He had just come from a meeting with President Obama, in which McClenahan's church was recognized for its commitment to serving the undocumented immigrant community and for its immigration reform advocacy efforts.

Despite the progress and attention, Juan-Daniel takes these markers of success with a measure of cautious optimism. He's happy about the burst of interest among the evangelical elite, though he can't help but wonder sometimes, "Wow, where the heck have you been in the last thirty years?" He knows there is still a long road ahead. But he's pleased with the bridges he and his colleagues have built between the white and undocumented immigrant evangelical communities. These relationships are the engine for change in the evangelical church, he said. "We start to see in each other what we are supposed to always see in each other: somebody made in the image of God."

FERGUSON

So God created mankind in his own image,
in the image of God he created them;
male and female he created them.
Genesis 1:27

Over the course of reporting this book, I've heard Juan-Daniel's sentiment—that we are all made in the image of God—echoed in conversations with countless evangelical racial justice advocates. It is their touchstone scripture, a verse stated plainly, yet beautifully, in the first chapter of Genesis. It is the human origin story that the Abrahamic faiths are founded on, and it's a theme that recurs throughout the Bible, from the Garden of Eden to Paul's proclamations of freedom through

Christ. When lived out, it is a powerful principle that can unite opposing groups and set individuals free from dehumanizing lies they have
learned from the world. It did this for Lisa, during her New York City
urban project when she was reintroduced to herself as a black person
and began to see herself as "someone made in the image of God."

Over the years, that realization became a driving force in her racial
justice career; it crystallized her mission: all people are made in God's
image, therefore all people are equally loved by God and equally deserving of just treatment, equal opportunity, and just social policies. To
push this conviction forward in the world, Lisa was willing to confront
powerful evangelical organizers, go without food for twenty-two days,
and, in 2014, join the chaotic street protests in Ferguson, Missouri.

In August 2014, after Darren Wilson, a white police officer, shot and
killed Michael Brown, an unarmed black teen in Ferguson, clashes between protesters and the police force erupted in the St. Louis suburb.
For a week and a half Lisa had been staying up late to follow the news.
The conflicts had escalated at a frightening speed, with local forces
moving in on protesters with armored vehicles, Kevlar vests, automatic
rifles, rubber bullets, and tear gas canisters tearing through night. Lisa
watched videos that showed young black men scattering through the
gas clouds, their faces wrapped in shirts, their screaming eyes baptized
with milk. Police arrested protesters and journalists. The National
Guard moved in. And some protests that lasted into the night, defying
curfew, ended in violence and mayhem.

PICO National Network, made up of faith-based organizations,
had been recruiting faith leaders from across the country to be peaceful
allies to youth protesters in Ferguson, marching alongside the young at
all hours of the day. When they reached out to Lisa, she knew she had
to be there. After convincing Sojourners to send her, she landed in St.
Louis on a sweltering August morning. Between e-mails and conference
calls from her rental car, Lisa and her assistant back at the office set up
a series of meetings and mobilizing events with local faith leaders. In
Ferguson, she quickly emerged as an influential evangelical voice in the

heart of the protests. Hours after Lisa arrived, protesters had gathered outside the office of Robert McCulloch, the St. Louis County prosecutor, demanding he recuse himself from the case due to his personal ties to the police force. The group had been chanting "We shall not be moved," and when another leader thrust the bullhorn into Lisa's hands, she echoed that chant. Then Lisa looked out at the chanting residents, the dozen clergy members, and the swarm of journalists surrounding her. She pointed to the second floor of the building, where she imagined McCulloch's office to be, and changed her protest. "Pro-se-cu-tor, you must move! Pro-se-cu-tor, you must move!" The sweaty crowd echoed her cry.

On Lisa's first evening, during her walk down to the protests, she struck up a conversation with a young man from Michael Brown's neighborhood. He had been a foster child and he told Lisa that he had been teargassed several times. Lisa asked him what tear gas felt like.

Your lungs feel like they're filling with fire.

Is that why you've wrapped a T-shirt around your head?

Yes, for protection from the tear gas, but also so the police can't identify me and target me later.

"There was a real sense of paranoia, justified or not, among the youth," Lisa said to me.

Ferguson epitomizes systemic inequality, the very kind that evangelical racial justice advocates want the church to help counteract. As one of the nation's most segregated metropolitan areas, St. Louis has a long history of racial inequality, made especially evident by the high levels of poverty among black residents and the overwhelmingly white city leadership and police departments.[17] The Ferguson Police Department has only three black officers out of a total of fifty-three, and its officers stop black residents at disproportionate rates, according to data kept by the state attorney general.[18] In 2013, blacks were subject to 86 percent of traffic stops and 93 percent of arrests by Ferguson police. For Lisa, this kind of rampant inequality called for evangelical action; Lisa believed the gospel demanded of people of faith righteous anger and active participation in upending the unjust power structure. And yet so many evangelicals had been silent. As Lisa waded among the throngs of battle-worn protesters, she prayed that the Holy Spirit would move her people.

WILL EVANGELICALS SHOW UP?

In a web discussion during late autumn of 2014, Lisa, Soong-Chan, and another E4J member, Troy Jackson, lamented the evangelical response during "this era of Mike Brown" and so many other black deaths from excessive police force.

For Soong-Chan, evangelical leaders have not provided a strong theological answer, and therefore have failed to motivate believers to solidarity or activism. "Power comes when we say, 'These are the words of the Lord,'" he said.

Lisa noted how, historically, evangelical justice efforts have paled in comparison to mainline Protestant justice efforts. Mainline Protestants organized by establishing offices of social engagement; they literally built social justice into the structure of their denominations. But when evangelicals sought to address race, only some opened offices of racial reconciliation, "but usually what they're focused on is, 'How do we get along?'" said Lisa.

Troy Jackson believes that this era has fundamentally shifted America and has thrust a big question in the face of the evangelical community: *Will the evangelical church show up and be counted in this moment?* Troy is a white evangelical pastor from Cincinnati who leads the AMOS Project, a coalition of local congregations actively addressing local racial injustices. Troy has mobilized the faith community to demand justice for John Crawford III, a young black man who, after picking up a toy BB gun from a shelf in a Walmart, was shot and killed by the police. Troy got white evangelicals to march, to join a forty-eight-hour police station sit-in, and to voice solidarity with the young people of color in their communities.

Speaking from his own experience as a white evangelical who works with white evangelicals, Troy believes his community faces many obstacles toward becoming substantial allies. "White evangelical arrogance plays a part in how we engage work for justice." He explained that his own growth curve has been steep, especially when it comes to understanding the kind of rubber-meets-the-road community organizing that creates change. "I think evangelicals are addicted to conferences, addicted to writing books about justice and experiencing moments of justice; we're really bad at strategically engaging in coalition and the hard work of doing justice." Oftentimes, when white evangelicals do engage justice, it's with a colonial mindset, Troy said—offering as a recent example "Rick Warren's five-point plan to save Africa"—or it's done in a way that's irrelevant, like one-off prayer meetings and press rallies.[19]

But that doesn't mean they don't want to help. Troy often hears those in the white evangelical community lament how the subculture was complicit during Jim Crow and absent during the civil rights movement. Today, with black life after black life ended by reckless law enforcement, Troy sees an opportunity for the evangelical church to act on its regret. The question that remains: Will they?

In many ways, the white evangelical church has not shown up. In the wake of the shooting death of Trayvon Martin, in February 2012, white evangelical leaders said little. Months later, the Southern Baptist Convention's Richard Land did speak out, by calling black political leaders "racial demagogues" and accusing them of exploiting the Trayvon Martin story to garner black votes, and by stating that a black man is "statistically more likely to do you harm than a white man." He later apologized for his comments. (Also, Land was found to have plagiarized his comments. This string of events led to his eventual resignation.)

But in 2014, the deaths of Michael Brown, Eric Garner, John Crawford III, and many other black men have awoken a more diverse response from the broader evangelical world. Nearly every major Christian publication covered these events. *Christianity Today* released a steady stream of articles highlighting "How Black and White Christians Think Differently about Race," about how "The System Failed Eric Garner," and about how "The Sin of Racism Made Ferguson Escalate So Quickly." The Southern Baptist Convention's Russell Moore, who replaced Land as the head of the denomination's Ethics & Religious

Liberty Commission, responded with grief and a call to action after a grand jury decided not to indict the officer who killed Eric Garner. He called this decision "not a government living up to a biblical definition of justice or any recognizable definition of justice." Moore, who says the African American community is one of the fastest growing groups in the denomination, indicated that the news motivated him to work on rescheduling an SBC conference on racial reconciliation from 2016 to 2015.

For Troy, hearing these sentiments from powerful leaders helps, but the real justice work gets hashed out on the ground, day to day, in uncomfortable conversations between neighbors of different stripes, far from the bright lights of conferences. This is the messy task the AMOS Project has taken on for decades. In addition to its direct advocacy work, the group brings white evangelicals and people of color together for monthly meetings where they tackle thorny racial justice questions. The group has grown out of two decades of work across racial lines, and has garnered a multiethnic coalition of local residents ready to do civil disobedience. Troy believes that this on-the-ground community-organizing work—the kind of work that makes evangelicals accountable to the people closest to the pain of injustice—is key for building a truly mobilized evangelical base.

"We have to begin to move, whether it's on the gun issue, whether it's on policing and criminal justice, whether it's on law enforcement, immigration, the environment," Troy said. "Are we going to actually build a base of people committed to this and do that hard work? Or are we going to have a strategy where we get amazingly powerful pastors to raise their voices, but they do it isolated from their actual daily ministry and leadership?"

MESSING WITH YOUR WORLDVIEW

There are so many chasms in evangelicalism: the chasm between black and white believers, millennials and their elders, progressives and conservatives. Over the course of Lisa's life, she's found herself routinely suspended between these worlds, acting as a bridge connecting disparate parties. When facing the challenges of mobilizing evangelicals, she has deployed her narrative to quell the hostility or the suspicions or the assumptions that brew beneath the surface.

Two days after arriving in Ferguson in August, Lisa took a break between protests and spoke at a gathering of a couple dozen local and regional evangelical leaders at Three Kings Pub, a bar near Washington University in St. Louis. She wanted to explain why she believed harnessing the evangelical community to join this long justice campaign was a gospel imperative.

When she looked out at her rapt audience in that crowded back room of the pub, she saw representatives from many major evangelical organizations: InterVarsity, Young Life, the Acts 29 Network, the Presbyterian Church of America, and the Baptist churches. That's when she realized, *My life has prepared me for this moment.* She had been involved in some of these groups in the past. They could not dispute that she was one of them, a bona fide evangelical Christian. Lisa had meant to simply say a few quick words about her background, but as she spoke she could feel the spirit moving her—to raise her voice, to *preach*. She spoke emphatically. She urged her listeners to join in the long, arduous journey of racial justice work. When some offered trite Christian-ese solutions, she forcefully rejected their Band-Aid suggestions like *I want to make sure we're not getting away from what really matters—the gospel* and *All the people of Ferguson need is Jesus.*

"No, they don't," Lisa shot back. "They need Jesus to work in us to press the powers to actually do justice. They need the powers to actually do justice. They need the police to stop targeting black people and stopping them and impoverishing them through all the fees."

What frustrated Lisa most about these comments was that they were coming from black men who had risen in the ranks of conservative evangelical outfits. "All I could think to myself was, 'Brothers, you're not helping,'" Lisa said with a chuckle. "But let me just say, I understand it. They had to give everything up to be [accepted into con-servative evangelicalism]. They kind of have to justify giving up their own ethnic identity. And in order to survive they have to distance themselves from it."

Lisa ended the meeting with a stirring question. She asked the pastors to think about the black people in South Africa under apartheid and about the community of enslaved Africans in Missouri only a handful of generations ago, "and ask yourself, would the Four Spiritual Laws be good news to them? 'Just get right with Jesus; just hold on until you get heaven in the end. And let's look at the Holy Spirit booklet, the one that tells you how to get all the circles of your life in order *while you are still in chains.*' Is this enough?" There was a rousing, "Noooo!" from the table. And immediately after the meeting, even the more conservative men were so moved that they reached out to her. "Can we meet?" their e-mails read.

The next day, when Lisa met with Darren Casper, a local pastor, their conversation brought him to tears. As Darren recalled, Lisa kept pressing the message that the gospel was "bigger than the salvation message" alone; in its entirety, the gospel called for social justice. Lisa's language made Darren uncomfortable, he admitted, and he did not adopt her wording. Nonetheless, he said, Lisa's message shook his world. "God used Lisa," to help him see that "the truth of the gospel demands that I am involved in the work of social justice," he said. Later, Darren told a mutual colleague that his chat with Lisa "messed him up." Since their conversation, Darren has become increasingly involved in justice initiatives across the city.

Lisa made the conversation bigger a few days later when she and other leaders gathered 250 St. Louis faith leaders and trained them in community organizing. She heard leaders talk about engaging with the community, about demanding justice alongside the protesters, about registering voters, and about using the power of the church to press for accountability and change. Over the course of that fall and winter, Lisa returned to Ferguson multiple times to help equip local leaders who had committed to keeping the religious community mobilized, so that "evangelicals are right there, involved."

Howie Meloch, a white St. Louis–based leader for InterVarsity's black campus ministries and a director of the organization's central region, said Lisa's presence helped empower and train local evangelical leaders, many of whom were white church planters (people who establish new churches) with little experience engaging with the questions raised in the wake of the fatal shooting of Michael Brown. Many of these leaders understood the gospel through the lens of "individual transformation," said Howie. In other words, they limited their Christian faith to salvation and personal piety. They did not include fighting institutional injustice, such as police brutality or racial profiling, as part of the gospel calling.

To that audience, Lisa's message struck a radical note. The work she described focused on the long-term commitment to action required for true justice; she did not speak about conversion or even doing charitable acts with an eye toward conversion. She made it clear that this moment did not call for Christian saviors, it called for solidarity, sacrifice, and hard work.

When these pastors heard Lisa's talk, many stepped away from her call to action. "There is a fear . . . that you're losing what is thought to be the core of the gospel when you talk about more than the individual transformation," Howie said, explaining that there's often an unnecessary division between adherents of the "social gospel" and the "salvation gospel." But many others joined the broader movement of faith leaders supporting youth protesters, which included marching, receiving training in nonviolent civil disobedience, and confronting police officers with prayer, even to the point of getting arrested. Howie, who was arrested while participating in the Moral Monday March that Lisa helped organize that October, said, "I would never have done that without Lisa's connection to me." Howie explained that Lisa has helped build that bridge between the "social gospel" and the "salvation gospel." "Her presence has really catalyzed a movement of people."

Nationally, big questions linger. Will the national evangelical church community join in or let the moment pass by as they have done so often in the past? "I don't know the answer to that question," said Lisa. But she does know that many want to be involved. She sits on conference calls with national faith leaders. An increasing number want to understand the conversation about criminal justice issues, and Lisa and Soong-Chan and others like them are poised to help them do so. Meanwhile, Lisa and Soong-Chan, their E4J colleagues, and the growing network of minorities and white allies continue their work in pressing for immigration reform and criminal justice reform.

Lisa knows this work will take many long, hard years. She knows she may never see the fullness of its rewards. She knows to temper her optimism and press forward with caution. But she also knows that despite all of these obstacles, she and her colleagues have helped carve out a new path for evangelicalism. They've changed the lives of fellow evangelicals, and even their own.

Still, so much of history suggests that the evangelical racial divide is irreconcilable. Minorities working to change the culture from within, like Lisa, Soong-Chan, and their colleagues, face a frequent barrage of microaggressions and outright exclusion. It's enough to make one wonder, why do they stay?

Most of the activists I spoke to did not define evangelical faith by their bad experiences with bigotry or by the misbehavior of other evangelicals; they saw past the politics and cultural blind spots to what they believe the faith truly is: good news. "It's a faith—a faith I believe in," Lisa said, recounting the strains of justice movements throughout history that have sprung from the evangelical church. "I haven't left because I have sensed a call on my life to help preserve that faith—to call the church back to that faith." Daniel Fan has stayed because he has found a unique subculture among other evangelicals of color where both his faith and identity as a Chinese American are affirmed. Elsewhere, he has felt pressure to subordinate one of these aspects of himself. Among white evangelicals, he is often asked, "Why do you have to be Chinese? Why can't you just be Christian?" In secular settings, he faces the opposite question, "Why do you have to be Christian?" Finding other minority Christians like himself has given Daniel a sense of belonging. "You want to be in a place that's OK with who you are, where you won't have to subsume that half of your identity under someone else." For Soong-Chan, political wrangling has tarnished the evangelical name, but "at its heart, there's an evangelical Christianity worth redeeming." That faith, centered on Christ, community, and scripture, drives him to reclaim evangelicalism and restore it to its original meaning. "If we get to define it, we would define it very differently than the way it's being tossed around now," he said, noting that changing demographics are making this more possible today. "And if we get to define it, then why would we abandon it?"

By staying, not only have these leaders witnessed the impact of their racial justice work on evangelical society, they've also seen the impact on their own sense of self. When Lisa addressed faith leaders in Ferguson, many of whom hailed from denominations that largely disallow female preachers, her mind flashed back to her years at Campus Crusade, where she had been told that her gender disqualified her from leadership. Now, more than two decades later, she has "experienced a freedom" from those gender constraints. Standing on that stage, facing hundreds of faith leaders, she made a bold proclamation about her view of the gospel: that it didn't simply call people to reconcile with God, but it called for the reconciliation of all things. "I know that for some here, those are controversial words," she said to her audience. "But I just want you to know, I don't care what you think. I know I'm right." As the crowd laughed, Lisa sensed they understood her message, "that a gospel that is only good news to the affluent is not good news at all."

Years ago, as a soft-spoken college girl in neutral-toned clothing, she never could have imagined herself being so bold. Even when she concluded her talk and stepped off the stage she could hardly recognize herself. She smiled and thought, *Wow, you've come a long way, baby.*

GOD SEES YOU

Back out on the streets of Ferguson, tension hung in the air. Though the throngs of protesters and police officers had not yet clashed that night, everything felt like it was on the brink of chaos. Protesters marched in circles on West Florissant Avenue. Police officers leveled machine guns at those who stopped to rest, ordering them to continue moving. It was another blistering August night in Ferguson, and as Lisa marched with her fellow protesters, she thought to herself, *This is insane.*

Lisa, then forty-five, had been marching with two other middle-aged black faith leaders, the Reverend Leroy Barber, a longtime community development leader addressing domestic and global poverty, and Bishop Dwayne Royster, who leads a Philadelphia-based interfaith group that works on combating poverty and systemic racial injustice.

"The old folks were getting tired," Lisa remembered. "Our knees were giving out and getting swollen." By 11:30 p.m., relieved that there hadn't been any violence and exhausted by the endless rounds they walked, Lisa, Leroy, and Dwayne hobbled to a parking lot that was a designated rest area.

As the three shook out their legs, they noticed a growing circle of young, mostly black, protesters collecting nearby. They spoke animatedly to each other about the injustice of their situation. *This is so cool,* Lisa thought to herself. *The young people are organizing.*

"Pray with us!" one young person called to the middle-aged faith leaders. The circle expanded to let them in.

As they were praying, a vision came to Lisa. She saw the elders—herself, Leroy, and Dwayne—praying individual blessings on each young person. The idea made her nervous, but "I also know to obey when I sense God's leading," she told me later. So when the prayer ended, Lisa stepped into the middle of the circle and shared her vision with the group. She asked permission to pray over each young person, and they nodded in agreement.

The first person she prayed for was a tall nineteen-year-old with a guarded look on his face. Lisa took his hands and the two bowed their heads. "The sense that I got when I was praying for him was, he doesn't see who he is. He doesn't see God's dream for his life yet. My personal sense was that he had been flooded with other people's perceptions of him. The angry black man. The dangerous black man. The thug. The gangster. All these different perceptions of black men. I prayed that

God would show him who he really was. That God would show him his dream for him."

Lisa hoped that, for this one young man, her prayer could help dislodge the racism he had internalized. The events at Ferguson had only intensified her understanding of how black men are systemically dehumanized from birth to death. So she prayed for him, earnestly and passionately, pleading for God's blessing upon him.

When Lisa closed her prayer, she felt the young man let go of her hands. She felt a pang of disappointment. *Oh, this didn't really touch him,* she thought. *He's just glad it's over.*

But that wasn't it at all. He lifted his head and looked at Lisa with teary eyes.

"Can I hug you?" he asked.

"Yes," Lisa said, and he wrapped his arms around her. He would not let her go. He began to weep, his body shaking against her tight embrace.

"It's OK," Lisa whispered. "God sees you. It's OK. God sees you."

EIGHT

Femmevangelical

JOURNEY OF THE FEMMEVANGELICAL

In the years after Jennifer Crumpton left her husband, a new life unfolded. Her cozy apartment saw the comings and goings of close friends who stood by her through her separation and divorce. Her church attendance faded, and the distance she put between herself and her Southern Baptist upbringing brought a wave of refreshment. As a single woman far from whispering church folk, she felt free to use her every spare moment to discover her interests. A vast horizon of alone time unfolded before her, which she embraced, restoring herself through long walks in nature, through luxurious afternoons reading spirituality books, and through exercising to stay healthy.

During these years, Jennifer's advertising job began taking off. What began as a postgraduation internship at a telecommunications company quickly became a career. "I just worked hard," she recalled. "That was the one thing I was trained to do as an evangelical Christian girl." Jennifer took direction, did everything she was asked, did it quickly, and did it well. Within a few years she nabbed a management position, running multimillion dollar campaigns, managing advertising agencies, and regularly launching new products.

In 2004, Jennifer moved to New York City, where her career soared. She eventually became the vice president of advertising at a major corporation. On the surface, Jennifer looked like the emblem of success, gliding between executive meetings, cocktail parties, and dates with similarly high-powered Manhattan singles.

But Jennifer still felt unsettled in her life. At her job, image was everything; she felt that her work simply advanced the shallowness that ruled her pageant days. Attractive models and actors always won out for the commercials her team put together. Their work exploited human fears and convinced viewers to buy products that promised to make them whole again. More broadly, Jennifer noticed the way the advertising and media industry reduced women to objects—again with the explicit goal of making them feel inferior—in order to sell goods. As the reality of her work crystallized in her mind, Jennifer faced a crisis of consciousness.

She noticed how these themes of inferiority played right into her personal life. As much as leaving her husband had empowered her, she still struggled against "this internal perception that I was always less important" than men. When it came to dating, she met men whom she described as "like the guys in *Mad Men* on steroids." They openly made women compete for their affection. Their phones buzzed with incoming sexts and naked photographs from the women they juggled. Even when she managed to avoid the playboys and find decent men, she'd quickly lose herself in the relationship. As she dated around, she didn't seek out an egalitarian relationship. "Sadly, I was looking for something much more simplistic: Sheer respect." *Does he let me talk? Does he respect my sexual boundaries?*

Jennifer's journey toward empowerment unfolded slowly over the years. She began by reading. She lingered in bookstores, plucked intriguing titles from the shelves, and spent hours poring over the opened books fanned out before her. Reading was, as it turned out, the first step in deprogramming. "My gut knew all along that I was seeking something out," she recalled. "I just didn't have the language to think about it. I just kind of crawled along grabbing at things that looked good, positive, affirming." She read Gloria Steinem, Naomi Wolf, and feminist theologians whose ideas blew her mind. Initially, these ideas—open indictments of patriarchy, female beauty standards, and gender inequality—scared her. They took her far outside of her comfort zone, far from that cocoon of evangelicalism that cast patriarchy as God's ordained way. For most of her life she had been taught that stepping outside these boundaries could cost everything—even her salvation. Exploring new ideas made her feel as if she were jumping blindly from a ledge. Who would she be at the end of this journey? Would it destroy her? She didn't know the answer to these questions. All she knew was that she had to press ahead.

With these new perspectives on her mind, Jennifer turned to the Bible and read its stories with fresh eyes. She reread the Old Testament story of Esther, an orphan Jew sent to serve as a concubine for the king of Persia. Esther finds favor in the king's eyes (translation: she's the hottest virgin) and is selected to be the new queen. For a long while she conceals that she is Jewish and remains the good obedient wife. When she learns of a plot to kill the Jews, she makes an appeal to the king and saves her people.

In the past, Jennifer had drawn the standard evangelical conclusion from this story: God used obedient, beautiful, and brave Esther to carry out his will. Esther's example has been used to instruct Christian women how to behave, how to submit, and how to endure oppression nobly. But Jennifer's fresh reading of Esther opened her eyes to the numerous injustices toward women in this biblical story *and* the way theologians had irresponsibly failed to address these issues. Like the evangelical feminists who came before her, she abandoned biblical inerrancy and she no longer views biblical stories like Esther's as models for female behavior. Instead, she says, they "should be something we use to interrogate the way human beings react and the way social structures are built."

Jennifer noticed how Christian books, such as Charles Swindoll's *Esther: A Woman of Strength and Dignity*, fail to comment on the exploitation of women in this story, focusing instead on how Esther and the many other virgins underwent beauty treatments and participated in festive pageantry to please the king. One chapter in his devotional is titled "There She Goes—Miss Persia!"[1]

For Jennifer, everything became clear: the traditional interpretation of biblical stories about women reinforced terrible lessons about gender, sex, and female agency. She realized how these warped Bible lessons directly fed into her feelings of being less worthy than men, voiceless and disempowered.

Jennifer felt her world rocked by these revelations, but she did not yet know what to do with them. Then one day in 2007, just as the country edged toward economic collapse, her company began slashing jobs. Her supervisors asked her to stay on, but as her advertising work had made her feel, as she put it, "dead inside," she realized this could be her chance to change her life. One Friday, Jennifer came home from work, locked the door of her apartment and didn't leave or speak to another person all weekend. She spent that time praying fervently, journaling, and thinking about her future. In a moment of spiritual revelation, she ended up, as she put it, "face-planted" on the floor of her apartment with a clear sense that she had to leave advertising. She wasn't sure what would come next, but she knew what she wanted: she wanted to attend Union Theological Seminary.

Jennifer took the severance check from her company and began mapping out a new future. She had recently begun attending Redeemer Presbyterian, a conservative evangelical church led by celebrity pastor Tim Keller. At the end of one church gathering, she mustered up the courage to introduce herself and tell Keller about her plans. *Maybe he could offer some wise advice,* she thought. But when she mentioned Union Theological Seminary, he stopped her. He told her that Union was outrageously liberal and discouraged her from going down that path, she recalled. Instead, Keller suggested she take a few seminary-like classes he was beginning to teach, and bid her goodbye.

That night Jennifer went home feeling conflicted. *Tim Keller just told me not to go to Union,* she thought. She turned his words over in her mind and then felt an unfamiliar shift. *Wait a minute,* she thought. *Yes, people put him up on a pedestal. But God is telling me something else.* In what amounted to a major turning point in her life, she realized she didn't need the approval of an authoritative male figure to make her decisions. So Jennifer applied to Union, got accepted, and awaited the start of her new life.

The summer before seminary began, Jennifer made that fateful journey back to Birmingham and found herself listening to celebrated megachurch pastor David Platt tell a room half-filled with women that they did not belong in leadership. She wondered if Platt understood the impact his words had on his female congregants, how his message could unleash years of self-doubt on the very people he cared for. Already, his words had begun to noodle their way into the cracks of her confidence. Had she made a huge mistake by quitting advertising to attend seminary? If so many churches, like Platt's, disqualified women from leadership, would she ever find work?

Jennifer took a deep breath and looked around at the women listening to Platt's message. *These women deserve so much more*, she thought. It bothered her that Platt and other young male evangelical leaders were gaining celebrity as the "new faces of evangelicalism" despite their, as she put it, "faux-progressive" posturing. Jennifer thought about her lifetime of letting men like this steal her agency and decided she would be a victim no longer.

It was in that moment that Jennifer decided to claim a new label—feminist—and reclaim another—evangelical. Because of Platt's message, Jennifer walked out the doors of his church emboldened with a clear goal for seminary: she would take back evangelical faith for herself, for feminism, and for the many women hurt by her faith tradition. She would become, as she put it, a femmevangelical.

RISE UP, WOMEN

Jennifer is part of a broad, though fragmented, movement of women and men advancing feminist values in evangelical society. Theirs is a disjointed party, coalescing in various communities and embracing disparate causes. Some, like Jennifer, openly identify as feminist. Others eschew the baggage that comes with the "f-word," preferring labels such as "Christian for biblical equality" or "gender justice advocate." Some point their focus to global women's issues, with sex trafficking leading their agenda, while others deal domestically with promoting gender equality in marriage and the church. Many care about reproductive rights, but they are still finding the language to express these concerns to their evangelical communities. A few try to tackle all of the above.

These evangelical feminists face a different landscape than their foremothers did. They run up against a robust complementarian culture, along with a complicated topography of evangelical women who are difficult to reach. For example, many in the younger generation may be leaders at work and share household responsibilities with their husbands, all the while objecting little to the complementarian theology of their churches. Taking broader feminist advances for granted, they may see no need to challenge this gender framework. Another audience less primed to join the egalitarian cause are the many women living in closed communities similar to Jennifer's childhood community, where women are so steeped in patriarchal culture that they are unaware of any other way of living. They may, in fact, support complementarian theology as advantageous to women, since it defines roles clearly and demands that men hold up their end of the bargain by providing for their families. Altogether, evangelical women make for a complicated and difficult community to mobilize behind an evangelical feminist movement.

Given the landscape, the online world has become a central gathering place for working out feminist theology. Major evangelical feminist outfits such as Christians for Biblical Equality and the Evangelical and Ecumenical Women's Caucus have transitioned much of their dialogue to their online platforms. Furthermore, independent feminist bloggers and authors are gaining even wider attention for their efforts to combat evangelical patriarchy. Sarah Bessey, author of *Jesus Feminist*, writes viral posts in which she dismantles Candace Cameron's biblical defense of male authority over women, extends compassion to those leaving evangelicalism, and critiques purity culture and the way it made her feel disqualified from true love since she had sex before marriage. When complementarian group The Gospel Coalition endorsed female subordination in the marriage bed (utilizing the following quote: "A man penetrates, conquers, colonizes, plants. A woman receives, surrenders, accepts.") evangelical feminist blogger Rachel Held Evans expressed her dismay to her 155,000 followers. "This is such an overtly misogynistic post that I wouldn't bother commenting on it had it not appeared on a mainstream complementarian site like The Gospel Coalition," she wrote, disputing the argument point by point. "I believe, with every bone in my body, that patriarchy is a result of sin," she concluded before exhorting her readers to get angry, call out the Gospel Coalition on its misogyny, and support egalitarian institutions like Christians for Biblical Equality.[2]

In 2012, Jennifer joined the evangelical feminist blogging sisterhood by launching *Femmevangelical: For Women Who Don't Submit* on the religion site Patheos. She was one year out of seminary and working as an associate pastor at Park Avenue Christian Church in Manhattan. She had spent her seminary years finding her tribe. She met others from conservative evangelical backgrounds who, like herself, were stripping fundamentalist theology away from their faith. Over drinks they would attempt to outdo each other with outrageous anecdotes from their past—the virginity pledges, the suppressed sexuality, the obscenely sexist messages from the pulpit. One friend from a Texas evangelical family shared traumatic tales about the ex-gay camps he attended. Another recounted the way her church community learned that her father, the church pastor, had been cheating on his wife for years, but ultimately had sided with him. The friends often gathered at nearby bars or in their apartments on Union's gothic campus, which resembles Hogwarts from the Harry Potter books, with its decorative scalloping and glowing cathedral towers. As they swapped stories, they'd often recall familiar evangelical camp songs and burst into chorus together, their glasses raised as they laughed at lyrics they now found ridiculous. At other times they'd confess the pain they had carried from their past and comfort each other.

Jennifer had hoped to knit a similar support network through her blog. "It's hard to be a rogue and redefine yourself," she said. The feminist journey for evangelicals can feel "like entering a whole new faith in God." Those women need support to grant validity to their questions and changing beliefs. For Jennifer, seminary had given her the training and the experience to do just that. After an internship at Park Avenue Christian church, a "pro-LGBTQ, pro-women" congregation, Jennifer underwent the long ordination process, emerged from seminary a newly ordained pastor, and served as an associate pastor at the same church for a few years.

But Jennifer wanted to extend her "femmevangelical" ministry beyond church walls. In addition to blogging, she began to forge partnerships with numerous religious and feminist women. Her blog garnered an outpouring of thanks from readers (mostly women who appreciated her candid writing about misogyny in the Bible) for criticizing the GOP's attempts to regulate women's bodies and for articulating a vision of a "creative, kick-ass but fair female God." After meeting at a gala and feeling an "instant connection," Jennifer gained as a mentor Robin Morgan, a secular feminist icon who cofounded the Women's Media Center with Gloria Steinem and Jane Fonda. Though Robin is an atheist and Jennifer is a pastor, the two saw their shared interest in "moving women ahead in history." Jennifer is now a part of the Women's Media Center and she also partners with other religious feminists who face similar hurdles in engaging their faith communities on gender equality.

The recent explosive popularity of feminist bloggers reveals a broad evangelical hunger for gender equality, but given the absence of a cohesive national movement, evangelical feminism as a whole appears to lack a solid strategy for widespread structural change.

Part of the problem stems from a common, but flawed, evangelical approach to complicated issues, an approach that values individual stories above collective action. The blogging realm is one example of how hundreds of thousands of evangelicals may gather around one person's narrative rather than around an organized strategy. Their followers may add a comment, or post a story to their social media feed, but that's not the same as sustained grassroots organizing, said former CBE member

Daniel Fan in an interview. On top of that, there are limits to how radical these bloggers can be. Daniel added, "By virtue of being authors, they are beholden to the Christian publishing industrial complex," where there is pressure to avoid hot-button feminist issues.

This highlights another major obstacle: trying to reach a community that has been conditioned to reject feminism. By branding feminism as antifamily, conservatives very effectively defanged the evangelical feminist movement over the past decades. In fact, much of today's popular evangelical feminist dialogue steers clear of truly radical proclamations. Leaders and bloggers alike have broached women's issues cautiously, even limiting their agenda to issues like women's ordination and egalitarian marriages, while leaving more controversial issues such as reproductive rights largely untouched.

Leaders should look to the racial justice and LGBTQ justice movements for lessons on collective action and bold advocacy. While individual narratives play a part in these campaigns, racial and sexual minorities, along with their allies, have intentionally focused on building robust national networks that drive collective mobilization. And their aim is systemic, as they fight to dismantle very real institutional injustices such as discrimination on the basis of race, sexual orientation, or gender identity. To many in these movements, their work is a matter of life or death: another black person dead in the street, another transgender life ended. While systemic threats to women, such as laws that restrict life-critical health resources, are equally dire, these are the very conversations many evangelical feminists shy away from.

ENDING PURITY CULTURE

Of course, just because evangelical feminism is fragmented doesn't mean that important, influential work isn't taking place. Groups like CBE and E4J, along with the growing number of egalitarians in evangelical institutions, are working to advance women's equality in a variety of ways. Generational shifts have also added momentum to the feminist cause. In fact some younger evangelicals have emerged as more willing to take risks by not only promoting egalitarian marriage and women's ordination, but also by speaking out on the contentious issues of reproductive rights and purity culture.

Krista Pedersen, a junior at Wheaton College, grew up hearing "the purity talk." She was raised in Miami, attended a nondenominational evangelical church, and learned the complementarian gender model from her Southern Baptist parents from an early age. Krista absorbed their lessons, but felt a disconnect between those values and her parents' push for higher education. She often wondered, *What's the point of going to college if my future holds only marriage, babies, and no career?*

But when Krista arrived at Wheaton College, she met "kick-ass" female professors who upended her complementarian beliefs. "They have three babies, they are tenured," and they are running their departments, she said with breathless admiration. "They're doing it all and they're like, *You can do this.*" Inspired by these professors, Krista spent her freshman year exploring feminism. She read its literature, history, and theory for classes and for pleasure. Krista soon identified as a feminist, an egalitarian, and a supporter of gender and LGBTQ equality.

Krista knows others just like her. Though Wheaton's administration leans conservative, Krista characterized its faculty and student body as mixed and increasingly resistant to the patriarchal system that underpins purity culture and complementarianism. Many students may shy away from identifying as "feminist" (the far Right has effectively redefined the label to mean man-hating, strident, and antifamily), but they *will* cry foul when Wheaton men ask women to dress modestly or when they cast women as "wifely material" as opposed to intellectual competitors, Krista told me. As her generation grows open to changing how Christians talk about sexuality, Krista envisions a future for young evangelicals that is focused on discussion of sex education, the definition of consent, and the diversity of opinion on how people should engage sexually. And she's helping build a path to that future.

At the start of her sophomore year, Krista became the vice president of the Christian Feminist Cabinet at Wheaton College. Noticing a lack of interest in feminist issues, she and her coleaders "kicked it up a notch" and quickly built a campus-wide dialogue around gender issues. They've hosted discussions about sexual consent and rape culture, female leadership, feminist issues in the developing world, and the history of feminism, among other topics, and have seen attendance grow rapidly. They noticed on social media that their peers increasingly engaged with "pop-culture feminism," posting feminist articles from *BuzzFeed* and *Jezebel* or commenting excitedly about Emma Watson's viral United Nations speech on ending gender inequality.

After Wheaton College filed a lawsuit (*Wheaton College v. Burwell*), in which it objected to compromises in the Affordable Care Act for religious institutions, colleges, and hospitals regarding coverage for certain forms of contraception—the case reached the Supreme Court in July 2014 and gender became a central issue of debate across campus.[3] Female faculty members who were frustrated with the lawsuit confronted the college president. They expressed disappointment in the administration's exclusion of their voices in a decision that directly affected their reproductive health. Professors brought up the subject in the classroom, broadening the conversation to issues of maternity leave policies and how the rhetoric of the lawsuit impacted women. Meanwhile, Christian Feminist Cabinet events "exploded," Krista recalled. Even though the lawsuit impacted health care for staff and faculty only, students packed every event. They flocked to lectures about the history of feminism. They read up on the lawsuit and buzzed with debate—was this a religious liberty issue or a women's rights issue? Are certain forms of contraception abortive and in conflict with the conservative Christian pro-life stance?

Krista does not see this as a religious liberty issue, nor does she view these birth control methods as abortive. And while this lawsuit applies only to faculty and staff, she takes issue with the larger message, a message that perpetuates a cycle of sexual shame. "There seems to be a lot of shame about having sex and there's shame about preventing pregnancy and there's also shame about terminating pregnancy, which leaves very little room for the Christian young adult" who may have unprotected sex because they are too ashamed to buy condoms or birth control.

This reflects the broader challenge young evangelicals face when contending with the demands of purity culture, Krista said, noting that the old damaged-goods metaphor, which ties a women's worth to her sexual experience, lives on today, reimagined in countless ways. Years ago, a youth pastor described to me a lesson on sexual purity he had given to his church's teens. First, he presented two cups of fresh water. Then, to a chorus of "ewwws," he released a single drop of toilet water into one cup. "Which cup would you drink from?" he asked his teens. They unanimously thrust their fingers toward the uncontaminated cup, laughing at the absurdity of drinking the defiled water. The youth pastor concluded, *Nobody wants the cup with even a drop of toilet water, because it is ruined. And that's exactly how even one drop of sexual impurity can ruin you.*

In response, Christian feminists like Krista have risen to oppose the damaged goods language, especially purity culture's emphasis on virginity. "I just want to get rid of that word," Krista said, noting that the focus on virginity "really prevents people from feeling like God loves them if they don't have virginity anymore." Oftentimes, young Christians who end up having sex before marriage believe "they're not valuable to God or valuable to their (future) partners because they got something taken from them, or they 'gave it away.' It's really detrimental and it's really bad for the gospel. My vision is that we no longer see virginity as a part of a woman's worth."

Although conservative evangelicals may dismiss such views as coming from the radical Left fringe, many others are echoing Krista's call. In a 2013 article for *Prodigal*, an online magazine targeting young people of faith, writer Emily Maynard declares that "I'm done with virginity."

"I'm done with that word and that idea," she goes on. "I'm done defining myself, my past and my future, in terms of who's [*sic*] what has been where, or hasn't. I'm done with stories of virgins and non-virgins, promises and praises, and sentiments of 'restoration' that just push forward bulldozer loads of this horrible twisted shame. . . . I'm not just a virgin or a non-virgin. And neither are you."[4]

EGALITARIAN PROGRESS

In April 2011, during her last semester of seminary, Jennifer attended a friend's fund-raising after-party at a crowded restaurant and nightclub in midtown Manhattan. The scene exhausted her. Music pulsated.

Crowds swarmed. Seated beside her, a wealthy real estate businessman leaned in too close, flirting with Jennifer. He tried feeding her a fried Oreo—a dessert favorite of hers—but she pushed his hand away.

Across the table, a man named Dave Ross watched the interaction with interest. Earlier, Jennifer and Dave had briefly locked eyes, noticing each other. Dave possessed the classic handsomeness of a fairy-tale prince: tall and lean, searching eyes and great hair, with flecks of gray at his temples. Jennifer liked his smile. Dave wondered if she was dating the flirtatious man seated beside her; he felt a jolt of hope when he saw her reject the man's advances.

Later that night, Dave made his way to Jennifer's side of the table and the two began chatting. When Jennifer mentioned she was attending seminary, she readied herself for an uncomfortable end to the conversation. She had gotten used to the awkward silences and ignorant questions that typically followed. *Seminary? Are you going to be a nun? Are you some religious weirdo?* But Dave found her studies fascinating and the two ended up deep in conversation. Jennifer was impressed that he understood her work and took her seriously. They both felt a spark, but in the eddy of party interruptions, they lost track of each other and did not exchange information.

Eventually, Dave found Jennifer through mutual Facebook friends and the two made a date for the following week. From there they grew close, sharing long phone conversations and heart-to-hearts over dinners and outings all over the city. Dave was different from the other men Jennifer had dated. He grew up with a strong mother and held firm feminist views. As a child, he helped with household duties and saw the roles of men and women as equal and shared. It took time for Jennifer to truly believe this. Memories of her first marriage and past bad boyfriends haunted her. If she changed something about herself, would she be shunned? If she disagreed with Dave, would he turn her away? (One boyfriend had threatened to break up with her because his best friend found her feminist views annoying.) So she spent the early part of her relationship with Dave bracing for rejection, but it never came.

At the heart of their relationship was mutual affirmation. Jennifer supported Dave's ambitions as a lawyer; Dave celebrated as Jennifer's fledgling femmevangelical ministry grew. When her blog took off and Jennifer faced criticism from folks back home, Dave backed her. "Jenny's one of the bravest people I've ever known," Dave said in an interview, recalling the way she left everything familiar in her life—her marriage, her hometown, and eventually her successful advertising career—to establish a life and identity entirely of her own making. "It takes a lot of guts to challenge everything you've been taught growing up." When her blog became a book and her subsequent research reshaped her theology once again, Dave acted as her sounding board and cheerleader. Even though their opinions diverged on a lot of issues (Dave is Jewish, Jennifer is evangelical; Dave is a fiscal conservative and social liberal, Jennifer is very liberal), their differences seemed only to bring about interesting conversations and greater understanding. Over the years they both changed and they both took risks, standing steadfastly by each other and falling more deeply in love.

When the two married in 2014, they held an interfaith ceremony at a progressive church with both a pastor and rabbi present. Breaking even further from tradition, Jennifer walked herself down the aisle. "I don't need or want to be given away," she explained. "It's so inauthentic to who I am." For a while, she worried that the decision would hurt her father's feelings and invite judgment from conservative guests. But to Dave, the decision just made sense: "At the end of the day, she walked herself down the aisle of life to become who she is; that's the way she should walk herself down the aisle at her wedding."

Today, Jennifer has the life she wants: a rewarding career, a supportive church community, and a loving, egalitarian marriage. But the journey she traveled along the way was marked by despair, rejection, heartbreak, judgment, and much confusion. Early in my conversations with Jennifer, I found it surprising that someone from Generation X with a college education, successful career, and experience living in a major metropolitan area would struggle for so many years to break free from the complementarian perspective. She reminded me of my bright college girlfriends who spoke enthusiastically about submitting to their future husbands. Why weren't younger evangelicals dismissing this outdated gender framework? After all, weren't younger generations more quick to adapt to social progress?

But of course, it's not so simple. The complementarian movement has strengthened in recent decades, said Letha Scanzoni, who cowrote *All We're Meant to Be* and who has examined evangelical feminist efforts since the 1960s. Women like Jennifer, who might be inclined toward gender equality, grew up facing harsh condemnation and shame for even questioning traditional gender roles. Expressing doubt put both their social status and their salvation at risk. That's why so many women simply play by the rules, Letha explained. "If you submit to the complementarian view you can just relax," she said. "Someone will take care of you. The evangelical subculture will love you. But once you step out of that, you're a pariah."

Christians for Biblical Equality has seen the consequences of this system firsthand and has played a leading role in combating it. Over the years women have turned to CBE with accounts of abuse, sexual violence, and domination in such great numbers and with such grisly details it has horrified CBE president Mimi Haddad. When Mimi took the job nearly two decades ago, she envisioned spending her days digging into church history and theology, but on day one, she awoke to a sobering reality. Phone calls and e-mails poured in with gruesome accounts of how patriarchal theology played out in the lives of evangelical women. Mimi encountered women who struggled in complementarian marriages and had come undone by the power their husbands held over them. "You would not believe what I have heard," she said sorrowfully, pointing to the many stories of Christian men behaving horribly. "The power that some men have in this country based on their wealth and prominence, and the way they've used that to abuse their daughters and wives . . . you would not believe it." In one extreme case, a woman who had once been a proponent of female submission later confessed to Mimi that her abusive husband controlled everything in her life; he even denied her the right to sleep with clothes on. For years, she saw his authority over her as "God's ideal," but as the abuse continued she eventually realized "how sick the whole system was," Mimi recounted. The all-male church leadership offered no help. Instead, they surrounded her husband and "she was systematically excluded from conversations which determined her future and her family's future." It's a pattern that plays out in so many Christian marriages, even among the nonphysically abusive. "So many evangelical women and men are in marriages that are wildly unhappy and destructive, where women have no voice," Mimi said. "By saying to a women that you have no voice in your marriage, based on the teachings of 1 Timothy, that's the same as saying you are not as valuable."

Today, CBE aggressively works to advance egalitarian marriage principles in evangelical culture. Oftentimes this means other feminist causes, such as advancing reproductive rights, don't take center stage. But to CBE, marriage is a central focus because of the sheer volume of calls it receives regarding abuse within marriage and the extreme consequences of patriarchy in marriage. CBE has led the way by organizing women nationally and by working directly with churches and some of the most influential evangelical groups out there. In addition to playing a leading role in major evangelical networks and institutions, and spreading its egalitarian mission statement to three hundred groups, CBE also promotes female leadership by quietly working beside leaders of denominations that are both supportive and opposed to women's ordination.

Despite the success of complementarian groups, Mimi insists that the egalitarian movement is anything but a lost cause. Younger evangelicals are increasingly rejecting patriarchal views and embracing gender equality. CBE has chapters at Christian colleges, the evangelical feminist blogosphere continues to gain attention, and young women like Krista Pederson at Wheaton College's Christian Feminist Club are challenging their generation to work toward gender equality.

In fact, a recent study showed sweeping support among evangelicals for women's equality and leadership in society.[5] The study, which surveyed more than six hundred leaders within roughly one hundred evangelical organizations (nonprofits and colleges), found that a whopping 94 percent of male and female respondents supported gender equality in society. However, that support dropped when it came to women's roles in the family and church, with just over 60 percent of men favoring an egalitarian view, compared to roughly 80 percent of women.[6] The data also showed that when asked to identify with labels along the gender equality spectrum (feminist, egalitarian, complementarian, and hierarchical), men evenly split between identifying as egalitarian and complementarian, whereas women were more likely to identify with terms that support gender equality, with nearly a quarter identifying as feminist and about two-thirds identifying as egalitarian.

The two most interesting aspects of this data: first, how overwhelming support of women's equality in society fails to translate to leadership roles in evangelical organizations and, second, how divergence over women's equality enters the picture when economics are involved. To the first point, the study found that despite evangelical support of women's workplace equality, female leadership in evangelical organizations significantly lags behind the broader nonprofit market. Women account for only 19 percent of top paid evangelical leaders, 21 percent of board positions, and 16 percent of CEOs, according to Gordon College's 2014 study of more than 1,400 evangelical organizations. These figures significantly trail the larger nonprofit world, where women make up 48 percent of board membership and 40 percent of CEOs. On top of that, women are more likely to hold leadership positions among organizations with the lowest budgets and smallest staffs.[7]

One of the most significant findings was that while women tended to hold more leadership roles in social services (25 percent) as well as in education and youth ministries (23 percent), those numbers sank markedly when it came to ministry positions (19 percent) and higher education (18 percent), meaning that among institutions where theology is shaped, female voices are barely present.[8]

To the second point, these results suggest that men are fine with sharing economic responsibility with women, despite the fact that the "traditional" model insists that men assume the full economic burden. But beyond economics, the data seem to say that men still want to retain dominance in the home and in the church. And they justify this dominance using scripture. Complementarian apologists insist that they affirm the equality of men and women; they simply see a difference in gender roles. But here they create a false equivalency. You cannot have an equal relationship when one member is assigned the role of authority and the other is assigned the role of submission. Complementarians argue that the kind of authority they refer to is not a domineering authority, instead it refers the authority Christ has over the church. What did Christ do for the church? He died for the Church, he sacrificed for the church. Complementarians say that by assigning the husband the role of Christ's authority, he is ultimately called to the greatest form of submission, he must sacrifice and die for his wife. This sounds generous, but in reality these men aren't dying for their wives. From the calls made to the CBE, from the e-mails Jennifer Crumpton has received, from the pastoral messages of complementarian leaders like Mark Driscoll, and from the many other stories of evangelical women, it is clear men are oftentimes controlling and in some cases abusive. Complementarians use rhetorical acrobatics to insist upon their belief in gender equality, but the inconsistencies in what they say versus what women experience underscore just how difficult true gender equality is under the complementarian model.

FINAL FRONTIER

Amidst all of the challenges facing evangelical feminism, perhaps the most contentious issue is reproductive rights. It's difficult to talk about reproductive rights because the pro-life/antichoice ethos has been so deeply instilled in evangelical culture. As mentioned in the introduction of this book, evangelicals still largely identify as "pro-life," but a new consensus on what "pro-life" should really mean is emerging, especially among the younger generation. Specifically, "life" issues are no longer limited to the womb; instead the pro-life umbrella has extended over concerns about supporting environmental justice, ending violence at home and abroad, and providing services to the poor. And when addressing issues of reproductive rights, this emerging group is not asking questions about how to overturn *Roe v. Wade*. Instead, this group is asking about how to help disenfranchised women access contraception and women's health care, and how to provide better pregnancy prevention education and resources. Leaders shaping this new pro-life framework are slowly presenting these ideas to the broader evangelical world, pushing these ideas cautiously, but holding back their message in certain contexts, when the stakes of losing their evangelical credibility are just too high.

Even leaders like Lisa, who write and speak openly about their views on reproductive rights, avoid broaching this subject in certain evangelical settings. For Lisa, race had been a primary factor in the bulk of her activism, but her gender has always played into her evangelical experience, and in interviews she has grown increasingly vocal about reproductive rights. (In 2010 Lisa identified as "100 percent pro-life," with an important caveat: "I do not think the way to protect [life] is to outlaw abortion." In 2013 Lisa would tell me, "I don't ascribe to either pro-life or pro-choice. I actually ascribe to both.") Though her labeling has widened, her reasoning has stayed the same: she objects to efforts to overturn *Roe v. Wade*, believing instead that the best way to combat abortion is to address the conditions (such as poverty, lack of access to contraception, etc.) that lead women to seek abortions. I've heard Lisa deliver these sharply articulated arguments in radio interviews, in articles, and in books, but from the main stage (at the many evangelical conferences I've seen Lisa speak at), I've noticed that she rarely speaks out on reproductive rights.

In July 2013, I attended a conference celebrating the forty-year anniversary of the historic 1973 Thanksgiving Workshop, which launched the progressive evangelical movement and Evangelicals for Social Action, or ESA. Lisa joined the conference, called ESA40, as a featured speaker, alongside the movement's aging forefathers. There was Ron Sider, organizer of the landmark workshop and founder of ESA, flashing a bright, white-mustached smile to everyone who greeted him. He gave a hearty embrace to his old friend Jim Wallis, no longer the youthful, shaggy-haired antiwar radical (but instead a graying spiritual advisor to Barack Obama now, a husband and father, and a recent survivor of prostate cancer). Behind Wallis ambled Tony Campolo, another progressive evangelical forefather, who described the weekend as "a reunion of a bunch of old soldiers."

The new generation of soldiers, which included a cast of energetic leaders like Lisa, Soong-Chan, and many others, spent the weekend hammering out a vision for a brighter evangelical future. Lisa gave presentations on immigration reform, led the audience in a moment of silent mourning after the George Zimmerman verdict was handed down, and spoke on a panel about how the next generation would "be a faithful witness in the public square." Time and time again, the audience looked to Lisa as someone shaping the trajectory of progressive evangelicalism's next era. While the 1970s efforts weakened under disagreements over how to handle identity politics, this gathering of several hundred seemed intent on prominently including the voices of women and people of color. From the front of the auditorium, I listened for a message about gender, but heard none. This baffled me, especially since, in our interviews, Lisa had expressed strong opinions about sexism in the evangelical church.

Lisa and other female leaders shared prominent positions on the stage, casting a vision for a new progressive future. But when the interests of women did arise, discussion was limited to the narrow scope of female leadership and the occasional mention of sex trafficking. Supporting reproductive rights seemed decidedly off the table—that is, until Lisa spoke up at a small workshop called "Abortion: Changing Views and Public Policy."

The workshop took place in a fluorescent-lit classroom, among a semicircle of sixteen participants sitting on black plastic chairs. Despite the group's progressive leanings—as expressed in participants' frustration with the pro-life movement's opposition to government-funded health care, and in the group's concerns about poverty—much of the conversation echoed the rhetoric of the Right. Only two women—Lisa and a twenty-something evangelical and US Agency for International Development family planning specialist named Kaitlyn Patierno—pushed back. When one man suggested that abortions caused long-term mental health issues and led to higher rates of substance abuse, Kaitlyn countered with data from the Guttmacher Institute that disproved his claim. "They have an agenda," he shot back. The discussion leader, Heidi Unruh, suggested that contraception covered under the Affordable Care

Act could be considered abortifacients. Again, Kaitlyn raised her hand to offer clarification.

"Not all morning-after pills are abortifacients," she said, adding that "ella and Plan B are not abortifacients; they are disrupting fertilization."

"I mean, some are calling Plan B an abortifacient," Heidi offered.

"They call it that, but it's a scientific inaccuracy," Kaitlyn said firmly.

A debate broke out, and Lisa listened from the back of the room, feeling increasingly vexed that she was hearing the "same old, same old" in a session purportedly about "changing views" on abortion. The discussion shifted to the language of abortion, and when Heidi expressed her discomfort with the term "war on women" ("No women have the same interests; therefore you can't conduct a war on all women."), Lisa felt sick to her stomach. Heidi went on to say that the "abortion discussion" so often excludes the needs of the father and the other family members affected by abortion, such as grandparents, aunts, and uncles. "Part of our paradigm in our country is to be so individualistic . . . [and] to see this, more than any other issue, as an individual right," Heidi said. "But God has created us to be members of families, to be members of communities. So we have to see abortion in a larger context."

At this point, Lisa's hand shot up. "Many of the laws that are [being] passed right now in regards to abortion—the mother is not a consideration. Earlier you said we have to consider mothers as individuals, not as a group of women. And I don't agree with that. Women have to be considered as a bloc."

When I spoke to Lisa later, she was exasperated by how the conversation seemed to diminish the role of women, how older men seemed to dominate the room, and how so few voices expressed outrage over the way state legislatures were systematically violating women's rights, privacy, and access to health care. "When you start talking about putting a probe up a woman's vagina and mandating that by the state . . . you're talking about invading a woman's body by order of the state." Lisa is aware of how her beliefs may cast her "outside the political boundaries of late twentieth-century evangelicalism." She insists that she believes abortion is a sin, but, she said, "I also believe that it is a sin, and maybe even biblically more sinful, to endanger the lives of grown women . . . [by] eliminating clinics that are expressly for pre-serving the health of women, especially poor women who can't afford a private doctor or to go to the hospital to get checkups." She went on to defend Planned Parenthood, which has become "the devil in evan-gelical circles, but the reality is that abortion is a very, very minuscule percentage of the work that they do." She also defended the term "war on women," because "all you have to do is watch the news, read a newspaper, and every single day there's a new state legislature that has moved legislatively to close women's health clinics. I'm sorry, but that is a war on women."

Lisa was happy that she spoke up at the workshop, but admits that outside of her writing and the occasional interview, she shies away from discussing reproductive rights. When Lisa stands before thousands of evangelicals, reproductive rights stay safely off the program. It's just an-other example of evangelical feminists torn between progressive con-cerns and their conservative audience. "To lead with that issue with my point of view would jeopardize my ability to speak to [evangelicals] on other things, and so I've chosen to be silent on that, mostly," she told me.

Jennifer Crumpton understands this impulse and is strategic in how she broaches the issue of reproductive rights. Like Lisa, Jennifer has spent years cultivating relationships with older, male evangelical stalwarts. What sets Jennifer apart from the larger evangelical feminist movement is how she has been intentional about making feminist issues, especially reproductive rights, a key evangelical priority. During her last year of seminary she spent a spent a semester in Atlanta studying with David Gushee, a leading evangelical ethicist at Mercer University. David in-vited Jennifer to help shape the vision of a newly formed evangelical organization called the New Evangelical Partnership for the Common Good. Along with David, founding members included Steven Martin, a pastor turned filmmaker; and Richard Cizik, who is considered to be one of the most influential evangelical lobbyists in the country. Rich-ard spearheaded the group after his three-decade-long career at the Na-tional Association of Evangelicals came to a crashing end following his public support for gay and lesbian civil unions and for Barack Obama. After losing his job as the NAE's chief lobbyist, Richard maintained his access to evangelical elites, congressional leaders, and Washington, DC, galas, and worked to craft a new, more progressive agenda for the evangelical community. Though once a self-described "reliable ally of the Religious Right," Richard has spent this new chapter of his life vocalizing his increasingly progressive views, even backing feminist causes, voicing support for Planned Parenthood, and crafting a strategy for dispelling myths in evangelical communities about contraception and family planning.

Despite the vitriol Richard faced from much of the conservative evangelical world, he did not give up on evangelicals. Instead, he pressed forward with the NEP and began mentoring younger believers like Jennifer. "There has never been a time I could not call on him for advice or encouragement, and big talks about the world," Jennifer told me, recalling the time he traveled from Virginia to New York City to watch Jennifer's ordination, and the way he helped launch her career and rallied behind her *Femmevangelical* blog. With feminist initiatives in mind, Richard and the others welcomed Jennifer as a coleader, seeking her expertise and folding her ideas into the mission of the NEP. To be taken seriously as an intellectual equal by older evangelical men—*this* was a twist in her journey that Jennifer did not see coming.

Of course, as Jennifer got to better understand the mission of the NEP, she saw that Richard and his colleagues were intent on reaching older, conservative evangelicals who had shaped the very culture Jennifer had run from. But she understood these men well and she, like the NEP leadership, understood that to draw the support of these older men, compromises to the NEP's message had to be made. For Jennifer's part, that meant striking a conservative tone in her quest to gain the older generation's support for family planning, something it's historically been against. In the run-up to the 2012 elections she and the other NEP leaders wrote a monumental thirteen-page statement in defense of family planning, calling on pro-life evangelicals to support family planning efforts globally and domestically. The statement, "A Call to Christian Common Ground on Family Planning, and Maternal, and Children's Health," distinguished family planning from abortion (the two are often conflated in evangelical circles), arguing that family planning would actually help prevent abortions. It also supported contraceptive access, though making clear that the NEP does not "offer moral support for sexual activity outside of marriage," while also defining marriage as between a man and a woman. To Jennifer, these are necessary concessions to win conservative evangelicals.

"The older generation is more entrenched in their ideology," Jennifer said, explaining that she personally does not condemn gay marriage or premarital sex. But she believes older conservatives remain important to reach because they hold enormous influence in politics and the church, even though a strong majority (86 percent) of white evangelical Protestants view contraceptives as morally acceptable[9] and some 74 percent use highly effective methods of contraceptives including the Pill, IUDs, and sterilization.[10] Nonetheless, it's the older conservatives who "are still in authority positions, whether they are affecting the minds of young women from the pulpit or from other positions of authority." To Jennifer, this is about playing the long game. By partnering with Richard, she's bridging a generational gap and helping gain support for family planning and eventually reproductive rights from the larger evangelical movement. By setting aside her differences to mobilize around common-ground causes, she hopes to influence evangelicals to vote and voice their support for policies that will make women's lives better.

These efforts culminated in a presentation of the NEP's statement at the National Press Club just weeks before the 2012 presidential election. As one of the keynote speakers, Jennifer stepped out before her audience, a packed room of journalists and Washington influencers, possessing all of the poise she gained from her beauty pageant days, but none of the baggage. She was no longer the insecure girl, looking to men for validation. She was no longer the wife trapped in a controlling marriage. She was no longer the scandalous divorcee, trying to outrun the shadow of shame and the message that her choices would send her to hell. She had conquered all of that, reinvented herself, gained confidence, and learned to do what David Platt and others told her she could not do: lead.

By breaking free from tradition and following her moral convictions, Jennifer has embarked on a new life, which she described as "coming full circle," bringing her back to that childhood feeling of being capable of anything. For the first time in decades, Jennifer has recaptured that sense of life's fullness, of God's love surrounding her, of endless possibilities. She no longer fears expressing her opinions, whether to her partner, to the men she works with, or to a room filled with journalists.

So that October morning in 2012, Jennifer took her place at the front of the room wearing a sharp black blazer and a determined smile. Armed with her iPad and months of research, she laid out a new mission for the evangelical community: to support and increase access to family planning for women across the country and globally. She knew she was making a controversial argument, but she was not worried. She was doing everything she was called to do.

NINE

Pride

BQU YEARBOOK

At 8:30 a.m., Will clutched a fistful of tiny fliers and looked up at his dormitory, a plain two-story building.

Dear God, let everyone be asleep, he prayed as he hurtled inside. The first few hallways were empty, and smelled of sleeping, unwashed college boys. Will scurried quietly past each room, dropping fliers announcing the BQU yearbook at the foot of each door. He moved swiftly from hallway to hallway, and twenty minutes in, when the dorms began to stir with beeping alarm clocks and shirtless guys returning from their showers, Will ran outside and went looking for his friends.

On his way to the center of campus, Will found Jason, who had just blanketed a handful of nearby dorms. It was 9 a.m. when the boys found Tasha waiting at the fountain with another BQU member, a straight ally whom everyone called Tavi.

"Ready?" asked Tasha, walking with a bounce in her step. The four exchanged giddy looks and braced themselves for the most challenging part of their mission: handing fliers to their fellow students. Their pockets filled with illegal leaflets, they walked four abreast, bravado masking their nervousness as they passed the hovering Jesus mural.

At the center of campus, students clustered at outdoor patio tables. Will, Tasha, Jason, and Tavi peeled off individually to cover more ground. While the others spoke to the people they approached, Will avoided eye contact and wordlessly distributed his fliers. A few friends asked what he was doing, but he just mumbled inaudibly and shuffled away, leaving them with bewildered looks.

Jason eyed the crowd and whispered to himself, "Breathe." He approached a woman sitting alone and handed her a leaflet.

"Hi, we're from the Biola Queer Underground and we're coming out," he declared. She looked up and smiled, squinting at the sun. "Oh, thank you." Jason's eyes began to well up, so he forced a quick smile and walked away to sob out of sight. I asked if he was OK.

"It's scary," he said, gasping. "But it feels like a relief to be able to bring our full selves to our school."

Jason ventured into the cafe, where he spotted Atticus, who was part of Jason's regular meetings with the dean of students first semester. Months earlier, when Jason dropped out of the Danny meetings, Atticus had wondered what happened to him. "One day he stopped showing up," Atticus recalled later. "We couldn't get a text or a phone call from him." Atticus didn't know about Jason's membership with the BQU.

"Biola Queer Underground," Jason said, plopping a flier down on Atticus's table "This is what I decided to do. This is who I am."

Atticus looked at the flier, then at Jason, then at the flier again.

"Oh. My. God?!"

Tasha could hear the shouts of disapproval as she walked away from another group of students.

"What *is* this?!" a few of them exclaimed, their wide eyes scanning her fliers. And when she gave one to a middle-aged man with a salt-and-pepper beard, he jumped out of his seat and chased her down. He was a school administrator.

"You need to stop," he said firmly. Tasha had just caught up with Jason and Will. They swapped quick, nervous looks, but Will tried to act casual.

"OK, we have a few more that we're going to pass out and then—"

"No," the administrator interjected. "You need to respect what I'm saying."

"Why—"

"You're not allowed to do this."

The administrator explained that because they didn't get approval from the school to distribute fliers, they needed to stop.

"How is it respectful to keep doing something that you were denied?" he asked, explaining that their activity amounted to littering that someone else would have to clean up. The students protested—there was nothing disrespectful about handing out fliers.

"So, so, just help me understand," the administrator said.

"I think you do understand," said Jason. "We're from the Biola Queer Underground. And we're handing out fliers right now. We're coming out. We want people to know who we are."

Jason thanked the administrator and turned on his heel.

"Please don't walk away from me," the administrator said, speed-walking toward Jason. "Because that feels really disrespectful."

Jason spun around, his face a mix of emotions—anguish, anger, frustration—but his voice steady.

"We're students here and we would also like to be respected. We don't like to be denied, just because we're queer, from putting up posters around here."

In fact, there were no posters, only palm-sized leaflets. It was strange that a scrap of paper could lead to a chase down and confrontation. The squabble continued fruitlessly for another few minutes, and when the students walked away, the administrator put his cell phone to his ear and began pacing. Jason guessed that he was contacting campus security to remove them from campus, so the four students passed out their remaining fliers and hurried away.

Tasha drove back to her school, Scripps College, where a final exam awaited her. Will and Jason speed-walked to Jason's truck, their emotions swinging between glee and dread.

"I hope this doesn't bite us in the ass," Will muttered, his mind racing with all the ways things could go wrong.

Jason tried to soothe Will's fears with mantra-like assurances.

"We're going to go to Starbucks. We're going to breathe. Your job is going to be OK. This is what we were made to do."

The two eventually made their way to the off-campus apartment of Sarah, Will's best friend. They parked in a modest, sun-washed suburban subdivision with neatly trimmed lawns and walked through her apartment complex, a low-slung maze of single-story units surrounded by tropical foliage.

Will knocked and cracked the door open. Sarah and Natalie, both straight allies in the BQU, were anxiously waiting for news of the year-book launch.

"Will!" they shouted in unison. Relieved to see his friends and wiped from the morning's events, Will didn't even walk in. He let out an exasperated sigh and fell forward, collapsing on the carpeted floor as his friends rushed to embrace him, laughing.

Sarah's apartment was completely bare—she had just moved out—so the four friends plopped down on the wiry brown carpet to debrief. Sarah and Natalie peppered Will and Jason with questions as the two regaled them with tales from their morning.

But after the storytelling and high fives, Will turned to me, confessing his self-doubt. The encounter with the school administrator had thrown him.

"We were already in a place of insecurity, and just being confronted made me feel wounded, like I wasn't doing the right thing anymore." Did Will feel guilty for handing out the fliers? Yes. "And even more than that, I feel guilty for who we are."

After a beat, Will reflected more. "I feel like that guilt doesn't come from God. It comes from the culture that Christians have created. I felt ashamed. But I know I shouldn't feel that way."

Later that day, I left the BQU students and ventured onto campus by myself. I wanted to talk to non-BQU students and the administration. At one point, I was chatting with a few students who happened to be selling the official Biola yearbooks. That's when I noticed something in the reflection of a large window: a group of burly, uniformed campus security officers and a short, stern-looking woman in a khaki getup were stalking toward me from behind. Something strange was about to happen.

The short woman's polo shirt identified her as Veronica, the school's private investigator. Veronica asked for my identification, and when I showed her my driver's license, she passed it to a security guard who—no joke—ran away with it. Veronica wouldn't let me follow him; instead, she nodded to the chief of campus safety, a towering man wearing a crisp uniform who walked with the swagger of a sheriff in a bad Western. I realized I was stuck.

The chief, John Ojeisekhoba, eyed me with suspicion and settled into interrogation mode. I explained that I was a journalist working on a book and public radio piece, but he didn't believe me. Over and over again, like a detective trying to rattle a suspect, he demanded, "Who are you with? Who sent you?" I learned that John had received complaints about the distribution of BQU fliers and was called to put a stop to it. He suspected that I was an outside gay activist—an infiltrator—likely responsible for the BQU and running its covert flier operations. It reminded me of the conspiracy theory–laden comments that flooded the BQU in-box and the comment section of the *Chimes* articles about the BQU. I was beginning to understand why the BQU students wanted to come out and put real Biola faces to their queer stories.

I explained my book project and public radio ties ad nauseam, but John called me a liar and persistently ordered that I show him the contents of my bag. When I refused, he took that as proof that I was concealing contraband BQU leaflets. I realized that it was the kind of questioning where, no matter what I said, he'd find a way to indict me. It reminded me of Rory, the transgender student whose was reported and questioned for engaging in "same-sex behavior." I realized I was experiencing the kind of antagonizing speech the BQU students had told me about, except I didn't have to lie about myself or risk losing anything.

My relationship with John flipped like a light switch when, forty minutes in, I convinced him that I was not an operative of the BQU or of any gay activist group. Once I had done so, his tone shifted from berating and threatening to respectful and accommodating. He even helped me line up an interview with the administration.

Earlier in the day I had written in my notes that the BQU's paranoia seemed a little overblown, but this experience helped me see that the things they feared—questioning, scrutiny, punishment for their sexuality—were very real. And when they did throw on an extra layer of paranoia, it was only for their protection.

That evening, Will, Tasha, and Jason met with Elizabeth Sallie, the editor in chief of the *Chimes*. Elizabeth had been working on a three-part series entitled "Homosexuality on Campus," which would explore the perspectives of a Side B student, a Side A student, and an administrator. Will was looking forward to representing the Side A position and proving, once and for all, that the BQU was run by a bona fide Biola student. But that evening, Elizabeth announced that her final story would focus on Tasha and exclude Will's story. She would name Will as the BQU cofounder but decided it was unwise to explicitly state his sexuality in print. Jason concluded that the administration had tied her hands.

"Administration hasn't tied my hands," Elizabeth asserted. "I sought [Danny Paschall's] advice. I sought Will's safety first. I said, 'I want my source to graduate, so tell me what I need to do to make that happen.' And he was very clear. He was very gracious. He was very open and willing to talk and discuss how we can make this happen. Because I went to them first, the administration would be able to give me a bit of an idea of what the ramifications might be, but at no point had they asked me to change my coverage, at no point had they asked me to not cover Will. I've made that decision on my own."

Tasha gave an understanding smile. Will was quiet, withdrawn. Jason grew aggravated. Was the administration's response a threat to Will's graduation? Why silence Will? Jason asked. Elizabeth wouldn't get into specifics—her talks with Danny were off the record—and she pushed back against the idea that she was silencing a voice.

"I really think that this is me stepping out on a very, very tiny, very dangerous limb," she said.

In my interview with Elizabeth, she explained that the campus conversation around the LGBTQ community was fragile and opinions were varied. There were those wary of the antigay rhetoric, but unsure of what they believed. There were the students who wanted more Side A representation at panels. But even they found the BQU "a little too rebellious . . . or a little too gay," Elizabeth said with a laugh. Then there was the vast cohort of students unaware of the issue's nuances. Side A, Side B, and Side X? Might as well be speaking a foreign language. "There are the kids who grew up in homes where gay marriage was the thing that we fought against, so we're just going to keep fighting against it," she explained.

This campus wasn't ready for Will's story, Elizabeth concluded. If she published it now, "it might damage the conversation more than it will help it."

The next morning, Tasha's story was up on the *Chimes'* website. Will and Tasha read the piece from their different campuses and pinged each other excitedly over instant message. Will raved about Tasha's photo and wished that his acne had been photoshopped out. They tried laughing off the critical comments. They watched their Facebook walls and in-boxes fill with more likes and comments.

As Will and Tasha reveled in the second day of their coming-out, I met with two Biola administrators and a public relations representative. There was Danny Paschall, nestled in a cushioned armchair. Across from him sat Vice President of Student Development Chris Grace, a sort of smiling enforcer who cut an imposing figure. And between them, the primly dressed Vice President of Communications Irene Miller, perched on her chair, armed with prepared statements she occasionally read from in response to my questions.

Unlike campus officials the previous day, these Biola representatives didn't rebuke the students' forbidden flier distribution or speak of the complaints called in. Instead, their answers came across as polite and polished, trained on a single message: the administrators are not the bad guys.

They expressed empathy for the tricky position queer Biola students find themselves in and promised that Biola treated queer students with respect. Irene used the transitive property (if A=B and B=C, then A=C) to prove her point: In the BQU yearbook Will and Tasha wrote that they love Biola. Love and respect go hand in hand. "And you love Biola when you've been treated respectfully," she reasoned.

When it came to discussing policy, Danny appeared visibly torn between his roles as counselor and sheriff to Biola students. He personally knew a handful of the fifteen students who came out in the BQU yearbook and wouldn't be expelling any of them because they didn't mention any "homosexual behavior." To me, this decision seemed to set a precedent, allowing students for the first time to be openly queer and Side A as long as they refrained from same-sex activity. I asked Danny, Was this the case?

But Danny and Chris's answers, often circular and indirect, suggested that this was an exception, rather than a precedent. When students want to advocate values that differ from Biola's (which is what the BQU had done), "then we're going to have a conversation with that student," Danny said, wary of using words like "expel" or "punish." But Chris Grace was more direct, explaining, as he had in previous statements, that even advocating against the school's policy would lead to dismissal.[1]

This should be no surprise, Chris said, as "we are very up front about this when we recruit faculty . . . and students." According to the logic of many Christian college administrations—and even some secular commenters—the solution to this conflict is obvious: if you're openly LGBTQ, don't go to schools like Biola. I'll admit, this line of reasoning occurred to me. *There's a whole world out there that will accept you,* I thought. *Why subject yourself to this?*

But for many LGBTQ Christian youth, it's not so simple. Students like Tasha have dreams of ministry; students like Will want to forge business ventures built on biblical principles. They can't find that at secular schools. They don't want to leave the conservative evangelical world they were raised in—they want to further its mission. For many, their family's financial support is contingent on attending a Christian college; a request to transfer to a secular school might force them out of the closet before they are ready and jeopardize their financial security.

On top of these complications, many LGBTQ Christian youths don't grapple with their sexuality until years into college. When I posed the administration's "know-before-you-go" argument to Josh Wolff, the faculty member at Adler University in Chicago and research psychologist studying LGBTQ youth at conservative religious schools, he replied, "To say to a seventeen-year-old or eighteen-year-old that 'you need to have this completely figured out—and nothing should change for the next four years—before you even come here,' I just think from a developmental perspective, that that's completely unrealistic." For many LGBTQ Christians, their journey toward understanding their sexuality is often a veering, halting experience. By the time they begin to accept themselves and, for some, identify as Side A, they may be juniors or seniors, too deeply invested to transfer schools. The prospect of "having a conversation" with the administration that could force them to start over is daunting.

Danny recognized this as a scary possibility, but continued to bill the school as a safe place for open exploration, even if that could lead to losing everything. He framed previous cases of gay students departing as volitional on the students' parts and ultimately positive.

"Some students are like, 'Thank you for how you've engaged this with me and I think, where I am right now, I wanna go to a place that aligns a little more with where I am,'" said Danny. "We've left on really good notes together. That to me is ideal. I love that. We have several students who come to that place."

But to many queer students I spoke to, the message they hear is: You can come here and have open dialogue about sexuality as long as you understand Biola's position, arrive at the same conclusion, and do not advocate for a competing message.

Weeks later, when the BQU leaders met with Danny and systematic theology professor Matt Jenson, Will explained that the school's dogma made authentic dialogue impossible. All they wanted was a safe space to be honest about themselves—contrary views and all—and for diverse opinions at campus panels.

"We need room to breathe. We're suffocating hiding a part of ourselves. We're called illegitimate from the pulpit from the president of our own school." Will seemed breathless, waiting for Danny's response.

"Hm . . . hm . . . ," Danny murmured. "I want to just hear you guys. You want the campus to engage this. What does this look like?"

Will asked for permission to advertise BQU events on campus.

"If BQU supports Biola's vision and mission and everything else, then yes," Danny replied. But the BQU is Side A, Tasha pointed out, so does that mean no?

Neither Danny nor Matt offered a direct answer. Matt suggested bringing the question to other administrators, but admitted that most "have thought zero about the issue . . . the sad reality is that some people aren't educating themselves."

In my meeting with the administration, Irene insisted that, behind the scenes, the administration was working very hard to educate itself and had intended to bring LGBTQ-affirming speakers to campus one day in the future.

"Folks don't know on the public side how much planning we have actually done this year," she said, adding that the issue comes up every month. "We just haven't gone public . . . because we want to do the homework."

Indeed, the Monday after my interview with the administration, roughly one hundred of the school's faculty and staff (students were not invited) gathered to hear three openly gay Biola graduates tell their stories. One of the speakers was Josh Wolff. When I spoke to Josh about the event, he told me he was astonished by the school's invitation.

Addressing the audience, Josh spoke candidly about his isolation as a gay Biola student and about his academic research, shining a light on the devastating mental health risks queer youths face in environments like Biola's. As the panel discussion wrapped up, the moderator, a Biola faculty member, surprised Josh by announcing to the audience, which included Biola's president and administrators, that she and many other faculty members agreed that much could be done to make Biola a more welcoming place. Those faculty members formed a crowd around the panelists after the talk, Josh recalled. Many thanked the panelists for coming and two quietly confessed to Josh their full support of LGBTQ students. Josh wished the school had invited Biola students. This, he said, was a message they needed to hear.

As the younger generation's call for equality, inclusive policies, and openness swells, and as traditionalist views lose footing, evangelical institutions are facing mounting pressure to take these conversations public. Places like Biola are trying to keep up and finding themselves stumbling through the debate, like so many other evangelical groups.

The BQU hoped this discourse would accelerate campus progress. And while it certainly sparked a flurry of activity—the administration's public statement, the school president's speech on sexuality, the panel discussion—after one year, the BQU took stock of the school's response and felt dejected. The school president had called same-sex relationships "illegitimate," and professor Erik Thoennes had made homosexuality analogous to racism and dishonesty. Even after they came out publicly and met personally with Danny Paschall, the BQU members felt like the administration still wasn't truly listening to their concerns. I debriefed with Danny and the BQU after their summit and saw just how disconnected the two sides were from each other.

The BQU wanted specifics on where the line for punishing LGBTQ students was, but Danny told me, "I think we all agreed that's not what this time was for." Danny left the conversation satisfied. But Tasha walked out frustrated, feeling that Danny had evaded their questions. Danny said he was glad to put faces to names and give them space to tell their stories. But that wasn't enough for the BQU. When Tasha told Danny about her unraveling OCD and the psychological stress she experience at Biola, Danny just nodded quietly. Tasha waited for a response. Nothing. Later, Tasha would turn that moment over in her mind. What did she want? And then it came to her. "He didn't even say 'I'm sorry.'"

I had many conversations with Danny, and I'm not sure it would have occurred to him to apologize to Tasha. As much as he had steeped himself in the stories of LGBTQ students over the years and expressed genuine concern, he ultimately focused on Biola's standards with a degree of legalism that seemed to blind him to the (often urgent) psychological plight of queer students. Since he could frame his students' well-being only in terms of Biola's standards, he did not seem to grasp the damage those standards were inflicting on his students' mental health.

Christian college administrators like Danny must also keep the school's practical interests in mind. As laws and social mores have changed around the issue of sexuality and gender identity, schools like Biola face real potential costs, including the loss of government financial aid for students and the loss of accreditation for the school, concerns addressed in a 2014 article by Brett McCracken in *Biola Magazine*.[2] Some government nondiscrimination policies have begun to cover sexual orientation and gender identity in an effort to protect sexual minorities from discrimination in employment and housing, and from other forms of bias. Religious exemptions vary by policy—some do not exempt faith-based groups—putting on edge administrators at tuition-dependent colleges like Biola, who worry about the impact to the school of students losing federal or state financial aid while facing steep tuition costs, writes McCracken. When it comes to accreditation, accrediting bodies have begun scrutinizing Christian colleges to check if school policies meet nondiscrimination standards. "Loss of accreditation would mean loss of credibility as a degree-granting institution, but it would also have a bearing on funding," he writes.

Despite the BQU's roadblocks with the administration, its efforts had a ripple effect across campus, oftentimes in ways its members didn't always see or recognize. Elizabeth, the editor of the *Chimes*, told me that the BQU transformed her college experience. Its stories compelled her to fight queer stigma on campus and commit to addressing the issue in her post-Biola years. The BQU also reached straight students who hadn't given much thought to queer issues.

To senior Heidi Hester, the BQU's coming-out "is a good thing," something she hoped would prompt more Christians to listen and love more. There were a handful upset by the BQU, but many more students were like senior Tiffany Pang, who had read the BQU blog with interest. It countered what she had learned in psychology class, she told me, explaining that her professor had taught that, as Tiffany put it, "it's not a sin in and of itself to have attraction toward the same sex, but it's a sin to act upon it, according to what the Bible says."

"Do you agree with that?" I asked.

"Mmm . . . ," Tiffany paused, casting a thoughtful sideways look. "I'm still in the middle."

Even those who spoke confidently about the school's right as a private institution "to restrict your behaviors and your lifestyles," as one student put it, and to expel those who violate code, shied away from fully backing the school. If the school's policy "doesn't line up with the Biola Underground then Biola does have the right to ask them to leave," said Jesse Bauder, a senior. "Do I think that needs to change? Possibly."

What surprised me the most was Danny's own microshift in our interviews over the span of a few weeks. In a later conversation, I brought up a contradiction from our first interview that I couldn't quite reconcile. He and Chris said that advocating a different position from the school's was a punishable violation of policy; but the BQU had done just that and the fifteen students who came out weren't facing scrutiny. A precedent had been set, and I wanted to know, would it hold? Will Biola no longer punish openly LGBTQ-affirming students as long as they abide by the school's behavioral standards? Danny thought about it. This time, he said, "Yeah, I would say that's correct."

SIDE UNKNOWN

Throughout the history of the progressive evangelical movement, the debate over sexual minorities in the church has divided even the most left-leaning leaders of the faith. As we saw in an earlier chapter, this issue split the evangelical feminist movement in the 1970s and 1980s; the feminists who condemned homosexuality prospered in the larger progressive evangelical community. (Professing a Side B or Side X theology has long been the not-so-secret handshake into evangelical acceptance.)

But in recent years, a handful of progressive evangelical leaders have crept along the Side X to Side B to Side A continuum. There was Richard Cizik, voicing support for civil unions in 2008 and for gay marriage in 2015; progressive Christian leader Brian McLaren leading his gay son's commitment ceremony in 2012; and former megachurch pastor Rob Bell publicly affirming same-sex marriage in 2013. And there was Sojourners' Jim Wallis's about-face, also in 2013, when—after years of opposing it—he voiced support for legalizing gay marriage (though he made no comment about the morality of it).

Progressive evangelical founding father and massively influential leader Tony Campolo admitted to me in 2013 that his long-held opposition to gay marriage had become, as he put it, "shaky." (Though hailed as a pioneer of progressive thought, Tony has fiercely asserted that same-sex relationships are sinful.) Sitting beside me in a hotel lobby, he noted that, at seventy-eight, he had a tally of issues he has been wrong about, like disallowing women preachers and excluding divorced and remarried people from church. As the years have passed, he has felt increasingly torn between his interpretation of scripture and the living witness of loyal gay Christian couples. "I've got this biblical admonition over here, and I've got the empirical evidence of what's happening to these people. And you become shaky, because the empirical evidence begins to challenge your biblical perspective." When Tony and I parted ways, I wondered if he might eventually change his mind.

As a young evangelical I was taught a battery of conversion techniques; the most powerful, according to leaders, was my testimony. The reasoning: my story would humanize Christianity. That logic seems to also apply to the testimonies of queer Christians. It explains, in part, the tide change in evangelicalism as more LGBTQ people come out and force their communities to reckon with their identities.

For Lisa Sharon Harper, it was her nephew who placed the firm stamp of humanity on this minority experience. Witnessing his testimony in real time moved her from the "it's a sin" camp to the "I don't know" camp, she told me, especially when she saw how his choice to embrace his gender identity had made his life more healthy and stable.

Lisa's nephew is a transgender man who grew up with a schizophrenic mother and bounced between relatives' homes and the streets for years. But after coming out and transitioning from female to male, he became settled, secure, and happily married. Lisa said that she is learning through her nephew. "Even the fact that I'm saying 'he' right now is really cool. I mess up sometimes. But you know, he's given me grace."

Like that of Tony Campolo and a growing number of evangelicals, Lisa's experience is complicated by longstanding doctrinal condemnations of homosexuality, placing her on the edge of what Baylor University researchers are calling the "messy middle," the 24 percent of evangelicals who morally oppose homosexuality but support gay civil unions.[3] And while Lisa shares many attributes of the so-called "messy middle," her category is even messier as she doesn't morally oppose *or* approve of homosexuality. After reexamining scriptural admonitions against homosexuality, "I've come to understand that there are question marks there. There are reasons to question those interpretations. So I just don't know."

This is a remarkable shift from evangelical sentiments a decade ago, but stops short of true justice in the eyes of queer advocates. OneEastern founder Ryan Paezold, who knows both Lisa and Tony personally, expressed his frustration with the way these leaders waver in the middle. When I spoke to Ryan in 2013, he pointed to the times he has seen Tony, in the company of queer Christian communities, wearing a rainbow stole to show his solidarity. "He's welcoming and affirming but won't publicly say that because he has an evangelical problem. As he's getting older, now is the time to speak out before he's no longer a part of [the conversation]." It wasn't until the summer of 2015 that Tony finally called for the full inclusion of gay couples in the church. And though it rocked much of the evangelical world, when viewed in the grand scheme of queer advocacy within evangelicalism, the announcement was simply an aftershock. People like Tony and Lisa, and institutions like Red Letter Christians and Sojourners, though frequently viewed as progressive pioneers, are not the leaders on issues of sexuality.

SIDE ALL

The real leaders have operated in obscurity for the past dozen years and are now gaining traction. There are groups like Soulforce, with programs both domestic and international, that address intersectional justice issues such as race, immigration, gender, and sexuality. Soulforce members have met with influential leaders, like Willow Creek megachurch pastor Bill Hybels, and have been credited (or blamed) for Willow Creek's subsequent decision to cut its two-decade-long ties with Exodus International, then the flagship ex-gay therapy organization.[4] Soulforce has also fought global efforts to criminalize sexual minorities by challenging the institutions that back such legislation as the Anti-Homosexuality Act in Uganda. Groups like Believe Out Loud have pressed for queer equality in mainline Protestant denominations and used their media platform to educate a spectrum of Christians interested in learning about faith and sexuality. Then there's the Gay Christian Network (GCN), with its distinct evangelical bent, fostering a vocal, organized cadre of queer Christians introducing a new, but theologically rigorous pro-LGBTQ interpretation of scripture to the broader evangelical community.

Curious to see the work of the real pioneers, I attended the 2014 GCN annual conference, which was held at a Westin Hotel ballroom in downtown Chicago. Days earlier, a polar vortex blew through, leaving the city snow-swept like a frozen wedding cake. But inside, the conference ballroom—complete with swirling purple lights and voices crooning pop praise songs—felt warm and alive with the sense of urgent acceptance, as if these six hundred LGBTQ and ally Christians were orphans knitting together a newfound family.

This was the tenth annual conference of a thirteen-year-old organization. GCN blossomed out of a decision by its founder, Justin Lee, to post his coming-out story online. Justin was a devout Southern Baptist teenager nicknamed "God boy," and his coming-out followed a path familiar to many LGBTQ kids in conservative churches. He confessed his same-sex attraction with trepidation. He wondered if he could change. He attended ex-gay conferences. He listened to leaders bill the ex-gay route or celibacy as the only acceptable Christian options. He felt torn between his faith and sexuality.

But in college he reexamined the scriptures, investigated the context of the condemning verses, and discovered the two core themes of Jesus's teachings: First, the spirit of the law trumps the letter of the law.[5] Second, the Holy Spirit guides believers to live out God's unconditional agape, or selfless, love.[6]

"With these standards in mind, it became much easier to interpret Scripture's difficult passages consistently," Justin writes in his book *Torn: Rescuing the Gospel from the Gays-vs.-Christian Debate*. "Yes, there were slaves in Bible times, but doesn't selfless agape love demand their freedom?"[7]

"If every commandment can be summed up in the rule to love one another, then either gay couples were the one exception to this rule, and Paul was wrong—or my church had made a big mistake."[8] After these revelations, Justin began to speak out, and over time an outpouring of support came from all corners of the country. Justin launched an online support group, which became GCN.

Over the years, GCN has forged a nationwide community of LGBTQ believers, Christian parents of LGBTQ children, and allies. It offers a space for Side A and Side B Christians to have open dialogue and, perhaps more important, be in community with each other. Eschewing culture war practices, GCN does not identify with one side or the other (though Justin identifies as Side A) and messaging consistently emphasizes that GCN is a space for Christians from across the theological spectrum.

"We all agreed that to call something sin that's not sin is wrong," Justin said on the conference's opening night. "And to call something not sin that is sin is also wrong. And so we agreed that it matters but we disagreed on what the answer was." The audience laughed. "But we also agreed that we needed to find a place to wrestle with these questions."

I'll admit that I was skeptical of this model. I've witnessed so-called bridge-building efforts that seem to dilute the message of both sides at the expense of justice. I wondered if GCN meetings were just strained exercises in Christian politeness. So over the course of the four-day conference, I watched this motley crew of outcasts worship, pray, discuss, listen, cry, and strategize.

Many in attendance were Christians, young and old, questioning their sexuality for the first time. Side A Christians and Side B Christians debated each other, sometimes affably, sometimes with an edge in their voices. Happy queer couples held hands during worship. Transgender believers served communion. Straight allies voiced their support. Pastors lamented their own role in ostracizing LGBTQ congregants. Folks in mixed-oriented marriages (for instance, a gay man married to a straight woman) weighed heavy questions, like whether their marriages would or should survive. Parents of newly out LGBTQ children sought advice on how to raise their sons and daughters and how to deal with judgment from their church communities.

From the start, attendees networked eagerly; they seemed like refugees from different lands, united by their exile. They spilled their stories readily, relieved to find a place where they didn't have to edit out their sexuality. Strangers struck up personal conversations with little preamble. "I had questions, but never felt welcomed to explore them," one young man said to someone he met in line. Samantha, an early-thirties web designer with kind eyes and a curtain of blond hair, told me she had only recently come out of the closet after she and her best girlfriend fell in love. But after a brief, blissful relationship, her girlfriend, overwhelmed by guilt, ended things. Samantha was confused. Was she gay or bi? Was she Side A or Side B? Was this sin or identity? Could she be a Christian and a lesbian? She hoped to find answers at the conference, because all she knew for certain so far was that her heartbreak hurt like hell.

The seminars were tailored for people like Samantha, queer Christians from conservative backgrounds who felt like outcasts in Christian and queer worlds. "We're not all naked, writhing people on floats," said one seminar speaker to murmurs of approval. Others bristled at the assumption that by embracing their queer identities they had abandoned rigorous theological thinking or conservative lifestyles. They flocked to seminars that addressed faith, theology, and sexuality, such as "Praying the Scriptures with a Gay Heart," "Coming Out in Faith" or "The Naked Truth about Keeping Your Clothes On."

Darren Calhoun, a photographer in his early thirties, left the "Naked Truth" seminar happy to have found a space to talk openly about his sexuality—he's gay—*and* his recent resolution to save sex for marriage, he told me. Here, his sexuality wasn't frowned upon and his vow wasn't an embarrassing declaration.

But Darren felt divided in other ways. As a black gay Christian, he has watched the LGBTQ movement fight for marriage equality while ignoring the unique challenges of queers of color, such as experiences involving racial profiling, police brutality, incarceration, and youth homelessness. In his own city of Chicago, he has seen a familiar pattern play out: low-income LGBTQ youth of color flock to wealthy, historic, white gay neighborhoods—in this case Boystown on Chicago's North Side—and affluent queer residents blame local crime on their presence. Darren wished LGBTQ advocates and Christian advocates would direct their energy toward helping minority queers facing poverty and systemic racism. But even at a place like GCN and among other Christian groups that trumpet justice-seeking, Darren says these issues are sidelined. For Darren, it's difficult to find a place—the church, the queer community, the black community—where all of his identities are embraced.

Another conference attendee, whom we'll call Kingsley, called this the dilemma of "triple consciousness," a play on W. E. B. Du Bois's writing in his book *The Souls of Black Folk* on "double consciousness," which expresses the psychological dissonance of a divided identity.[9]

It is a peculiar sensation, this double-consciousness, this sense of always looking at one's self through the eyes of others, of measuring one's soul by the tape of a world that looks on in amused contempt and pity. One ever feels his two-ness,—an American, a Negro; two souls, two thoughts, two unreconciled strivings; two warring ideals in one dark body, whose dogged strength alone keeps it from being torn asunder.[10]

For Kingsley, an early-twenties interfaith justice advocate who is also black, gay, and Christian, these three identities feel constantly disjointed. In the secular LGBTQ community he feels fetishized. "I become this thrill," he said. "My humanity gets lost and I just become this 'BBC'—big black cock." And at his liberal, LGBTQ-friendly Methodist church, which tried addressing racial injustice, the nearly all-white congregation lacked minority voices and struggled to unite around these initiatives. Yet, in African American churches, where the worship style was to his liking and the community grappled daily with systemic racism, Kingsley always wondered, *How out can I really be?*

Kingsley came to the GCN conference "to find a community where I don't have to choose [between my identities]," he said. He had interacted with GCN members on message boards, occasionally feeling "like I'm problematic" for bringing up race issues, but he had hoped that meeting folks in person would help him spot people he could identify with and forge deeper friendships. But when he arrived and saw few attendees who looked like himself and found no seminars that addressed the unique challenges he faced, "I just felt like I didn't belong."

So he did what many minorities tend to do; he adapted to the culture available to him. He looked for Christians his age. He engaged in common-ground issues. This wasn't a sufficient answer, of course, but it was all he could do that weekend at the predominantly white GCN conference.

At lunchtime, Kingsley befriended a group of young, white attendees who shared his interest in wrestling over biblical truths. Samantha, from earlier, was among the group, as was her friend Joe, and another attendee named Jonathan. Despite the denominational diversity of the attendees (Kingsley doesn't identify as evangelical), what made Kingsley's group and the conference *feel* so deeply evangelical was the heightened focus on scripture and theological wrangling. Seminars about bullying and LGBTQ health garnered modest crowds, but the presentation on applying scripture to LGBTQ issues drew over a hundred people. At that seminar, a rapt audience listened as James Farlow, a theologian who grew up in the Southern Baptist tradition, pointed out the flaws in the common assumption among conservative evangelicals that "The Bible + Exegesis = Moral Absolute Law."

"This is not how the Bible interprets itself. This is not how the apostles interpreted scripture," said Farlow, taking issue specifically with how this equation has been applied to queer issues. "If we only say that we can only get meaning from the text from the exact original literal composition, we will be forever dependent on academics and the intelligentsia, which—if you read scripture—it's very clear that that's not what Paul and the others thought it needed to be."

Over lunch, as Kingsley, Samantha, Joe, and Jonathan moved deeper into their conversation, they each struggled against conservative biblical interpretation, revealing the deep-seated nature of the homosexuality-is-sin narrative. Joe, Samantha, and Kingsley each were in various stages of sorting out the Side A and Side B debate. Kingsley explained himself this way, "I want to be Side A, but I'm so immersed in shame and guilt. . . . Side B is a safer route. As Side B, my parents and church are more likely to accept me."

But Jonathan confidently laid out his interpretations. He identifies as Side A, but with a twist. To him, homosexuality is still a sin, but one that's just as "covered in grace" as any other sin, which is why he freely pursues relationships with other men. The group was confused. Didn't Side A Christians view same-sex relationships as *not* sinful?

"According to the Word, [gay marriage] is still sinful, but it's biblical." We all raised our eyebrows. "Marriage is biblical," he clarified. "But it's still sinful" when it involves two people of the same sex. "But overall, I think grace has covered everybody. I sin, everybody sins. The only difference between my sin and someone else's sin is I'm open about it."

But this approach—essentially a Side B view on the sinfulness of homosexuality with a Side A approach to openly pursuing same-sex relationships—felt inconsistent to Joe.

"My perspective on sin, though, is sin is something that separates us from God," Joe said. "And if something is sinful, I don't want to do it."

"So for you, homosexuality is sin," Jonathan replied.

Joe tilted his head, uncomfortable with that assessment.

"Uhhhheeeeeeee . . . that's what I'm wrestling with and studying, going back to some of the original texts."

"Aren't you supposed to repent from your sin?" I asked Jonathan.

"Absolutely. And that's a continual, daily going to the Lord and saying, 'God, I love you. You made me new every day. Your grace is renewing every day.'"

"But repentance means we should learn from it," Samantha said. "Not just ask for forgiveness."

The argument went on like this for some time and Jonathan repeatedly came back to his view. "I believe that homosexuality is a sin but I'm completely forgiven. I don't know how else to describe it." In his own life, that means he is out to a select group of people while remaining closeted in certain communities, like his church.

As Jonathan spoke, I saw people exchange glum looks across the table. I understand that people come out of the closet in different ways, but it made me sad to think about how much the homosexuality-is-sin concept limits the geography of where queer Christians can be their whole selves.

It's this kind of compartmentalization that made so many GCN conference attendees struggle with accepting themselves and feeling known by their own communities. At the seminar on supporting LGBTQ students at conservative Christian colleges, a crowd of about forty attendees lamented the lengths some administrations went to keep queer students and alumni underground.

They name-checked the administrations that denied club status to groups, the ones that ignored the presence of LGBTQ students on campus, and the others, like Biola's, that simply suggested queer students leave campus altogether. The seminar host, a diminutive lesbian and a graduate of Wheaton College, explained how this exclusion intensified after graduation. Alumni magazines "try to erase the existence of gay alumni" by refusing to include their stories or cutting them—or their children—out of reunion photographs, she said.

But other attendees spoke about the signs of hope, calling out the schools that are giving official club status to LGBTQ groups or the administrations that are more open to engaging the issue. An alumnus from an Assemblies of God–affiliated college shared, "I've actually had the opportunity to speak personally with the administration and even get vocal, very specific admissions that they have really legitimate concerns and fears about things like losing money." To this alum, that conversation, and a subsequent exchange he had in the school newspaper with the university president, demonstrated "a . . . significant first step" in the "recognition of (queer) students' existence."

A middle-aged woman with a soft British accent introduced herself as an administrator at Calvin College, a Christian college in Grand Rapids, Michigan. "Things are possible," she assured the crowd. "We have an LGBTQ and allies group that is funded through donor funding. I do programming on sexuality. We have donor funding from gay alumni. Officially our college holds a Side B position, but there are things that are possible. LGBTQ students do peer education around the dorms every year around safety, antiharassment, and basic terminology. And I know that's probably not possible at a lot of these Christian colleges right now. But don't turn your backs on all the administrators," she pleaded gently. "I am here today and where I am at in my job because I got to know gay students and gay alums. So, administrators are not necessarily the enemy."

A young, straight woman with a neat bob haircut and delicate features rose slowly from her seat, revealing a nearly full-term pregnant belly. She praised the work of campus LGBTQ advocates and wished they had been around when she was a Wheaton College student a decade ago. "My husband is gay. He came out to me six months ago," she said. The audience looked at her face, then her belly, stunned. She smiled knowingly and wondered aloud about what life would look like if Wheaton College had been more open about discussing queer issues when she and her husband had attended.

"I wish if *that* had been going on [then] I would have been less naive, more people would have been aware of the issue, he would have been supported and . . . ," her voice trailed off. "All of us straight spouses in Chicago, whenever we get together . . ." She paused a beat and looked around the room. "We just want everyone who is gay to just come out!" The crowd burst with laughter as the woman carefully lowered herself back into her seat.

RYAN

As I bounced between seminars, worship sets, speeches, and intense conversations, my mind kept returning to the students I met at the Biola Queer Underground. When compared to secular LGBTQ advances, the BQU's victories may seem minor, but to the queer students on campus, they are life changing, life saving, and history making. If Will had attended Biola a decade ago, he might well have become the recently out husband with a stricken pregnant wife. Tasha's OCD might have gotten the better of her. Students struggling with suicidal thoughts might have acted on them. In fact, before 2012, the BQU did not exist. In the eyes of one Biola family, if the club launched just a few years earlier, it could have saved their gay son's life.

I met Linda and Rob Robertson at the GCN conference. They serve on the Biola University Parent Council. Linda is a Biola alum and three of their four children graduated from Biola. Their fourth child, Ryan, had been accepted to Biola and its Torrey Honors Institute for the fall of 2006, but his college plans had been derailed by a crippling drug addiction.

The Robertsons, who were keynote speakers at GCN, have told huge crowds of evangelicals across the country about the years leading up to Ryan's drug problems. Linda typically does most of the talking in a cracked, quavering voice, always on the verge of crying. As she tells it, when her twelve-year-old son Ryan came out of the closet, Linda and her husband Rob guided him down the destructive path of reparative therapy. Ryan tried this until, six years later, he snapped. He ran away and turned to drugs—cocaine, crack, heroin—quickly falling down the rabbit hole of addiction and Seattle street life. The Robertsons went from praying that Ryan would be straight to praying that Ryan would know he was loved and that he'd come home safe.

One day, Ryan called his parents wanting to reconcile and get clean. Over the next few months they experienced the miracle of forgiveness and restoration. They met his boyfriend. They checked him into rehab. They had long, late-night conversations, rebuilding their love for each other. They bonded with Ryan's boyfriend during the three-hour drive to and from the rehab center, alternating between swapping Ryan stories and listening to the *Twilight* series audiobooks. Linda and Rob learned to love their son and his boyfriend and accept them completely.

But the consequences of addiction were more difficult to remedy. Ryan made strides in rehab, until he didn't. Linda and Rob watched him relapse three times. The first time, he spent a week in the ICU. The second time, he lost his hearing and awoke with permanent brain damage. The third time, he was with friends who didn't call 911 until he had been unconscious for nearly forty-eight hours. His litany of ailments was too long to list and too severe to offer hope. Linda and her family gathered in Ryan's hospital room for seventeen days, riding the roller coaster of emotions as Ryan's body flicked between life and death. On July 16, 2009, Ryan died.

As Linda and Rob spoke, they cried with regret. The GCN attendees sobbed with them, many hearing their own stories in the Robertsons'. When I spoke to Linda after her talk, she told me that she often wondered if Ryan's life might have been saved if the BQU had existed. At eighteen, he had been accepted to Biola. Instead of befriending junkie street kids, Ryan might have attended school, eager to find his tribe in the BQU. Maybe BQU friends would have helped him overcome his self-rejection and shown him that he was loved.

It's an alternate timeline that Linda has turned over in her mind and in conversations with Biola's president, Barry Corey. She has urged him to sanction the BQU and open up Biola to alternative perspectives. Linda and Rob have befriended the BQU, publicly supported them, and given talks at their events, actions that have put them at risk of being kicked off the Biola University Parent Council, Linda told me. But Linda and Rob aren't backing down. They continue to support the BQU and are calling on others, especially straight people, to "all join together and ask Biola to not be afraid of different perspectives," said Linda at a BQU panel discussion.

CREEPING ALONG THE CONTINUUM

At the start of the GCN conference, I was a skeptic of the organization's dual embrace of Side A and Side B. I worried that giving the Side B argument equal weight would perpetuate the shaming of sexual minorities. Telling people that "God called them to celibacy," that they were required to deny themselves intimacy and sexual expression for life, felt cruel and harmful. I still feel that way and I still worry about the consequences of these demands. But I've begun to understand why the strategy made sense for this audience. For one, it fostered open dialogue and diminished culture war rhetoric. Secondly, it offered a place of belonging to people who felt marginalized by the church and the LGBTQ community. Lastly, as I saw it, it facilitated the transition from Side X to Side B to Side A.

Many of the LGBTQ Christians I spoke to were raised in Side X communities. They couldn't make the leap to Side A without first wrestling with the thorny Side B questions of celibacy and biblical interpretation. For many, like Will, they needed to slowly move through the stages of self-hatred and cautious acceptance before they could arrive at total affirmation of their sexuality. As Will told me, it took him years of questioning and batting between the two sides before he fully embraced his sexuality.

It's easy for me to look at this issue through a lens of straight privilege and secular progressiveness, and grow impatient. Even with my evangelical background, I don't carry nearly the amount of cultural baggage that more entrenched evangelicals bear. For them, process, self-discovery, and theological wrangling are crucial to deprogramming from such deep-seated homophobia and transphobia. They need support as they tease out the particulars of their minority identity.

They shouldn't be shamed for how they come out of the closet or how they identify, or if their coming-out process takes multiple stages.

For some, it might mean identifying as bi before identifying as gay. For others, it might mean identifying as lesbian before identifying as trans. And for others, it might mean baby steps along the theological spectrum. Some may leave ex-gay therapy and find their comfort zone in the out-but-celibate camp. Others may take this further and years later embrace their desire for romantic love.

This transition also applies to straight evangelicals and their journey toward accepting their LGBTQ brothers and sisters. Countless parents and straight allies spoke about how they needed time to process their loved ones' coming-out. They asked for patience, forgiveness for their ignorance, and most of all, grace through the messiness. Maybe one day, after a generation of grace and processing, there will be evangelical spaces where the forces of heterosexism won't make the transition so difficult, or even necessary. Skeptics may dismiss this possibility, but this growing network of LGBTQ evangelicals and their allies are working to make this a reality.

DANNY CORTEZ

The GCN conference closed its last night with an intimate three-hour open mike sharing session, which ended with a stunning confession that, months later, would make church history.

It was late, nearing midnight, and for several hours the audience had cried with, applauded, and amen'd the dozens of attendees brave enough to share their stories. During what felt like an enormous group therapy session, one woman spoke about the slurs hurled her way after she accidentally came out to her church community. Others shared about rising from the ashes of suicide attempts, addiction, or body-image issues to find healing in this rare community of LGBTQ Christians. "You all have helped me feel so normal," said one college student, explaining that she has always felt like an outsider: gay in a Christian setting, black but ridiculed for talking "like a white girl" at her mostly African American school. Parents confessed their own screwups and their fear of community rejection; they thanked the audience for giving them strength to cast that aside. "I'm so proud of my son," one mother said softly, her voice cracking. A younger woman offered a stunning story: when denominational authorities threatened to shut down her church after it embraced her and her wife as members, the church stood by the couple. A married gay man thanked his pastor, his pastor's wife, and his own wife—all in attendance—for supporting him after he came out. Addressing his wife, he wept. "I do regret all the pain that I have caused, that I am causing, that I will be causing as we finish walking through this process."

Then, as the night was winding down, as the emotional whiplash had pushed the audience to the brink, a soft-spoken, straight middle-aged preacher with a mop of dark hair, round cheeks, and a salt-and-pepper soul patch introduced himself.

"My name is Danny Cortez and I'm a pastor of a Southern Baptist church," he said, his voice shaking slightly. Danny, a Filipino American husband and father of four, is the founding pastor of a multiethnic church located across the street from his seminary alma mater, Biola University. Since founding his own church and becoming its teaching pastor, Danny has confronted a new reality: LGBTQ Christians in his congregation. He confessed to the GCN crowd that in his fifteen years as a pastor, he always pushed them toward celibacy or reparative therapy. That is, until a lesbian congregant pleaded with Danny to educate himself on LGBTQ issues, and he embarked on years of intense, scholarly research.

Then, in the summer of 2013, he explained, "I finally came to realize, dear God, I've been wrong."

The GCN audience murmured with surprise. Coming from a straight, conservative, Southern Baptist, evangelical pastor, this story had special weight.

"So now we find ourselves here—my wife and I," Danny continued. "And every session we go to . . . I realize that I've contributed to your hurt." A few audience members began to cry. "As a pastor, and on behalf of pastors, I want to apologize to you. I want to say I'm sorry for the way we've treated you. I want to say I'm sorry for making you feel like you weren't part of the body of Christ and that you didn't have a voice and that you were somehow evil because of your identity."

Danny explained that after his epiphany, he kept it a secret for a bit. He knew it could cost him everything—his career, his community, possibly even his family. But weeks later, when he was driving his fifteen-year-old son Drew to school, Macklemore's song "Same Love" began to hum through the speakers. Something about it gave Danny the courage to tell Drew about his change of heart. Drew sat quietly, looking puzzled. They stepped out of the car and Danny asked Drew what he thought.

"And he looked over at me and said, 'Dad, I'm gay.'"

The GCN audience let out a collective gasp.

"And I realize," Danny said to his stunned audience, "for the fifteen years of his life and the fifteen years I've been pastor of this church, God had been preparing me for that moment."

Danny closed by asking for prayer; his life was about to change drastically. "My son is about to create this coming-out video in the next few weeks. And I'm about to tell my church." He was preparing to lose his job, and preparing for Drew to face rejection and for his family to have to rebuild their lives. As he walked away from the microphone, the crowd leapt to their feet, in a roaring standing ovation.

DANNY'S GAMBLE

In the weeks that followed the GCN conference, Drew came out of the closet to his family and friends and, in a way, so did Danny.

Drew posted a fourteen-minute coming-out video. In it, his black hair stood straight up and his youthful, handsome face cried and cracked shy smiles as he talked about rising from a life of pain to a place of peace.

Danny told the three other pastors at his church, New Heart Community. They all expressed their love for Danny, but also predicted a schism. They couldn't envision a future with Danny in leadership, but offered him one last Sunday sermon in February so that he could share his transformation with the congregation. The stress of preparing to come out publicly as a queer ally overwhelmed Danny so much that in the week leading up to that service, his doctor, alarmed by a sudden turn in Danny's health, prescribed blood pressure medication and warned that a systolic blood pressure reading over 180 could lead to a stroke or worse. *If that happens, you must go to the emergency room,* his doctor urged.

Then, just hours before Danny broke the news to his congregation, with his body feeling "ready to explode," he took another blood pressure reading and saw that his systolic blood pressure was 196. Danny's mind raced. *I should drive to the emergency room,* he thought. But then he thought about Drew and his congregation, and decided to take the biggest gamble of his life. He climbed into his car and drove to church.

"JESUS SAYS, YOU LOOK AT THE FRUIT"

Standing at the pulpit, Danny could feel the blood coursing through his body. He was nervous, and from the looks on his congregants' faces, so were they. Danny let his story unspool. He told his congregation that church teachings should not destroy human dignity the way so-called biblical values have done to the LGBTQ community.

He backed up his claims with scholarship: *Arsenokoites,* the Greek word used in scripture, has only recently been translated to mean "homosexual," he argued. When the rarely used word appeared in Greek literature, he explained, it was to describe a wide spectrum of sexual activity, typically involving nonconsensual, violent sex to establish power—not homosexual sex.

"I thought, *you know what? That's a different world.*" The world Paul had been writing about has no connection to today's gay community, he told his congregation.

He backed up his reasoning with Jesus's teachings. You don't need all this scholarship to know the will of God, he said. "Jesus says, you look at the fruit. Is it bad or is it good? Because a good tree bears good fruit. A bad tree bears bad fruit. And everybody knows we're wired to recognize hatred. We're wired to recognize injustice. We're wired to recognize things that are evil. So we don't have to have all that knowledge."

He backed up this analogy with anecdotes from his own son's life. Traditional teachings had driven Drew to isolation. Every birthday before Drew had come out, Drew would wake up saddened that he was still gay, Danny told the congregation. Only after he came out did he feel peace. And even after his family embraced his sexuality, Drew couldn't shake the sense that he was somehow broken. "Dad," he said one day, "I want you to know, if someone gave me a pill right now that could change my gayness, I would take it right now." Danny mulled Drew's statement and found him the next day. "Drew," Danny said to his son, "I want you to know that if I had a pill that could change you, I wouldn't give it to you, because you're perfect just the way you are. No more fighting, Drew. No more fighting. Accept the way God has made you. I love you just the way you are.'"

From the back of the sanctuary, Drew cried as he listened to his father recount that conversation. The two had locked eyes in what Danny would later call "a beautiful father-and-son moment." Looking at his congregation, Danny's voice rose: "I felt like I was giving him life! For the first time, I was actually offering words of life. And I thought: the fruit of this feels familiar."

AFTERMATH

The reaction to Danny's sermon was a total messy mix. After Danny stepped away from the pulpit, the other pastors took the stage and warned that Danny's course change had led the church into "dangerous waters." One of the pastors, Matthew, addressed Danny's son directly, saying, "The most abundant life for Drew or anyone dealing with a minority sexual orientation or identity issue . . . could be sixty to seventy years of not choosing to fulfill that desire . . . for a life of eternity, beyond this life."

As Danny described it, his congregation looked disoriented after the service ended, some tearful, others dazed. One man angrily called the other church pastors judgmental. A woman accused Danny of heresy. "You've gone off the deep end, Pastor." But many simply hugged him.

In the weeks that followed, the church hosted discussions, brought in speakers from across the theological spectrum, and held prayer meetings to come to an educated community decision about how to respond.

Danny mentally prepared for his inevitable firing and grew convinced that he should start an LGBTQ-affirming church on his own.

In a few months, New Heart's discussion and speaker series had concluded, and it was time to vote. In May 2014, New Heart made a historic departure from its Southern Baptist denomination's tradition by voting to affirm the LGBTQ community. Danny kept his job, but nearly half of the congregation and the three other pastors left the church a month later. Danny began rebuilding his church as a "third-way church," a new church model that eschews the progay/antigay binary and welcomes people from across the spectrum to deepen their understanding of LGBTQ issues. Much like the Gay Christian Network, New Heart Community Church's leader is Side A; the community welcomes and affirms LGBTQ people, but it also welcomes a diversity of opinions. In September of that year, the Southern Baptist Convention Executive Committee voted unanimously to expel Danny's church from the denomination.

Danny calls this point in church history a place of transition, where "there's always collateral damage. For better or for worse, this is where we're at." According to Danny, the third-way church model is the best place to work out that transition, to keep LGBTQ Christians from leaving the church and to bring straight Christians into the conversation. This might be one of the most powerful tools to push those in the "messy middle" along the continuum to total affirmation and acceptance.

As Danny and his church venture into uncharted territory, they're finding a growing community of Christians just like them, conservative evangelicals with a deep commitment to biblical authority who believe that Christians have been misinterpreting biblical passages about homosexuality all along.

The same year of Danny's church split, several evangelical leaders emerged voicing support for LGBTQ equality. Pastor Ken Wilson published his book *A Letter to my Congregation*, in which he documents his journey, both scholarly and spiritually, toward embracing sexual minorities in the church. Months later Matthew Vines, a young gay evangelical, published his book *God and the Gay Christian*, which provides a theological argument to affirm same-sex relationships. Vines also launched the Reformation Project, a nonprofit aimed at training

Christians and their leaders to affirm sexual minorities in the church. Vines attracted the support of David Gushee, a renowned evangelical ethicist who, also in 2014, shook the evangelical world by publicly supporting full LGBTQ equality. Meanwhile, 2014 also brought the launch of Evangelicals for Marriage Equality, a group formed with the explicit agenda of changing the minds of anti-equality believers. Megachurch leaders have also joined the movement. EastLake Community Church has recently affirmed full inclusion of LGBTQ people, while Willow Creek's Bill Hybels, who hasn't made any declarations yet, has reportedly been meeting and listening to the stories of his queer congregants.[11]

In early 2015, the Gay Christian Network hosted its annual conference, attracting its largest audience yet, a reported 1,400 attendees.

Experts watching this shift say that it has staying power. "What's clear is that there's been movement toward much greater acceptance," said Jeremy Thomas, sociologist and expert on evangelical perspectives on sexuality. Despite conservative resistance, Thomas predicts a loss of energy in the policy fights against homosexuality and, down the road, "pretty significant acceptance" of the LGBTQ community among congregations.

CLOSING TIME

It's this momentum toward LGBTQ progress that points to a hopeful future for the BQU leaders and those who will follow them. It will be a long journey, to be sure. After the big BQU yearbook launch and the conversations with Danny Paschall, the BQU leaders felt let down. They had expected a more startling conclusion—a policy change, an apology, a marked shift among the administration signaling a new beginning. In the coming year, the BQU would feel further sidelined after NakID, Atticus's school-sanctioned Side B group, began to draw members away from the BQU. That same year, Biola lawyers would notify the BQU that its use of the Biola name violated the school's trademark rights, and insist that the group stop using the Biola name and Listserv. Despite the challenges, there was much about the BQU that the school could not take away from the group. During my week with the BQU, watching members come out publicly and, days later, watching them gather for their final meeting of the year, there was an undeniable sense that something entirely new and entirely lasting had been built.

Their last gathering was on a Friday night at their secret undisclosed location off campus. Will assumed it would be a normal year-end meeting, but the rest of the group had planned a surprise party to send him off properly. I arrived early with Jason, and before we went in, Jason pulled out a letter he had written to Will in which he listed all the ways he admired him. The letter was written on a folded piece of paper that had been burned at the edges. Jason loved Will. Earlier in the year they had a few "romantic moments," as Jason put it, until Will had gently let him down. But college was ending and Will was moving away; the time seemed ripe for one last romantic confession.

Inside the party room, speakers blared LMFAO's "Party Rock Anthem" and a few dozen college kids grabbed handfuls of chips, cracked open cans of soda, and did little shimmies next to their friends until everyone was dancing.

They were a vibrant group, ethnically diverse and representative of the whole spectrum of gender and sexuality. Later they'd hold hands in a big circle, thank the group for saving them from loneliness, whisper their fears through teary eyes, and pray together with an urgent, fervent kind of plea.

As they danced, I looked at their smiling faces and found it hard to believe that so many of them had contemplated suicide. One gorgeous, bubbly transgender woman from Asia later told me that she used to purposefully linger in her city's danger zones, hoping to be attacked because she did not believe her life was worth saving. I spoke to other members who recalled suicidal thoughts or deep, long depressions, but everyone spoke in the past tense. I asked about their struggles now, and no one could offer recent stories. They were happy, resilient, restored. I asked again and again, *But didn't you say Biola had hurt you?* They said yes, but the BQU had saved them.

"Will's here!" someone called before killing the lights and music. The door opened slowly and Will's silhouette filled the frame. A moment later, someone threw on the lights, the crowd screamed "Surprise!" and Will, startled and overjoyed, covered his face and laughed. Then he looked around the room, quiet now that every face had turned expectantly to him, and he began speaking. He was confident, happy, charming, and funny. I realized that I didn't recognize him. For so many days, he had seemed fragile, struggling to break free from his old self—the scrawny high school kid who hated himself, the insecure college freshman tortured by his lies, the ex-boyfriend heartbroken over his disastrous breakup, the campus activist, suddenly out yet still feeling ashamed. But here, in front of the peers he had helped over the past year, he was the man all his friends knew him to be. He was the clever one. The comedian. The crush. The bravest of them all. He was their leader.

Despite all the letdowns from the school and concerns about what was to come, victory was in the room. In the years that followed, the BQU would live on in their absence. There would be new members, new tears, new triumphs, new loves for them all.

But at that party, they thought nothing of the future. Jason slipped Will his love letter. Tasha kissed her girlfriend. They all danced until they were breathless. And looking into each other's eyes, they caught a wave of something sort of new, something that was becoming more familiar; it was the feeling of being completely known and still completely loved.

The Future

While researching this book, I rode many waves of emotions: excitement, surprise, disappointment, fascination, painful familiarity, hope, and curiosity for what the future might hold.

Many signs point to a radically different evangelical tomorrow. Demographic shifts—along with the vigorous mobilization behind justice issues that impact people of color, women, and queer Christians—appear to be widening the doors of the church. Evangelicals are positioned to contribute to social change in a powerful, positive way.

But change is complicated; progress for each group is uneven, jolting backward as often as it seems to be moving forward. Evangelical feminists remain so fragmented that it's difficult to predict their future. Social progress plays heavily in their favor, with feminist advances on clear display in certain evangelical circles. Generational changes and a growing consensus around redefining the "pro-life" label have begun to weaken conservative efforts to retain abortion as a wedge issue.

Still, given the highly patriarchal environment, some activists feel they must shy away from addressing reproductive rights, supporting queer equality, or even identifying as feminist. Their silence allows the conservative attack on women to go unchallenged by fellow evangelicals. When it comes to reproductive rights, the economic factor cannot be ignored: conservative efforts to deny women access to funded health services, education, contraception, prenatal care, and abortion strike a particular blow to low-income women. These disenfranchised women need evangelical feminists to represent their needs with as much passion, organization, and theological rigor as they extend to efforts supporting egalitarian marriages and women's ordination.

LGBTQ evangelicals face the most vocal objections and hostility to their equal civil rights. Add to that the grave mental health consequences and suicide risks they face in nonaffirming communities, and the landscape can seem downright hopeless. Nonetheless, the queer justice movement appears poised to achieve the most significant gains. The past couple of years have witnessed unprecedented change. Evangelicals from all corners of the culture are voicing support for LGBTQ equality: pastors, parents, evangelical leaders, straight allies, Christian college alumni, and queer Christians themselves. The networks they are building and the impact they have had already suggest that it may be only a matter of time before opposition to LGBTQ equality becomes the minority opinion in the evangelical world.

Despite verbal support offered by the evangelical community, the racial justice movement continues to deal with the steepest systemic challenges. On a rhetorical level, the evangelical world finds racism unacceptable, but beyond grand sermons about inclusivity, there remains serious systemic discrimination within evangelicalism that stands in the way of real progress. The church has not only inherited the country's legacy of racism, it has also perpetuated its own version of it by building segregation into its foundation through the homogenous unit principle. Even as multiethnic churches become more popular, experts suggest that oftentimes bringing diverse congregants into the fold is simply another church-growth scheme. As long as multiethnic churches perpetuate racial hierarchy—with white leaders collecting minority followers—it will not matter how much the evangelical church "browns." Authentic racial reconciliation will follow only actions that correct for the past and that fix today's unjust systems. For the evangelical church to arrive at true inclusivity, white leaders and followers must commit to learning about the policies and institutional barriers that devastate communities of color.

Pointing conservative evangelicals toward fixing systemic injustice for people of color, women, and the queer community is a daunting task. Because evangelicals tend to live and worship in fairly insular communities, a crucial component to success is fostering personal relationships between conservative evangelicals and evangelicals who are also members of these minority communities. But the pursuit of justice should not stop at simply getting along with "the other"; it requires deeper understanding and work toward systemic change.

In a sense, the queer Christian movement may serve as a model. Once LGBTQ people began coming out of the closet en masse, droves of straight evangelicals became allies. Many Christian advocates of inclusion and same-sex marriage are parents, relatives, pastors, or friends of queer people. These personal relationships force loved ones to grapple with struggles they once felt comfortable judging from afar, building empathy and activism. In many cases, this relational process translates to gender as well—the presence of women and girls in white evangelical families has prompted many communities to embrace policies that promote female advancement. As this has become the norm in certain evangelical circles, progress on women's equality has come so far that it is sometimes even taken for granted.

But with race, these bonds of familiarity rarely exist. Divisions within the church and segregated neighborhoods make cross-racial relationships challenging among evangelicals. As Soong-Chan put it, "A white family can give birth to a homosexual child. A white family can give birth to a girl. But a white family cannot give birth to a black child." This reality is changing slowly as interracial marriage and interracial adoption, and a multiethnic younger generation, build more cross-racial relationships. But, as in the broader American society, diversity does not often translate to systemic change. Getting along with people of other races does not necessarily translate to whole communities advocating for policies that actually help level the playing field.

Despite the obstacles, there is no question that communities of color, women, and queer Christians have a greater voice in evangelicalism than ever before. They are well aware of the aforementioned blind spots, and as their numbers and clout increase within the church, they are well positioned to guide mainstream leaders and the broader evangelical church toward a better future. Their shared spiritual heritage gives them credibility among white, heterosexual, evangelical men in power. And as they network with each other and hammer out a clear theological and practical vision for their movements, their influence will only grow. The work of minority communities has loosened the conservative grip on evangelicalism. A new era is truly upon us.

COMING HOME

Over the course of reporting this book, I spoke to hundreds of people across the faith and politics spectrum. The diversity of thought was wide, but one common theme that everyone shared was a desire for belonging. Whether we were leaving evangelicalism or staying in it, whether we claimed to have an abiding faith or no faith at all, whether conservative or liberal or somewhere in between, everybody had that same tug in the heart, that longing for a place to call home. I saw how we are all on a journey, carving out a space in the world where we can love, be loved, and thrive.

Lisa found her home on the front lines of racial justice activism and in the heart of American evangelicalism. She has become a reconciler of groups otherwise at odds, and her work has even helped her reconcile with her own family, especially her mother, Sharon. When I spoke to Sharon in early 2015, she recalled the tension in their relationship during Lisa's conservative evangelical years. But when she looks at her daughter today, she sees someone who has carried on her family's legacy of civic action. "Lisa has carried on far beyond what I was able to do," she said. "Lisa stayed in the fight. She carried the banner. Lisa has been the warrior. I'm in awe of her."

Jennifer found her home bridging a gap between young feminist evangelicals and the older, white male-dominated faith community she had originally fled from. After healing from her own troubled encounters with patriarchal Christianity, she is using her seminary pedigree, pastoral position, and "femmevangelical" platform to build an online community with women still bound by the faith's patriarchal culture.

For Will, Tasha, and Jason—they found their home in the enduring friendships they built on campus. Even after graduation, their legacy lives on at Biola. In October 2014, Biola hosted its first-ever Christian LGBTQ-affirming speaker on campus, Justin Lee, who spoke alongside Side B proponent Wesley Hill. Students filled every seat in the Sutherland lecture hall as well as overflow seating in Calvary Chapel.

Tasha attended, overwhelmed by the turnout and thrilled to see that the BQU's hard work from the previous years had paid off. Even her parents have come around somewhat: her dad has expressed his unconditional acceptance of Tasha and her sexuality, and her mom, while not going quite that far, has come to regret her past disparaging remarks.

Will moved to Colorado to face the postcollege challenges of paying off his Biola debt, finding his first jobs (at a bank, then at a flower shop), and building community in a new place. He described his new relationship in an e-mail to me as "quite fun :)" and said he often reminisces about the movement he started with Tasha.

After graduation, Jason attended the last Exodus International conference just in time to witness its president, Alan Chambers, announce the shuttering of the group, disavow ex-gay therapy, and apologize for the harm Exodus had inflicted. Then Jason formally came out to his parents, absorbed their rejection, and spent the following months drifting in and out of homelessness. He led the BQU with Tasha briefly, until financial constraints forced him to take a job on the East Coast. He is happy to have a job and a steady relationship. The BQU lives on under the leadership of Tasha's girlfriend. Both Tasha and Jason are making plans for law school, with dreams of one day representing sexual minorities facing discrimination.

At the start of this project, I found myself among the orphans of evangelicalism, holding on to something I still called faith but feeling estranged from the establishment that taught me about it. I did not set out to find a home for myself in writing this book, but I did. I found that I have, in fact, many homes: places of belonging among my husband, my family, and a community of friends who support me. I also found a home in journalism, which gave me permission to ask questions, challenge trite answers, and get to the bottom of what people really thought—all things I was too polite to do as an insider. Journalism allowed me to reconcile with my past—with Charlie, who showed me grace and forgiveness, as well as Toby and Rebecca, with whom I spent a four-hour-long Skype chat revisiting the painful moment (the mocking dance incident) that drove a wedge between us. Our long-overdue conversation allowed us to finally discuss how that experience shaped us. Toby and Rebecca offered heartfelt apologies for what had happened. I explained how that experience played a role in my departure from evangelicalism. Rebecca explained that she faced her own inner conflict over whether the dance was appropriate. They both shared all the ways that experience had sent them on a deeper, years-long journey of understanding white privilege and systemic discrimination, and ways their faith demanded racial justice. Despite the discomfort of confronting our past, it was a healing, restorative conversation.

By interrogating the faith and my evangelical past, I came to appreciate the complexities of evangelicalism and its people in a way I hadn't before. The process also helped me knit together a virtual community of other ex-evangelicals, orphans like myself, who did not judge me and who made me feel less alone.

As for my faith, I did not return to evangelicalism. I have traveled too a great distance theologically. But much of the time, my sense of faith feels strong, if vagrant and nameless.

Of course, some of the namelessness comes from how conservatives have defined what it means to be a "true Christian." In recent years, I have decided that they do not have the authority to disqualify me from the faith. Through my reporting for this book, I have witnessed profound grace and beauty and strength among marginalized believers who, in the face of hostile exclusion, have held on to their faith and changed their communities. Their lives have reminded me that God is so much bigger than the limitations set by the far Right or by anyone else. In God's house, there is room for everybody. There is room even for me.

Author's Note

I began my research for *Rescuing Jesus* in 2007. My reporting draws from my firsthand interviews with hundreds of sources; original reporting from various events; data from surveys, studies, and research papers; books by experts, journalists, and everyday evangelicals; and thousands of articles from a range of periodicals.

My sources include lay evangelicals, movement leaders, activists, scholars, theologians, historians, sociologists, demographers, academics, lawyers, analysts, outsiders, insiders, and everybody in between. For practical purposes, not every source made it into the book by name, but their influence permeates this book as their insights shed light on the breadth and nuances of this movement. I identify sources by their real names, unless otherwise noted.

Acknowledgments

I owe enormous thanks to the hundreds of people whose insights and support helped bring this book to life. My gratitude reaches wider than these incomplete acknowledgments allow.

I am especially grateful to the evangelicals who trusted me with their stories. They laid bare the complexities of faith and identity, breathing life into this book. My primary sources—Lisa Sharon Harper, Soong-Chan Rah, Jennifer Crumpton, Will Haggerty, Tasha Magness, and Jason Brown—all let me shadow them over years of their lives. For that privilege and honor, I am deeply thankful.

Others deserving of my thanks include my college friends Toby and Rebecca, who revisited a painful memory from our past with honesty and grace. Peter Heltzel and Rita Nakashima Brock urged me to write this book early on and introduced me to helpful sources. Richard Cizik offered invaluable insights into the evangelical establishment. My reporting relied on much past and present research by scholars, to whom I am indebted, including Randall Balmer, Pamela Cochran, Seth Dowland, Michael Emerson, Christian Smith, David Swartz, Jeremy Thomas, and Joshua Wolff. I'm thankful to those who gave me leads or made introductions, including journalists Sarah Pulliam Bailey and Bob Smietana, and sources Scott Calgaro, Marg Herder, Haven Herrin, Ben Lowe, Ryan Paetzold, Matthew Soerens, and many others.

This book is anything but a solo project. I'm lucky to have fantastic agents, Larry Weissman and Sascha Alper, who believed in this project when it was just the germ of an idea and steered me in the right direction so it could see the light of day. My wise editor at Beacon Press, Amy Caldwell, gave me encouragement, incisive feedback, and patience, and gently guided this book at every step. Thanks also to Will Myers, Susan Lumenello, Beth Collins, Caitlin Meyer, and everybody at Beacon Press.

I would not be where I am today without the encouragement from teachers and more experienced journalists who believed in me early in my career. I began to find my writing voice in college under the instruction of Julie Price, Matt Mitchell, and Brigit Pegeen Kelly. Years later, when I decided to become a journalist, I received tremendous guidance from Shawn Allee, Lynette Kalsnes, Adriene Hill, Sonari Glinton, and Mike Rhee at WBEZ Chicago Public Media, as well as Alex Kotlowitz, and the tremendous professors at the Columbia University Graduate School of Journalism, namely Dale Maharidge, Alissa Quart, Ari Goldman, and Stephen Fried.

I owe so much to my friends in the journalism and writing community who have become my family over the years. A very special thanks goes out those who read through the muddy drafts of this book and offered wisdom, questions, honest feedback, and sharp insights, including Katie Gilbert, Sushma Subramanian, Wailin Wong, Alec Nevala-Lee, Zainab Zakari, Kassi Underwood, Alison Bowen, and Minal Hajratwala.

During the production of this book, several friends, old and new, gave advice, helped me, encouraged me, housed me, fed me, or simply offered up kindness, dessert breaks, or late-night confabs, including Jessica Bruder, Chris Richards, Mitch Bach, Sarah Morgan, Jed Kim, Megan Hazle, Carol Kim, Eldwin Thay, Christina and Jake Johnson, Christine Huck, Luis Bacca, Silvia Vera, Jennifer Miller, John Corrigan, Martin Szeto, Nadja Drost, Sarah Elizabeth Richards, and Scott Carney.

I am blessed with lovely in-laws. Rita Porter, Tom Hjelle, Marcia Miller-Hjelle, Kate Barr, Justin Barr, and little Sophia have been consistent supporters, cheering me on at every stage. I'm grateful for their insights, including reflections from their own stories of faith.

My parents, Stephen and Sandra Lee, gave me the great gift of a loving, open, nonreligious upbringing from which I could chart my own spiritual path. I am profoundly thankful for their steadfast love through the years and the wisdom they have imparted. I am also thankful to my brother Dan Lee, my sister-in-law Michelle Hart, and their munchkins, Serena, Kian, and Torin, who gave me much needed play breaks from my book work.

I thank Kai, my sweet baby boy, who pencefully and patiently napped on my shoulder as I copyedited this book. Most of all, I thank Andrew Hjelle, my husband and best friend. For his unwavering belief in me and this book, for his humor, and for his boundless love, I am so thankful. I cherish every moment of our journey together. With him, I am always at home.

Notes

Unattributed quotes come from the author's personal interviews, conducted from 2007 to 2015.

Introduction

1. Nancy Gibbs and Michael Duffy, "How the Democrats Got Religion," Time.com, July 12, 2007, http://content.time.com/time/subscriber/article/0,33009,1642890,00.html.
2. Dan Cox, "Young White Evangelicals: Less Republican, Still Conservative," Pewforum.org, September 28, 2007, http://www.pewforum.org/2007/09/28/young-white-evangelicals-less-republican-still-conservative/.
3. Robert P. Jones et al., *Do Americans Believe Capitalism & Government Are Working? Religious Left, Religious Right & the Future of the Economic Debate* (Washington, DC: Public Religion Research Institute, July 18, 2013), http://publicreligion.org/site/wp-content/uploads/2013/07/2013-Economic-Values-Report-Final-.pdf.
4. Pew Research Center, *Religion Among the Millennials*, February 17, 2010, http://www.pewforum.org/2010/02/17/religion-among-the-millennials/.
5. Pew Research Center, *America's Changing Religious Landscape*, May 12, 2015, http://www.pewforum.org/files/2015/05/RLS-05-08-full-report.pdf.
6. "Six Reasons Young Christians Leave Church," news release, Barna.org, September 28, 2011, https://www.barna.org/teens-next-gen-articles/528-six-reasons-young-christians-leave-church.
7. Pew Research Center, *America's Changing Religious Landscape*.
8. Soong-Chan Rah, *The Next Evangelicalism: Freeing the Church from Western Cultural Captivity* (Downer's Grove, IL: InterVarsity Press Books, 2009), 14.
9. Laura R. Olson and Melissa Deckman, "The Times, Are They A-Changin'?," news release, PublicReligion.org, April 10, 2013, http://publicreligion.org/2013/04/the-times-are-they-a-changin/.
10. Tobin Grant and Sarah Pulliam Bailey, "How Evangelicals Have Shifted in Public Opinion on Same-Sex Marriage," ChristianityToday.com, May 11, 2012, http://www.christianitytoday.com/ct/2012/mayweb-only/evangelicals-shift-same-sex-marriage.html.
11. Robert P. Jones and Daniel Cox, *American Attitudes on Marriage Equality: Findings from the 2008 Faith and American Politics Study* (Washington, DC: Public Religion Research Institute, February 2008), http://publicreligion.org/site/wp-content/uploads/2011/06/American-Attitdues-on-same-sex-marriage-2008.pdf.

12. "How Many Evangelicals Are There?," Institute for the Study of American Evangelicals, accessed January 26, 2015, http://www.wheaton.edu/ISAE/Defining -Evangelicalism/How-Many-Are-There.

13. Pew Research Center, *America's Changing Religious Landscape*.

14. Quoted in David R. Swartz, *Moral Minority: The Evangelical Left in an Age of Conservatism* (Philadelphia: University of Pennsylvania Press, 2012), 1.

15. Ibid., 6.

Chapter 1: Assimilate to Survive

1. Lisa Sharon Harper and D. C. Innes, *Left, Right, and Christ: Evangelical Faith in Politics* (Boise, ID: Russell Media, 2011), 34.

2. New Jersey Division of Labor Market and Demographic Research, New Jersey State Data Center, *Population by Race and Hispanic or Latino Origin New Jersey Counties and Selected Municipalities: 1980, 1990 and 2000*, accessed January 22, 2015, http://lwd.dol.state.nj.us/labor/lpa/census/2kpub/njsdcp2.pdf.

3. Lisa Sharon Harper, *Evangelical Does Not Equal Republican . . . or Democrat* (New York: New Press, 2008), 4–5.

4. Campus Crusade for Christ recently changed its name to Cru.

5. Michael O. Emerson and Christian Smith, *Divided by Faith: Evangelical Religion and the Problem of Race in America* (New York: Oxford University Press, 2000), 25.

6. Ibid., 27–29.

7. Ibid., 32–33.

8. Ibid.

9. "Andrew Bryan, 1737–1812," *Africans in America*, PBS.org, accessed January 22, 2015, http://www.pbs.org/wgbh/aia/part2/2p28.html.

10. Julian Gotobed, "Walter Rauschenbusch (1861–1918)," in the *Boston Collaborative Encyclopedia of Western Theology*, ed. Wesley Wildman, http://people.bu.edu /wwildman/bce/rauschenbusch.htm (accessed January 22, 2015).

11. "Fundamentalism and the Social Gospel," *American Experience*, "Monkey Trial," PBS.org, accessed January 22, 2015, http://www.pbs.org/wgbh/amex/monkeytrial /peopleevents/e_gospel.html; "Scopes Trial," *Evolution Library*, PBS.org, accessed January 22, 2015, http://www.pbs.org/wgbh/evolution/library/08/2/l_082_01.html; Ernest R. Sandeen, "Christian Fundamentalism," Britannica.com, accessed January 22, 2015, http://www.britannica.com/EBchecked/topic/222234/Christian -fundamentalism#toc252659.

12. Emerson and Smith, *Divided by Faith*, 18–19.

13. Ibid., 79.

14. Max Blumenthal, "Agent of Intolerance," TheNation.com, May 16, 2007, http:// www.thenation.com/article/agent-intolerance#.

15. Emerson and Smith, *Divided by Faith*, 47.

16. Randall Balmer, *Thy Kingdom Come: An Evangelical's Lament; How the Religious Right Distorts the Faith and Threatens America* (New York: Basic Books, 2006), 17.

17. Emerson and Smith, *Divided by Faith*, 22.

18. Harper and Innes, *Left, Right, and Christ*, 33.

19. "Latinos, Religion and Campaign 2012: Catholics Favor Obama, Evangelicals Divided," news release, PewForum.org, October 18, 2012, http://www.pewforum .org/2012/10/18/latinos-religion-and-campaign-2012/.

20. "Asian Americans: A Mosaic of Faiths," news release, PewForum.org, July 19, 2012, http://www.pewforum.org/2012/07/19/asian-americans-a-mosaic-of-faiths -overview/.

21. Swartz, *Moral Minority*, 189.

22. Chicago Declaration of Social Concern, November 25, 1973, Chicago, IL, http://
www.evangelicalsforsocialaction.org/about/history/chicago-declaration-of-evangelical
-social-concern/

23. Ibid., 192.

24. Swartz, *Moral Minority*, 192.

25. Ibid., 194.

26. Ibid.

27. Lisa Sharon Harper, "By Any Other Name: Campus Crusade for Christ Becomes
Cru," HuffingtonPost.com, July 22, 2011, accessed January 26, 2015, http://
www.huffingtonpost.com/lisa-sharon-harper/campus-crusade-for-christ-cru_b
_906732.html

28. John M. Perkins, *With Justice for All: A Strategy for Community Development*
(Ventura, CA: Regal Books, 1982), 16.

29. John M. Perkins, *Let Justice Roll Down* (Ventura, CA: Regal Books, 1976), 16.

30. Emerson and Smith, *Divided by Faith*, 54.

31. Ibid., 64.

32. Ibid., 63.

Chapter 2: Good Christian Girls

1. Harold Lindsell, "The Suicide of Man," speech delivered at International Congress
on World Evangelization, Lausanne, Switzerland, July 1974, p. 421, http://www
.lausanne.org/docs/lau1docs/0421.pdf.

2. Ibid., 424.

3. Harold Lindsell, *The Battle for the Bible* (Grand Rapids, MI: Zondervan Publishing
House, 1976), 25.

4. Seth Dowland, *Family Values and the Rise of the Christian Right* (Philadelphia:
University of Pennsylvania Press, 2015), 165.

5. Quoted in Michael G. Long, *The Legacy of Billy Graham: Critical Reflections on
America's Greatest Evangelist* (Louisville, KY: Westminster John Knox Press, 2008), 79.

6. Dowland, *Family Values and the Rise of the Christian Right*, 213–14.

7. Stephen Arterburn and Fred Stoeker, *Every Man's Battle: Winning the War on Sexual Temptation One Victory at a Time* (Colorado Springs, CO: WaterBrook Press,
2009), 81.

8. Letha Scanzoni, "Part 1: Coauthoring 'All We're Meant to Be'—The Beginning,"
Letha Dawson Scanzoni (blog), January 7, 2011, http://www.lethadawsonscanzoni
.com/2011/01/part-1-coauthoring-all-were-meant-to-be-the-beginning/.

9. Letha Scanzoni and Nancy Hardesty, *All We're Meant to Be: Biblical Feminism for
Today* (Grand Rapids, MI: W. B. Eerdmans, 1992), 19.

10. Ibid., 32–33.

11. Ibid., 35.

12. Nancy Hardesty, "Blessed the Waters That Rise and Fall to Rise Again," speech
transcript, *Christian Feminism Today*, 2004, http://www.eewc.com/Articles/blessed
-the-waters/.

13. Swartz, *Moral Minority*, 198.

14. Dowland, *Family Values*, 197.

15. "The Top 50 Books That Have Shaped Evangelicals," *Christianity Today*, October
6, 2006, http://www.christianitytoday.com/ct/2006/october/23.51.html; Pamela
Cochran, *Evangelical Feminism: A History* (New York: New York University Press,
2005), 25.

16. Dowland, *Family Values*, 208.

17. Reta Finger, former editor, *Daughters of Sarah*, interview with the author, November 20, 2014.

Chapter 3: Safety in the Closet

1. Not her real name.
2. "CCCU Responds to Equality Ride," news release, May 1, 2006, http://www.cccu .org/news/articles/2006/cccu_responds_to_equality_ride. The Council of Christian Colleges and Universities, one of the most influential umbrella groups—representing 121 member campuses, including Biola's, in North America (as well as sixty affili- ates globally)—routinely defends campuses' guidelines against homosexual practice as biblical, even though Christian biblical interpretations on the issue vary widely among Christians and their denominations. Also, most of these schools accept stu- dents from affirming Christian denominations, such as the Episcopal Church, the United Church of Christ, the Presbyterian Church (USA), and others.
3. Sadie Whitelocks, "'I could be fired because I'm transgender': Female Theology Professor Risks Job at Christian College and Marriage After Revealing New Male Identity," DailyMail.co.uk, September 24, 2013, http://www.dailymail.co.uk/femail /article-2430674/Transgender-Azusa-Pacific-University-professor-reveals-male -identity.html.
4. As it stands, public schools are barred from discriminating against a number of pro- tected classes, and while certain laws have been used to prevent discrimination on the basis of sexual orientation and gender identity, LGBTQ people are not explicitly designated members of a protected class. In the workplace, no federal laws protect against discrimination on the basis of sexual orientation in the private sector, but close to half the states offer protection in both public and private jobs.
5. "DWT Pursues 'Enormously Significant' Discrimination Claim on Behalf of Trans- gender Student Expelled from California Baptist University," news release, DWT. com, Fall 2013, http://www.dwt.com/DWT-Pursues-Enormously-Significant -Discrimination-Claim-On-Behalf-of-Transgender-Student-Expelled-From-California -Baptist-University-Davis-Wright-Tremaine-Pro-Bono-Report-08–29–2013/; Michael Gryboski, "California Baptist University Sued by Expelled Transgender Student," ChristianPost.com, February 27, 2013, http://www.christianpost.com /news/california-baptist-university-sued-by-expelled-transgender-student-90934/.
6. William H. Green et al., Plaintiffs, v. John B. Connally et al., Defendants, v. Dan Coit et al. Intervenors, Findacase.com, 17–20, http://dc.findacase.com/research /wfrmDocViewer.aspx/xq/fac.19710630_0000050.DDC.htm/qx.
7. Bob Jones University v. United States, 639 F.2d 147 (4th Cir. 1980), http://caselaw .lp.findlaw.com/cgi-bin/getcase.pl?court=US&vol=461&invol=574.
8. Randall Balmer, "The Real Origins of the Religious Right," Politico.com, May 27, 2014, http://www.politico.com/magazine/story/2014/05/religious-right-real-origins -107133.html#.
9. Ibid.
10. Balmer, *Thy Kingdom Come*, 13–15.
11. Ron Sider, "Bearing Better Witness: Evangelicals Need to Rethink What They Do and Say About Gay Marriage," FirstThings.com, December 2010, http://www .firstthings.com/article/2010/12/bearing-better-witness.
12. Craig Osten and Alan Sears, *The Homosexual Agenda: Exposing the Principal Threat to Religious Freedom Today* (Nashville: Broadman & Holman Publishers, 2003), 148.
13. William Martin, *With God on Our Side: The Rise of the Religious Right in America* (New York: Broadway Books, 1996), 348.
14. Family Research Council and Focus on the Family, amicus brief: Lawrence & Gar- ner v. Texas, February 18, 2003, Texas Court of Appeals for the Fourteenth Dis- trict, http://findlawimages.com/efile/supreme/briefs/02–102/02–102.mer.ami.frc.pdf.
15. James Dao, "Same-Sex Marriage Issue Key to Some G.O.P. Races," NYTimes.com, November 4, 2004, http://www.nytimes.com/2004/11/04/politics/campaign/04gay.html.

16. Balmer, *Thy Kingdom Come*, 10.
17. This study looks only at lesbian, gay, and bisexual youths. Laura Kann et al., *Sexual Identity, Sex of Sexual Contacts, and Health-Risk Behaviors Among Students in Grades 9–12*, Centers for Disease Control and Prevention, June 6, 2011, p. 14, http://www.cdc.gov/mmwr/pdf/ss/ss60e0606.pdf.
18. Ann P. Haas, Philip L. Rodgers, and Jody L. Herman, *Suicide Attempts Among Transgender and Gender Non-Conforming Adults*, American Foundation for Suicide Prevention and the Williams Institute on Sexual Orientation and Gender Identity Law and Public Policy at UCLA School of Law, January 2014. http://williams institute.law.ucla.edu/wp-content/uploads/AFSP-Williams-Suicide-Report-Final.pdf.
19. Nicole Legate, Richard M. Ryan, and Netta Weinstein, "Is Coming Out Always a 'Good Thing'? Exploring the Relations of Autonomy Support, Outness, and Wellness for Lesbian, Gay, and Bisexual Individuals," *Social Psychological and Personality Science* 3 (2011), http://spp.sagepub.com/content/early/2011/06/10 /1948550611411929.full.pdf.
20. "Is Coming Out Always a Good Thing?," press release, University of Rochester, June 20, 2011, http://www.rochester.edu/news/show.php?id=3869.
21. Robert-Paul Juster et al., "Sexual Orientation and Disclosure in Relation to Psychiatric Symptoms, Diurnal Cortisol, and Allostatic Load," *Psychosomatic Medicine Journal of Biobehavioral Medicine* 75, no. 2 (2013), http://journals.lww.com /psychosomaticmedicine/pages/articleviewer.aspx?year=2013&issue=02000&article =00003&type=Fulltext.
22. Mark L. Hatzenbuehler, Katherine M. Keyes, and Deborah S. Hasin, "State-Level Policies and Psychiatric Morbidity in Lesbian, Gay, and Bisexual Populations," *American Journal of Public Health* 99, no. 12 (2009).
23. Mark L. Hatzenbuehler et al., "Effects of Same-Sex Marriage Laws on Health Care Use and Expenditures in Sexual Minority Men: A Quasi-Natural Experiment," *American Journal of Public Health* 102, no. 2 (2012).
24. Mark L. Hatzenbuehler, John E. Pachankis, and Joshua Wolff, "Religious Climate and Health Risk Behaviors in Sexual Minority Youths: A Population-Based Study," *American Journal of Public Health* 102, no. 4 (2012), http://ajph.aphapublications .org/doi/abs/10.2105/AJPH.2011.300517
25. Joshua Wolff, Heather Himes, Sabrina Soares, and Ellen Miller Kwon, "Sexual and Gender Minority Students in Religious Higher Education: Mental Health, Outness, and Identity," unpublished manuscript submitted for review to *Psychology of Sexual Orientation and Gender Diversity*.

Chapter 4: Racial Awakenings

1. Harper, *Evangelical Does Not Equal Republican*, 8.
2. "The History of InterVarsity's Multiethnic Journey," InterVarsity.org, http://mem .intervarsity.org/mem/about-mem/history.
3. "Vital Statistics," InterVarsity.org, http://www.intervarsity.org/about/our/vital-statistics.
4. Lisa Sharon Harper, "The Church Has Left the Building," Sojo.net, August 15, 2014, accessed January 26, 2015, http://sojo.net/blogs/2014/08/15/church-has-left -building.
5. Soong-Chan Rah, "'The Line,' the 47 Percent, and the Food Stamp Professor," Sojo .net, October 26, 2012, accessed January 26, 2015, http://sojo.net/blogs/2012/10/26 /line-47-percent-and-food-stamp-professor.
6. Emerson and Smith, *Divided by Faith*, 80.
7. Donald McGavran, *The Bridges of God: A Study in the Strategy of Missions* (London: World Dominion Press, 1955), 10.
8. Rah, *The Next Evangelicalism*, 77.

9. Albert Raboteau, *Slave Religion: The "Invisible Institution" in the Antebellum South* (Oxford, UK: Oxford University Press, 2004), 137.

10. Curtiss Paul DeYoung, Michael O. Emerson, George Yancey, and Karen Chai Kim, *United by Faith: A Multiracial Congregation as an Answer to the Problem of Race* (New York: Oxford University Press, 2003), 61.

11. Ibid., 54.

12. Ibid., 60.

13. Ibid., 66.

14. Ibid., 69.

15. Ted Olsen, "Promise Keepers: Racial Reconciliation Emphasis Intensified," Christianity Today.com, January 6, 1997, http://www.christianitytoday.com/ct/1997/january6/7t1067.html (accessed January 26, 2015).

16. Gayle White, "Clergy Conference Stirs Historic Show of Unity," ChristianityToday.com, April 8, 1996, http://www.christianitytoday.com/ct/1996/april8/6t4088.html.

17. Emerson and Smith, *Divided by Faith*, 67.

18. Ibid., 68.

19. "America the Diverse—Race and Religion by Generation," graphic, PublicReligion.org, February 6, 2014, http://publicreligion.org/research/graphic-of-the-week/american-the-diverse/.

20. Ibid.

21. Bob Smietana, "Are Millennials Really Leaving the Church? Yes—But Mostly White Millennials," FaithStreet.com, May 16, 2014, http://www.faithstreet.com/onfaith/2014/05/16/are-millennials-really-leaving-church-yes-but-mostly-white-millennials/32103.

22. Jonathan Merritt, "Are Christian Conferences Racially Exclusive?" ReligionNews.com, Nov 20, 2013, http://jonathanmerritt.religionnews.com/2013/11/20/christian-conferences-racially-exclusive/.

23. "Billy Kim - Thu, Feb. 5 - 2015 Moody Founder's Week," YouTube video, 38:36, posted by "Moody Bible Institute," February 6, 2015, https://www.youtube.com/watch?v=boLeAWnm4Qw.

24. Ken Walker, "Vacation Bible School Wars," ChristianityToday.com, March 1, 2004, http://www.christianitytoday.com/ct/2004/march/29.26.html.

25. Kathy Khang, "Dear Pastor Rick Warren, I Think You Don't Get It," *More Than Serving Tea* (blog), September 24, 2013, https://morethanservingtea.wordpress.com/2013/09/24/dear-pastor-rick-warren-i-think-you-dont-get-it/.

26. Karen Grigsby Bates, "Asian-Americans to Evangelicals: We're Not Your Punch Line," NPR.org, October 18, 2013, http://www.npr.org/blogs/codeswitch/2013/10/17/236380656/asian-americans-to-evangelicals-were-not-your-punchline.

27. Full disclosure: she was briefly my priest when I attended her church in New York City.

28. "Exponential Addressing Asian-American Leaders' Concerns," Exponential.org, updated October 15, 2013, http://www.exponential.org/exponential-addressing-asian-american-leaders-concerns.

29. "Events Leading Up to the Open Letter," AsianAmericanChristian.org, January 28, 2014, http://asianamericanchristian.org/2014/01/events-leading-up-to-the-open-letter/.

Chapter 5: Submit No More

1. According to India Ramey, another contestant and a friend of Jennifer's. Interview with the author February 7, 2015.

2. Amanda Barbee, "Naked and Ashamed: Women and Evangelical Purity Culture," TheOtherJournal.com, March 3, 2014, http://theotherjournal.com/2014/03/03/naked-and-ashamed-women-and-evangelical-purity-culture/.

3. Life Way Student Ministry, "A History of True Love Waits," LifeWay.com, accessed January 26, 2015, http://www.lifeway.com/Article/true-love-waits-history.

4. Barbee, "Naked and Ashamed."

5. Claire Gordon, "How the 'Fortress of Fundamentalism' Handles Sexual Assault," AlJazeera.com, November 5, 2013, http://america.aljazeera.com/watch/shows /america-tonight/america-tonight-blog/2013/11/5/addressing-sexualassaultona fundamentalistchristiancampus.html.

6. Kiera Feldman, "Sexual Assault at God's Harvard," NewRepublic.com, February 17, 2014, http://www.newrepublic.com/article/116623/sexual-assault-patrick-henry -college-gods-harvard.

7. Ibid.

8. Dowland, *Family Values*, 217.

9. Jonathan Dudley, "How Evangelicals Decided Life Begins at Conception," Huffing-tonPost.com, November 5, 2012, http://www.huffingtonpost.com/jonathan-dudley /how-evangelicals-decided-that-life-begins-at-conception_b_2072716.html.

10. Ibid.

11. Ibid.

12. Ibid.

13. Ibid.

14. Cochran, *Evangelical Feminism*, 54.

15. Ibid., 93.

16. Ibid., 98.

17. Ibid., 103

18. Ibid., 150.

19. Ibid., 150–56.

20. Ibid.

21. According to CBE president Mimi Haddad. From interview and e-mails with the author.

22. "Comparison of 1925, 1963 and 2000 Baptist Faith and Message," SBC.net, accessed January 26, 2015, http://www.sbc.net/bfm2000/bfmcomparison.asp.

23. Julia Lieblich, Associated Press, "Southern Baptist Convention Passes Resolution Opposing Women as Pastors," NYTimes.com, June 15, 2000, http://www.nytimes .com/2000/06/15/us/southern-baptist-convention-passes-resolution-opposing-women -as-pastors.html.

24. "Mars Hill Pastor Responds to Uproar over Blog Posts on Women," Seattlepi.com, December 3, 2006, http://www.seattlepi.com/local/article/Mars-Hill-pastor-responds -to-uproar-over-blog-1221412.php#ixzz1izSLMaZt.

Chapter 6: Coming Out

1. Matt Comer, "A Second Christian College Changes Anti-Gay Policy, After Visit from Equality Ride," InterstateQ.com, August 27, 2007, http://interstateq.com /archives/2309/.

2. Rachel Zoll, "Gay, Evangelical and Seeking Acceptance in Church," AP.org, June 30, 2013, http://bigstory.ap.org/article/gay-evangelical-and-seeking -acceptance-church; Sarah Parvini, "LGBTQ Group Finds Acceptance at Evangelical College," USAToday.com, July 13, 2013, http://www.usatoday.com/story /news/nation/2013/07/13/LGBTQ-group-finds-acceptance-at-evangelical-college /2514629/.

3. "Biola University Statement on Human Sexuality," May 2012, http://studentlife .biola.edu/page_attachments/0000/1641/Sexuality_May_2012.pdf.

4. Via a spokeswoman (Brenda Velasco), Biola Campus security confirmed that this call took place.

5. "Three Spiritual Journeys of Millennials," news release, Barna.org, May 9, 2013, https://www.barna.org/barna-update/millennials/612-three-spiritual-journeys-of -millennials#.

6. Jonathan Merritt, "Evangelicals and the New Wave of Gay Acceptance," Huffington Post.com, June 25, 2011, http://www.huffingtonpost.com/jonathan-merritt/ evangelicals-gay-acceptance_b_882079.html.

7. Jonathan Merritt, "A Thread Called Grace," ChristianityToday.com, March 28, 2014, http://www.christianitytoday.com/ct/2014/april/jonathan-merritt-thread-called -grace.html.

8. Jonathan Merritt, "Why I Shared My Sexuality Story," Religion News Service, March 31, 2014, http://jonathanmerritt.religionnews.com/2014/03/31/shared -sexuality-story/.

9. Justin Lee, *Torn: Rescuing the Gospel from the Gays-vs.-Christians Debate* (New York: Jericho Books, 2012), 56.

10. The American Psychological Association, the American Psychiatric Association, the National Association of Social Workers, and the American Academy of Pediatrics have all released statements to this effect.

11. Lee, *Torn*, 57.

12. Molly Ball, "Hobby Lobby Is Already Creating New Religious Demands on Obama," TheAtlantic.com, July 2, 2014, http://www.theatlantic.com/politics/archive/2014/07 /hobby-lobby-is-already-creating-new-religious-demands-on-obama/373853/.

13. Gabe Lyons, "Bullied on the President's Stage," *Q Ideas* (blog), http://qideas.org /articles/bullied-on-the-presidents-stage/.

14. Sarah Posner, "'New Evangelical'-Progressive Alliance? Not So Fast," January 28, 2013, http://religiondispatches.org/new-evangelical-progressive-alliance-not-so-fast/.

15. Laurie Goodstein, "Christian Charity Backtracks on Gays," NYTimes.com, March 27, 2014, http://www.nytimes.com/2014/03/28/us/christian-charity-backtracks-on -gays.html.

16. Jones and Cox, *American Attitudes on Marriage Equality*.

17. "A Shifting Landscape: A Decade of Change in American Attitudes about Same-Sex Marriage and LGBTQ Issues," news release, PublicReligion.org, February 26, 2014, http://publicreligion.org/research/2014/02/2014-LGBTQ-survey/.

18. Rachel Held Evans, "World Vision Update," *Rachel Held Evans* (blog), March 26, 2014, http://rachelheldevans.com/blog/world-vision-update.

19. Julia Henning, "'Sexuality Matters' Panel Draws More Than 500 Students, Discusses Biola Policy," Chimes.Biola.edu, September 28, 2012, http://chimes.biola.edu /story/2012/sep/28/sexuality-matters-discussion-homosexuality-biola-a/.

Chapter 7: Made in the Image of God

1. The content of this meeting was initially confidential. Participants agreed to let me record the meeting and approach individuals afterward to obtain permission to include their identities and stories in this book.

2. Daniel Fan, "Social Justice (Made in America): For Export Only," *Ethnic Space and Faith* (blog), February 27, 2011, https://ethnicspace.wordpress.com/2011/02/27 /social-justice-made-in-america-for-export-only/.

3. Rah, *The Next Evangelicalism*, 77.

4. Emerson and Smith, *Divided by Faith*, 96.

5. Ibid., 97.

6. Ibid., 110.

7. "Brown Signs Bill Cutting Language on Undocumented Immigrants," California-Healthline.org, September 16, 2014, http://www.californiahealthline.org/articles /2014/9/16/brown-signs-bill-cutting-language-on-undocumented-immigrants.

8. Wes Granberg-Michaelson, "The Hidden Immigration Impact on American Churches," Sojo.net, September 23, 2013, http://sojo.net/blogs/2013/09/23/hidden -immigration-impact-american-churches.

9. Matthew Soerens and Jenny Hwang Yang, *Welcoming the Stranger: Justice, Compassion & Truth in the Immigration Debate* (Downer's Grove, IL: InterVarsity Press Books, 2009), 163.

10. Paul Djupe, "Evangelicals and Immigration—A Sea Change in the Making?," news release, PublicReligion.org, March 22, 2013, http://publicreligion.org/2013/03 /evangelicals-and-immigration-a-sea-change-in-the-making/.

11. "Survey: Republicans and Evangelicals Support a Path to Citizenship with Basic Requirements for Immigrants Living in Country Illegally," news release, PublicReligion .org, April 16, 2013, http://publicreligion.org/research/2013/04/april-2013-religion -politics-tracking-survey/.

12. Ibid.

13. Djupe, "Evangelicals and Immigration."

14. Robert P. Jones, Daniel Cox, Juhem Navarro-Rivera, E. J. Dionne Jr., and William A. Galston, *What Americans Want from Immigration Reform in 2014*, PublicReligion.org, June 10, 2014, http://publicreligion.org/research/2014/06/immigration -reform-06–2014/.

15. Emma Green, "The Evangelical Slide on Immigration Reform," TheAtlantic.com, June 11, 2014, http://www.theatlantic.com/politics/archive/2014/06/the-evangelical -slide-on-immigration-reform/372541/.

16. Michele Margolis, "What Are the Reaches and Limits of Religious Influence? Religious Messages and Immigration Attitudes," PowerPoint presentation, Massachusetts Institute of Technology, April 3, 2014.

17. "The Death of Michael Brown: Racial History Behind the Ferguson Protests," editorial, NYTimes.com, August 12, 2014, http://www.nytimes.com/2014/08/13 /opinion/racial-history-behind-the-ferguson-protests.html.

18. "Racial Profiling Data 2013, Agency: Ferguson Police Department," Missouri Attorney General's Office, accessed January 26, 2015, http://ago.mo.gov/VehicleStops /2013/reports/161.pdf

19. "What Is the Peace Plan?" ThePeacePlan.com, accessed January 26, 2015, http:// www.thepeaceplan.com/what-we-do.

Chapter 8: Femmevangelical

1. Jennifer D. Crumpton, *Femmevangelical: A Modern Girl's Guide to the Good News* (Atlanta: Chalice Press, 2015), 70.

2. Rachel Held Evans, "The Gospel Coalition, Sex, and Subordination," *Rachel Held Evans* (blog), July 18, 2012, http://rachelheldevans.com/blog/gospel-coalition -douglas-wilson-sex.

3. Robert Barnes, "Supreme Court Sides with Christian College in Birth Control Case," *Washington Post*, July 3, 2014, http://www.washingtonpost.com/politics /courts_law/2014/07/03/622f7b12-02f8-11e4-8572-4b1b969b6322_story.html.

4. Emily Maynard, "The Day I Turned in My V-Card," ProdigalMagazine.com, January 31, 2013, http://prodigalmagazine.com/?s=the+day+i+turned+in+my+v -card.

5. Amy Reynolds and Janel Curry, *Gender Dynamics in Evangelical Institutions: Women and Men Leading in Higher Education and the Nonprofit Sector* (Boston: Gordon College, 2014), https://xythos.gordon.edu/Projects/WebsiteChangeProjects /webforms/WILNSPhase12Report_Nov2014.pdf?uniq=h4i10j.

6. Ibid., 15.

7. Ibid., 3–5.

8. Ruth Moon, "What the Largest Study of Women Leaders at Evangelical Nonprofits Has Learned So Far," ChristianityToday.com, May 29, 2014, http://www .christianitytoday.com/gleanings/2014/may/what-largest-study-women-leaders -at-evangelical-nonprofits.html.
9. Robert P. Jones, Daniel Cox, Juhem Navarro-Rivera, E. J. Dionne Jr., and William A. Galston, *How Catholics and the Religiously Unaffiliated Will Shape the 2012 Election and Beyond: The 2012 American Values Survey*, PublicReligion.org, October 23, 2012, p. 53. http://publicreligion.org/site/wp-content/uploads/2012/10/AVS -2012-Pre-election-Report-for-Web.pdf; Guttmacher Institute, "Contraceptive Use Is the Norm Among Religious Women," news release, Guttmacher.org, April 13, 2011, http://www.guttmacher.org/media/nr/2011/04/13/.
10. Guttmacher Institute, "Contraceptive Use Is the Norm Among Religious Women."

Chapter 9: Pride

1. Amy Seed, "Christian Universities Face Mounting Concerns over Homosexuality [Part Two]," Chimes.Biola.edu, May 11, 2011, http://chimes.biola.edu/story/2011 /may/11/christian-universities-homosexuality/.
2. Brett McCracken, "As Religious Convictions Are Met with New Legal Challenges, What's at Stake for Schools Like Biola?," *Biola Magazine*, Fall 2014, http://magazine .biola.edu/article/14-fall/the-freedom-to-be-a-christian-college/.
3. Terry Goodrich, "The 'Messy Middle': Many Evangelicals Are Ambivalent about Homosexuality and Civil Unions for Gays, Baylor Study Shows," news release, Baylor.edu, August 12, 2013, http://www.baylor.edu/mediacommunications/news .php?action=story&story=131931.
4. Chris Norton, "Willow Creek Splits with Exodus International," ChristianityToday .com, July 21, 2011, http://www.christianitytoday.com/ct/2011/julyweb-only /willowcreekexodus.html.
5. Lee, *Torn*, 202.
6. Ibid., 204.
7. Ibid., 205.
8. Ibid., 206.
9. Kingsley is not his real name. He asked to remain anonymous; although Kingsley has lived in the United States most of his life, homosexuality remains illegal in his native African country, where much of his family still resides. He is not out to most of his family, both in the United States and abroad.
10. W. E. B. Du Bois, *The Souls of Black Folk* (Chicago: A. C. McClurg and Co., 1903), 2.
11. Elizabeth Dias, "How Evangelicals Are Changing Their Minds on Gay Marriage," Time.com, January 15, 2015, http://time.com/3669024/evangelicals-gay-marriage/.

Selected Bibliography

Arterburn, Stephen, and Fred Stoeker. *Every Man's Battle: Winning the War on Sexual Temptation One Victory at a Time*. Colorado Springs, CO: WaterBrook Press, 2009.

Ball, Molly. "Hobby Lobby Is Already Creating New Religious Demands on Obama." TheAtlantic.com, July 2, 2014. http://www.theatlantic.com/politics/archive/2014/07 /hobby-lobby-is-already-creating-new-religious-demands-on-obama/373853/.

Balmer, Randall. *Thy Kingdom Come: An Evangelical's Lament; How the Religious Right Distorts the Faith and Threatens America*. New York: Basic Books, 2006.

———. "The Real Origins of the Religious Right." Politico.com, May 27, 2014. http:// www.politico.com/magazine/story/2014/05/religious-right-real-origins -107133.html#.

Barbee, Amanda. "Naked and Ashamed: Women and Evangelical Purity Culture." TheOtherJournal.com, March 3, 2014. http://theotherjournal.com/2014/03/0 3/naked-and-ashamed-women-and-evangelical-purity-culture/.

Blumenthal, Max. "Agent of Intolerance." TheNation.com, May 16, 2007. http:// www.thenation.com/article/agent-intolerance#.

Campolo, Tony. "My Response to *Sojourners*' Article About 'The Family.'" Sojo.net, June 10, 2011. http://sojo.net/blogs/2011/06/10/my-response-sojourners-article -about-family.

Christianity Today. "Walter Rauschenbusch: Champion of the Social Gospel." August 8, 2008. http://www.christianitytoday.com/ch/131christians/activists/rauschenbusch.html.

Cochran, Pamela. *Evangelical Feminism: A History*. New York: New York University Press, 2005.

Comer, Matt. "A Second Christian College Changes Anti-Gay Policy, After Visit from Equality Ride." InterstateQ.com, August 27, 2007. http://interstateq.com/archives /2309/.

Cox, Dan. "Young White Evangelicals: Less Republican, Still Conservative." Pewforum .org, September 28, 2007. http://www.pewforum.org/2007/09/28/young-white -evangelicals-less-republican-still-conservative/.

Crumpton, Jennifer D. *Femmevangelical: A Modern Girl's Guide to the Good News*. Atlanta: Chalice Press, 2015.

Dao, James. "Same-Sex Marriage Issue Key to Some G.O.P. Races." NYTimes.com, November 4, 2004. http://www.nytimes.com/2004/11/04/politics/campaign/04gay.html.

DeYoung, Curtiss Paul, Michael O. Emerson, George Yancey, and Karen Chai Kim. *United by Faith: A Multiracial Congregation as an Answer to the Problem of Race.* New York: Oxford University Press, 2003.

Dias, Elizabeth. "How Evangelicals Are Changing Their Minds on Gay Marriage." Time.com, January 15, 2015. http://time.com/3669024/evangelicals-gay-marriage/.

Djupe, Paul. "Evangelicals and Immigration—A Sea Change in the Making?" Public Religion Research, March 22, 2013. http://publicreligion.org/2013/03/evangelicals -and-immigration-a-sea-change-in-the-making/.

Dowland, Seth. *Family Values and the Rise of the Christian Right.* Philadelphia: University of Pennsylvania Press, 2015.

Du Bois, W. E. B. *The Souls of Black Folk.* Chicago: A. C. McClurg and Co., 1903.

Dudley, Jonathan. "How Evangelicals Decided Life Begins at Conception." Huffington Post.com, November 5, 2012. http://www.huffingtonpost.com/jonathan-dudley /how-evangelicals-decided-that-life-begins-at-conception_b_2072716.html.

Emerson, Michael O., and Christian Smith. *Divided by Faith: Evangelical Religion and the Problem of Race in America.* New York: Oxford University Press, 2000.

Eskridge, Larry. "How Many Evangelicals Are There?" Institute for the Study of American Evangelicals, 2012. http://www.wheaton.edu/ISAE/Defining-Evangelicalism /How-Many-Are-There.

Fan, Daniel. "Social Justice (Made in America): For Export Only." *Ethnic Space and Faith* (blog), February 27, 2011. https://ethnicspace.wordpress.com/2011/02/27 /social-justice-made-in-america-for-export-only/.

Feldman, Kiera. "Sexual Assault at God's Harvard." NewRepublic.com, February 17, 2014. http://www.newrepublic.com/article/116623/sexual-assault-patrick-henry -college-gods-harvard.

Gibbs, Nancy, and Michael Duffy. "How the Democrats Got Religion." Time.com, July 12, 2007. http://content.time.com/time/subscriber/article/0,33009,1642890,00.html.

Goodrich, Terry. "The 'Messy Middle': Many Evangelicals Are Ambivalent About Homosexuality and Civil Unions for Gays, Baylor Study Shows." Baylor.edu, August 12, 2013. http://www.baylor.edu/mediacommunications/news.php?action=story &story=131931.

Goodstein, Laurie. "Christian Charity Backtracks on Gays." NYTimes.com, March 27, 2014. http://www.nytimes.com/2014/03/28/us/christian-charity-backtracks-on-gays .html.

Gordon, Claire. "How the 'Fortress of Fundamentalism' Handles Sexual Assault." AlJazeera.com, November 5, 2013. http://america.aljazeera.com/watch/shows /america-tonight/america-tonight-blog/2013/11/5/addressing-sexualassaultona fundamentalistchristiancampus.html.

Gotobed, Julian. "Walter Rauschenbusch (1861–1918)." In *Boston Collaborative Encyclopedia of Western Theology*, edited by Wesley Wildman. Accessed January 22, 2015. http://people.bu.edu/wwildman/bce/rauschenbusch.htm.

Grant, Tobin, and Sarah Pulliam Bailey. "How Evangelicals Have Shifted in Public Opinion on Same-Sex Marriage." ChristianityToday.com, May 11, 2012. http:// www.christianitytoday.com/ct/2012/mayweb-only/evangelicals-shift-same-sex -marriage.html.

Green, Emma. "The Evangelical Slide on Immigration Reform." TheAtlantic.com, June 11, 2014. http://www.theatlantic.com/politics/archive/2014/06/the-evangelical -slide-on-immigration-reform/372541/.

Gryboski, Michael. "California Baptist University Sued by Expelled Transgender Student." ChristianPost.com, February 27, 2013. http://www.christianpost.com/news /california-baptist-university-sued-by-expelled-transgender-student-90934/.

Guttmacher Institute. "Contraceptive Use Is the Norm Among Religious Women." April 13, 2011. http://www.guttmacher.org/media/nr/2011/04/13/.

Haas, Ann P., Philip L. Rodgers, and Jody L. Herman. *Suicide Attempts Among Transgender and Gender Non-Conforming Adults.* American Foundation for Suicide Prevention and the Williams Institute on Sexual Orientation and Gender Identity Law and Public Policy at UCLA School of Law, January 2014. http://williamsinstitute .law.ucla.edu/wp-content/uploads/AFSP-Williams-Suicide-Report-Final.pdf.

Harper, Lisa Sharon. "By Any Other Name: Campus Crusade for Christ Becomes Cru." HuffingtonPost.com, July 22, 2011. http://www.huffingtonpost.com/lisa-sharon -harper/campus-crusade-for-christ-cru_b_906732.html.

———. "The Church Has Left the Building." Sojo.net, August 15, 2014. http://sojo.net /blogs/2014/08/15/church-has-left-building.

———. *Evangelical Does Not Equal Republican . . . or Democrat.* New York: New Press, 2008.

Harper, Lisa Sharon, and D. C. Innes. *Left, Right, and Christ: Evangelical Faith in Politics.* Boise, ID: Russell Media, 2011.

Hatzenbuehler, Mark L., Katherine M. Keyes, and Deborah S. Hasin. "State-Level Policies and Psychiatric Morbidity in Lesbian, Gay, and Bisexual Populations." *American Journal of Public Health* 99, no. 12 (2009).

Hatzenbuehler, Mark L., Katie A. McLaughlin, Katherine M. Keyes, and Deborah S. Hasin. "The Impact of Institutional Discrimination on Psychiatric Disorders in Lesbian, Gay, and Bisexual Populations: A Prospective Study." *American Journal of Public Health* 100, no. 3 (2010).

Hatzenbuehler, Mark L., Conall O'Cleirigh, Chris Grasso, Kenneth Mayer, Steven Safren, and Judith Bradford. "Effects of Same-Sex Marriage Laws on Health Care Use and Expenditures in Sexual Minority Men: A Quasi-Natural Experiment." *American Journal of Public Health* 102, no. 2 (2012).

Hatzenbuehler, Mark L., John E. Pachankis, and Joshua Wolff. "Religious Climate and Health Risk Behaviors in Sexual Minority Youths: A Population-Based Study." *American Journal of Public Health* 102, no. 4 (2012).

Henning, Julia. "'Sexuality Matters' Panel Draws More than 500 Students, Discusses Biola Policy," Chimes.Biola.edu, September 28, 2012. http://chimes.biola.edu /story/2012/sep/28/sexuality-matters-discussion-homosexuality-biola-a/.

Jones, Robert P., and Daniel Cox. *American Attitudes on Marriage Equality: Findings from the 2008 Faith and American Politics Study.* Public Religion Research Institute, February 2008. http://publicreligion.org/site/wp-content/uploads/2011/06 /American-Attitdues-on-same-sex-marriage-2008.pdf.

Jones, Robert P., Daniel Cox, Juhem Navarro-Rivera, E. J. Dionne Jr., and William A. Galston. *Do Americans Believe Capitalism & Government Are Working? Religious Left, Religious Right & the Future of the Economic Debate.* Public Religion Research Institute, July 18, 2013. http://publicreligion.org/site/wp-content/uploads /2013/07/2013-Economic-Values-Report-Final-.pdf.

———. *How Catholics and the Religiously Unaffiliated Will Shape the 2012 Election and Beyond: The 2012 American Values Survey.* Public Religion Research Institute, October 23, 2012. http://publicreligion.org/site/wp-content/uploads/2012/10/AVS -2012-Pre-election-Report-for-Web.pdf.

———. *What Americans Want from Immigration Reform in 2014*. Public Religion Research Institute, June 10, 2014. http://publicreligion.org/research/2014/06 /immigration-reform-06-2014/.

Juster, Robert-Paul, Nathan Grant Smith, Émilie Ouellet, Shireen Sindi, and Sonia J. Lupien. "Sexual Orientation and Disclosure in Relation to Psychiatric Symptoms, Diurnal Cortisol, and Allostatic Load." *Psychosomatic Medicine Journal of Biobehavioral Medicine* 75, no. 2 (2013). http://journals.lww.com/psychosomaticmedicine /pages/articleviewer.aspx?year=2013&issue=02000&article=00003&type=Fulltext.

Kann, Laura, Emily O'Malley Olsen, Tim McManus, Steve Kinchen, David Chyen, William A. Harris, and Howel Wechsler. *Sexual Identity, Sex of Sexual Contacts, and Health-Risk Behaviors Among Students in Grades 9–12—Youth Risk Behavior Surveillance, Selected Sites, United States, 2001–2009*. Centers for Disease Control and Prevention, June 6, 2011. http://www.cdc.gov/mmwr/pdf/ss/ss60e0606.pdf.

Kinnaman, David, and Gabe Lyons. *unChristian: What a New Generation Really Thinks About Christianity . . . and Why It Matters*. Grand Rapids, MI: Baker Books, 2007.

Lee, Justin. *Torn: Rescuing the Gospel from the Gays-vs.-Christians Debate*. New York: Jericho Books, 2012.

Legate, Nicole, Richard M. Ryan, and Netta Weinstein. "Is Coming Out Always a 'Good Thing'? Exploring the Relations of Autonomy Support, Outness, and Wellness for Lesbian, Gay, and Bisexual Individuals." *Social Psychological and Personality Science* 3 (2011). http://spp.sagepub.com/content/early/2011/06/10/1948550611411929 .full.pdf.

Lieblich, Julia, "Southern Baptist Convention Passes Resolution Opposing Women as Pastors," NYTimes.com, June 15, 2000, http://www.nytimes.com/2000/06/15/us /southern-baptist-convention-passes-resolution-opposing-women-as-pastors.html.

LifeWay Student Ministry. "A History of True Love Waits." LifeWay Christian Resources. http://www.lifeway.com/Article/true-love-waits-history.

Lindsell, Harold. *The Battle for the Bible*. Grand Rapids, MI: Zondervan Publishing House, 1976.

Long, Michael G. *The Legacy of Billy Graham: Critical Reflections on America's Greatest Evangelist*. Louisville, KY: Westminster John Knox Press, 2008.

Marin, Andrew. "Why Gabe Lyons and Others Are Wrong About the Louie Giglio Aftermath." Patheos.com, January 11, 2013. http://www.patheos.com/blogs /loveisanorientation/2013/01/why-gabe-lyons-and-others-are-wrong-about-the -louie-giglio-aftermath/.

Martin, William. *With God on Our Side: The Rise of the Religious Right in America*. New York: Broadway Books, 1996.

McCracken, Brett. "As Religious Convictions Are Met with New Legal Challenges, What's at Stake for Schools Like Biola?" *Biola Magazine*, Fall 2014. http://magazine .biola.edu/article/14-fall/the-freedom-to-be-a-christian-college/.

McGavran, Donald. *The Bridges of God: A Study in the Strategy of Missions*. London: World Dominion Press, 1955.

Merritt, Jonathan. "Are Christian Conferences Racially Exclusive?" ReligionNews.com, November 20, 2013. http://jonathanmerritt.religionnews.com/2013/11/20 /christian-conferences-racially-exclusive/.

———. "Evangelicals and the New Wave of Gay Acceptance." HuffingtonPost.com, June 25, 2011. http://www.huffingtonpost.com/jonathan-merritt/evangelicals-gay -acceptance_b_882079.html.

———. "A Thread Called Grace." ChristianityToday.com, March 28, 2014, http:// www.christianitytoday.com/ct/2014/april/jonathan-merritt-thread-called-grace.html.

Miller, Kevin A. "NBEA Hears Promise Keepers' Message." ChristianityToday.com, June 19, 1995. http://www.christianitytoday.com/ct/1995/june19/5t7043.html.

Missouri Attorney General's Office. "Racial Profiling Data 2013, Agency: Ferguson Police Department." Accessed January 26, 2015. http://ago.mo.gov/VehicleStops/2013 /reports/161.pdf.

Monk, Bethany. "Take Action: Violence Against Women Act Misleading." February 4, 2013. http://www.citizenlink.com/2013/02/04/take-action-violence-against-women -act-misleading-harmful/.

New Jersey Division of Labor Market and Demographic Research, New Jersey State Data Center. *Population by Race and Hispanic or Latino Origin New Jersey Counties and Selected Municipalities: 1980, 1990 and 2000.* Trenton, June 2001. http:// lwd.dol.state.nj.us/labor/lpa/census/2kpub/njsdcp2.pdf.

Olsen, Ted. "Promise Keepers: Racial Reconciliation Emphasis Intensified." Christianity Today.com, January 6, 1997. http://www.christianitytoday.com/ct/1997/january6 /7t1067.html.

Olson, Laura R., and Melissa Deckman. "The Times, Are They A-Changin'?" PublicReligion.org, April 10, 2013. http://publicreligion.org/2013/04/the-times-are-they-a -changin/.

Osten, Craig, and Alan Sears. *The Homosexual Agenda: Exposing the Principal Threat to Religious Freedom Today.* Nashville: Broadman & Holman Publishers, 2003.

Parvini, Sarah. "LGBT Group Finds Acceptance at Evangelical College." USAToday. com, July 13, 2013. http://www.usatoday.com/story/news/nation/2013/07/13/lgbt -group-finds-acceptance-at-evangelical-college/2514629/.

Perkins, John M. *Let Justice Roll Down.* Ventura, CA: Regal Books, 1976.

———. *With Justice for All: A Strategy for Community Development.* Ventura, CA: Regal Books, 1982.

Pew Research Center. *America's Changing Religious Landscape.* May 12, 2015. http:// www.pewforum.org/files/2015/05/RLS-05-08-full-report.pdf.

———. *Latinos, Religion and Campaign 2012: Catholics Favor Obama, Evangelicals Divided.* Pew Hispanic Center and Pew Forum on Religion and Public Life, October 18, 2012. http://www.pewforum.org/2012/10/18/latinos-religion-and-campaign -2012/.

———. *Religion Among the Millennials.* February 17, 2010. http://www.pewforum.org /2010/2/17/religion-among-the-millennials/.

Piper, John, and Wayne Grudem. *Recovering Biblical Manhood & Womanhood.* Wheaton, IL: Crossway, 1991.

Posner, Sarah. "'New Evangelical'-Progressive Alliance? Not So Fast." January 28, 2013. http://religiondispatches.org/new-evangelical-progressive-alliance-not-so-fast/.

Public Religion Research Institute. *A Shifting Landscape: A Decade of Change in American Attitudes about Same-Sex Marriage and LGBT Issues.* February 26, 2014. http://publicreligion.org/research/2014/02/2014-lgbt-survey/.

———. "Survey: Republicans and Evangelicals Support a Path to Citizenship with Basic Requirements for Immigrants Living in Country Illegally." April 16, 2013. http:// publicreligion.org/research/2013/04/april-2013-religion-politics-tracking-survey/.

Raboteau, Albert. *Slave Religion: The "Invisible Institution" in the Antebellum South.* Oxford, UK: Oxford University Press, 2004.

Rah, Soong-Chan. "'The Line,' the 47 Percent, and the Food Stamp Professor." Sojo.net, October 26, 2012. http://sojo.net/blogs/2012/10/26/line-47-percent-and-food-stamp -professor.

———. *The Next Evangelicalism: Freeing the Church from Western Cultural Captivity*. Downer's Grove, IL: InterVarsity Press Books, 2009.

Reynolds, Amy, and Janel Curry. *Gender Dynamics in Evangelical Institutions: Women and Men Leading in Higher Education and the Nonprofit Sector*. Boston: Gordon College, 2014.

Sandeen, Ernest R. "Christian Fundamentalism." In *Encyclopaedia Britannica Online*, accessed January 22, 2015. http://www.britannica.com/EBchecked/topic/222234 /Christian-fundamentalism#toc252659.

Scanzoni, Letha. "Part 1: Coauthoring 'All We're Meant to Be'—The Beginning." *Letha Dawson Scanzoni* (blog), January 7, 2011. http://www.lethadawsonscanzoni.com /2011/01/part-1-coauthoring-all-were-meant-to-be-the-beginning/.

Scanzoni, Letha, and Nancy Hardesty. *All We're Meant to Be: Biblical Feminism for To-day*. Grand Rapids, MI: W. B. Eerdmans, 1992.

Schaeffer, Francis. *A Christian Manifesto*. Wheaton, IL: Crossway Books, 1981.

Seed, Amy. "Christian Universities Face Mounting Concerns over Homosexuality [Part Two]." Chimes.Biola.edu, May 11, 2011. http://chimes.biola.edu/story/2011/may /11/christian-universities-homosexuality/

Sider, Ron. "Bearing Better Witness: Evangelicals Need to Rethink What They Do and Say About Gay Marriage." FirstThings.com, December 2010. http://www.firstthings .com/article/2010/12/bearing-better-witness.

Smietana, Bob. "Are Millennials Really Leaving the Church? Yes—But Mostly White Millennials." FaithStreet.com, May 16, 2014. http://www.faithstreet.com/onfaith /2014/05/16/are-millennials-really-leaving-church-yes-but-mostly-white-millennials /32103.

Soerens, Matthew, and Jenny Hwang Yang. *Welcoming the Stranger: Justice, Compassion & Truth in the Immigration Debate*. Downer's Grove, IL: InterVarsity Press Books, 2009.

Swartz, David R. *Moral Minority: The Evangelical Left in an Age of Conservatism*. Philadelphia: University of Pennsylvania Press, 2012.

Walker, Ken. "Vacation Bible School Wars." ChristianityToday.com, March 1, 2004. http://www.christianitytoday.com/ct/2004/march/29.26.html.

White, Gayle. "Clergy Conference Stirs Historic Show of Unity." ChristianityToday.com, April 8, 1996. http://www.christianitytoday.com/ct/1996/april8/6t4088.html.

Zoll, Rachel. "Gay, Evangelical and Seeking Acceptance in Church." AP.org, June 30, 2013. http://bigstory.ap.org/article/gay-evangelical-and-seeking-acceptance-church.